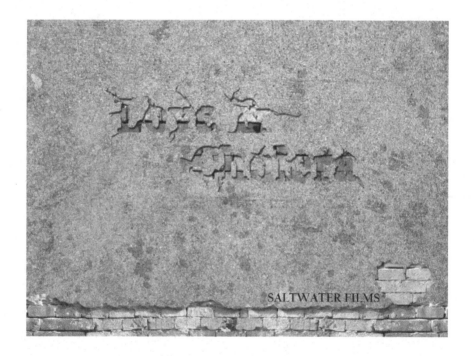

SALTWATER FILMS

# LOVE & CHOLERA

## Amour et le Choléra

## JEFF BENJAMIN

Published by AuthorHouse  09/16/2014

ISBN: 978-1-4969-3833-6 (sc)
ISBN: 978-1-4969-3832-9 (hc)
ISBN: 978-1-4969-3831-2 (e)

Library of Congress Control Number: 2014915759

# INDEX

# PREFACE

FOR LOVE- FOR FAITH-
FOR HOPE-FOR HAITI

AMOUR ET LE CHOLERA

# HAITI EARTHQUAKE
# (90 DAYS OF HELL)

The chronology of the 90 days following the 12 January 2010 earthquake provides valuable information about the events and their sequence.

This chain of events reinforces the concept that while hazards such as earthquakes can trigger a crisis, the disasters themselves are not natural but rather the result of a series of human actions.

This annex collects the main facts recorded in one of the few reports available from the day of the quake, known as the Haiti Earthquake Situation Report (Sitrep), prepared by the United Nations Office for the Coordination of Humanitarian Affairs (OCHA), with support from national and international agencies and NGOs. The review covers the first 33 Sitreps, from 12 January to 12 April 2010.

The chronology is organized around four issues:

1. Security and access
2. Official figures issued by the Government of Haiti
3. Emergency management
4. Health situation

**12 Jan Day 1 Earthquake Situation Report #1:** The capital of Haiti, Port-au-Prince (PAP), has been severely affected including critical city infrastructure components such as electricity, water and phone services.

Electricity is not available and communications are difficult. At this stage there is very limited access because of debris and other obstacles on the roads. The airport of PAP is reported to be closed. The Presidential Palace and Government buildings are reported to have been seriously damaged.

According to preliminary reports, several UN as well as other national buildings have collapsed or have been damaged. Populations may also be affected in Carrefour and Jacmel. There are no impact figures nor estimates. Initial reports indicate a large number of casualties and widespread damage with an urgent need for Search and Rescue (S&R).

**13 Jan Day 2 Situation Report #2:** The airport in PAP is reportedly operational, under control of the U.S. troops, and only open for humanitarian air flights. Roads to the capital are partly blocked. The UN Headquarters at the Christopher Hotel collapsed in the earthquake. There are no official reports. "The number of people in need of humanitarian assistance will not be determined until the extent of the damage is known. The death toll is unknown but is expected to be high." "S&R teams are arriving from Guadeloupe, the Dominican Republic and the United States. They are being deployed to major public buildings, hotels and hospitals." "The hospital in Petionville, a hillside PAP district, is destroyed and most of the medical centers have collapsed." "MSF has reported treating about 600 people in the affected area and is looking at sending additional medical supplies."

**14 Jan Day 3 Situation Report #3:** "The airport is operational for humanitarian and military flights. Air Traffic Control is responding to incoming aircraft, but with limited capabilities. There is very limited aircraft-handling capacity." "The port is not operational." "The Government is setting up an operations site close to the airport."

Situation Report #3: "A helicopter assessment by the UN Mission ...found some areas with 50 percent destruction or serious damage, with many buildings completely collapsed. PAP and other urban centers, such as Jacmel and Carrefour, are affected." "The death toll remains unknown." "There is no water supply." "Communications are down and there is no electricity." The Health Cluster is led by the World Health Organization. Most of the health resources and supplies need to go to the Dominican Republic and then by land to Haiti.

**15 Jan Day 4 Situation Report #4:** "Operations are heavily constrained due to the lack of fuel, transport, communications and handling capacity at the airport.

Some flights are being re-routed through Santo Domingo airport, which is also becoming congested." "The port remains non- operational." There were no official reports. Situation Report #4: "Identification of bodies remains a problem, in conjunction with assigning responsibility for the recovery of bodies. The Government is identifying various grave sites. No reliable figures are available on the extent of fatalities." "Phone communication remains difficult in most of the capital. However, text messages are getting through. Internet connections are possible in some areas, but constant access remains difficult." "The Pan American Health Organization is establishing a field office in Jimaní (Dominican Republic) to serve as a permanent bridge between this border city and to PAP (approximately a 90-minute journey).

The office will be a staging/transfer point for emergency humanitarian supplies and personnel needed in the Haiti response operation."

Health status

**16 Jan Day 5 Situation Report #5:** "The limited capacity of the airport combined with heavy and unplanned air traffic remains a challenge, resulting in many flights being detoured and delayed.... However lack of transport and fuel remain a problem making it difficult to move goods to other locations. With no storage facility, the airport is now packed with goods and teams. Safety and security remains an important concern." "PAP seaport is still non-operational.""The Ministry of Interior estimates that one million people have been severely affected by the earthquake and that 250,000 are in urgent need of assistance. Authorities believe that 50,000 people have died, but so far 13,000 bodies have been ac- counted for." Situation Report #5: "There have been 58 live rescues so far by these teams (Search & Res- cue International Teams).... Approximately 60% of the worst affected areas of PAP and surrounding communities have been covered." The major constraints for the USAR operation are security, transport, communications and fuel.

Estimates are that the number of dead ranges between 40,000 and 50,000 people. A mass burial of 3,000 bodies was reported yesterday. . . .(In PAP) at least eight hospitals and/or health centers have collapsed or sustained serious damage. ...At least five hospitals are functioning. "A dialysis center with 8 units was operational.

**17 Jan Day 6 Situation Report #6:** "The PAP airport is heavily congested. . . . Fuel remains an issue for humanitarian operations. . .

The port remains unusable." Situation Report #6: "S&R teams extracted 13 live rescues on 16 January bringing the total number of lives saved by these teams to 71." "The Health Cluster reports that seven field hospitals have arrived and three are fully operational. . . Handling of dead bodies remains an issue."

**18 Jan Day 7 Situation Report #7:** "MINUSTAH reports that the overall security situation in PAP remains stable, with limited, localized violence and looting occurring." "Twenty-six countries, including Argentina, Canada, France, Russia and the USA, have provided significant military assets towards the emergency response. These assets included field hospitals, troops, military aircraft, hospital ships, cargo ships and helicopters. MINUS- TAH currently has 3,400 troops and police on the ground." "The Government has further advised severely affected populations to leave the city if they have family or friends in non-affected areas. To this end, it provided cash and fuel to a transport company to pro- vide free transport. . . . thousands of displaced are leaving PAP for rural areas." Situation Report #7: "Urban Search-and- Rescue teams have saved 90 lives. Two more live rescues were reported on 18 January." "An initial assessment by the United Nations.

Environment Programme, from 13 to 17 January, indicated no major acute environmental emergencies, but enormous issues for the anticipated recovery phase. The most urgent issues include waste management, medical waste, disposal of corpses and disposal of demolition material." "All hospitals within the PAP area are overwhelmed with incoming patients.

Many fracture cases need urgent surgical intervention due to extended periods without care."

"Major gaps include surgical capacity, follow-up of surgical patients, maternity care, and coverage of areas of population displacements.... There is some coordinating between the health sector response from operation bases in PAP and Santo Domingo. An operations centre is also being set up in Jimaní, in the Dominican Republic."

**19 Jan Day 8 Situation Report #8**: "Despite logistical and security constraints, the affected population is receiving an increasing number of relief supplies, including medical assistance, food, water and shelter." "The Government has devised eight zones for the distribution of humanitarian assistance. A main concern for the Government continues to be the revitalization of economic activities." Situation Report #8 "The revised total of lives saved by international search-and-rescue teams is over 121 people... At the peak of the search-and-rescue effort, there were 52 teams on the ground with 1,820 rescue workers and 175 dogs." "Water distribution has been constrained by limited fuel supplies. Distribution was planned for 176 distribution points on 19 January." Haiti has "49 hospitals nationwide... including 11 hospitals in PAP. Eight hospitals and health-care facilities in and around PAP are damaged." "The Minister of Interior has started spraying caustic soda over bodies and buildings where bodies have still not been recovered." "The provision of water to hospitals, gathering sites and common areas are the priorities for distribution."

**20 Jan Day 9 Situation Report #9:** The PAP airport reports about 150 planes are landing daily. Finding free slots for large aircraft is still a challenge. "DPC has estimated that the earthquake resulted in 75,000 persons killed, 200,000 injured and one million displaced." Situation Report #9: "IOM estimates that there are more than 300 makeshift settlements scattered throughout the city, with an estimated 370,000 people living under improvised shelter with no access to water supplies, according to recent assessments." "Assessments of hospital facilities will continue to look at hospital infrastructure, referral systems and the organization of transportation of patients."

"As of 19 January, the WASH Cluster has established 82 distribution sites for water, and has 180 water trucks with a total capacity to provide water to 180,000 people."

**21 Jan Day 10 Situation Report #10**: "The road from the Dominican Republic remains the best option for the majority of incoming cargo." "The PAP port is functional." "The security situation in PAP remains stable although there are isolated cases of looting and violence. MINUSTAH currently requires military escorts for the delivery of aid by UN agencies." Situation Report #10: "The [UN] cluster estimates that the number of displaced people is between 500,000 and 700,000 (current planning figure).... Of the 508 makeshift sites identified by the Government, some 350 have been assessed (68%) by cluster partners. These 350 sites currently accommodate around 472,000 people and only six sites have access to water sources. A new 400-person site was established on 21 January in Del- mas." "PROMESS, the main medical storage and distribution facility is providing medicines and medical supplies for free to 50 organizations working in hospitals and clinics. The supplies have been offered since 13 January and each day the number of requests increases." The removal of medical waste from hospitals and wherever health care is provided is a challenge.

**22 Jan Day 11 Situation Report #11:** "The security situation remains stable but the potential for unrest remains. There is concern that in some Port-au-Prince neighborhoods (Belair, Martissant and Cité Soleil), formerly incarcerated criminals have returned and are attempting to reconstitute gangs." "As of 22 January, the Government has accounted for 111,481 confirmed deaths in four departments (South East, West, Nippes and West)." Situation Report #11: "The Government has declared the S&R phase over. There were 132 live rescues by international S&R teams." "So far, more than 130,000 people have been assisted... with transportation to leave the city, according to DPC."

Artibonite department has received 50,573 people; North West department 30,000; Centre department; 20,530; North department 12,500; Grande Anse 9,000; and South department 9,000. The total number of people leaving PAP by private means remains undetermined. "Currently there are 40 functioning health facilities in PAP, 8 of which are field hospitals. Urgent surgical interventions are decreasing and the follow up of the post-surgical patients is a problem that needs to be solved. Information management is a challenge for all clusters/ sectors." At present, Haiti's immunization program is not functioning and tetanus is the disease of most immediate concern.

**23 Jan Day:**   Improved waste management (solid and health care) is taking place in hospitals, including the appropriate disposal of amputated body parts.

**24 Jan Day 13 Situation Report #12:**   "The Government estimates the death toll from the 12 January earthquake at 112,250 deaths and 194,000 injured. The number of people in need of shelter ranges from 800,000 to one million." Situation Report #12: "The Government estimates that 235,000 people have left PAP using the free transportation being provided by the Government." "Water continues to be distributed daily at 115 sites in PAP reaching an estimated 235,000 people." "43 hospitals are functioning in the PAP area, 12 field hospitals (half of which are military hospitals) and two hospital ships (US and Mexico). There is a need for more information from areas outside of PAP. . . Important challenges remain especially in the areas of post-operative care and the adaptation of thousands of people who have lost limbs... No reported outbreaks of communicable diseases."

**25 Jan Day 14 Situation Report #13:**   The security situation in PAP remains stable but there have been isolated instances of looting and a recent incident where MI- NUSTAH troops fired warning shots and used tear gas. "More and more police officers are reporting for duty, increasing capacity to an estimated 60-70 percent of pre-earthquake levels in PAP." The Ministerial Conference on Haiti took place in

Montreal on 25 January. Situation Report #13: "The distribution of assistance continues in PAP and other affected areas such as Jacmel, Carrefour, Léogâne and Petit Goâve. Tents, food, health (post-operative care and epidemiological surveillance), sanitation and hygiene are the priorities for assistance." "The Ministry of Health of the Dominican Republic estimates that as of 22 January, 495 Haitian patients are in nine hospitals in the Dominican Republic. The majority (247 people) are in the Buen Samaritano Hospital in Jimaní. The influx of patients requiring emergency care in these hospitals is declining."

**27 Jan-Day 16 Situation Report #14:**  Commercial activities have resumed in many parts of the country. The security situation in PAP and other affected areas remains stable. Military escorts are required for UN relief distributions. "The Government is reporting that 112,392 have died and 196,501 people have been injured by the earthquake. The number of displaced people ranges from 800,000 to one million." Situation Report #14: "An increase in commodity prices has been reported further increasing the number of people who are dependent on humanitarian assistance. . . . Cash-for-work and cash-for-food programmes are starting to be used to engage Haitians in the recovery effort and to help stimulate the local economy.... All schools remain closed but schools in non-affected departments will reopen on 1 February." [18] Cases of tetanus and suspected cases of measles have been reported in Léogâne. A vaccination campaign against diphtheria and tetanus, DTT and measles will begin on February 2.

Water is reaching 308,000 people through 133 distribution points in PAP. The coverage in Léogâne and Jacmel has been expanded also. Additional boreholes and new contractors are being identified to increase production and distribution capacity.

**28 Jan Day 17:**   Health report indicates people with injuries have received medical attention, even though some require surgical care. Turning point between the life-saving and the post-operative care phases.

**29 Jan Day 18 Situation Report #15:**   "The port has been declared unsafe for incoming ships. PAP airport is operating at peak capacity with an average of 120 incoming flights per day." "While the overall security situation in PAP remains stable, crowd control at aid distribution points."

Situation Report #15: "As of 28 January, the Government reported that more than 341,000 persons have departed PAP for locations outside the capital.... Over a third of the total – some 133,000 individuals – have arrived in Artibonite department." "Several organizations have reported cases of tetanus and chicken pox. An isolated case of typhoid has been reported. ... In terms of medical supplies, crutches and x-ray equipment are in short supply and specialists in orthopedic and internal medicine are in high demand, according to the Cluster."

**1 Feb Day 21 Situation Report #16:**   "The PAP airport is handling approximately 120-150 planes per day. . . . The overall security situation across the country remains stable but potentially volatile." Situation Report #16: "The Government has revised the number of people leaving PAP for outlying departments to 482,349 people, as of 31 January." "The need for the establishment of post-operative care facilities and mobile clinics persists. Due to the large numbers of patients who are now homeless, hospitals are challenged with where to discharge patients. In collaboration with the regional waste-hauling authority, The World Health Organization has set up a collection system to remove medical waste in all hospitals and dispose them in safe and organized landfill sites."

**3 Feb Day 23 Situation Report #17:** "Growing gang rivalries remain a concern in PAP. UNPOL and HNP continue to maintain increased patrols in Cité Soleil and Marché de Fer. The Government decided to extend the state of emergency which was due to expire on 1 February for a further two weeks." Prime Minister says, "as angry pro- tests over the slow arrival of aid flared on the rubblestrewn streets," to the Agence France-Presse "There are more than 200,000 people who have been clearly identified as people who are dead," same report indicates "aid agencies have sounded the alarm that donations for Haiti relief have been desperately low.

Compared to after the 2004 Asian tsunami, which had a death toll of about 220,000." "Situation Report # 17: Sanitation is becoming a major concern at many of the temporary sites. . . . The WFP food surge continues. Some 1 million people have been reached since the onset of the emergency; 338,000 people have received two-week rations of rice over the past 3 days." "Health Cluster partners have recorded over 1,000 amputations in PAP.

There are also reports that some 50 people have been paralyzed from spinal cord injuries." "Medical waste management services are reportedly only being used by two hospitals in PAP. Some hospitals appear to be sending waste on their own to the landfill site." "Many medical supplies are still in large containers in PAP and need to be sorted and prioritized. This process is causing some delays in getting supplies distributed."

**5 Feb Day 25 Situation Report #18** "Some 80 to 90 flights per day are landing at PAP airport, down from the peak of 120-150 flights per day." "Contingency planning is underway to prepare for the upcoming rainy season, taking into consideration displaced populations and logistic shortcomings." "The DPC is verifying the latest figures for dead and injured (Declared by the Prime Minister on Feb 3) but has not issued an official update since 28 January when it reported that 112,405 had died and 196,595 were injured." Situation Report #18: "Seven organized settlements have been established for 42,000 displaced people; some 460,000 people remain in 315 spontaneous settlements throughout PAP, according to IOM." "Sanitation and vector control is becoming a major concern...." "... no notification of events with epidemic potential. Disease surveillance continues. There are 52 government-defined sentinel sites, 12 of which are located in the metropolitan PAP area. Investigations are also being conducted by three mobile teams from the Ministry of Health and the US Centers for Disease Control.

**8 Feb Day 28 Situation Report #19**   "The security situation remains unchanged but there is growing concern over potential restiveness and crime prompted by shortages of shelter, jobs and sanitation." Situation Report #19: "Contingency planning is underway to prepare for the upcoming rainy season, taking into consideration displaced populations and logistic shortcomings." Safe drinking water litres per person per day) is provided to over 780,000 people through water tankering and water treatment plants at 300 sites across Port au Prince, Léogâne, and Jacmel.

**11 Feb Day 31 Situation Report #20**   "Commercial cargo flights have started arriving at PaP airport." "The security situation throughout the country remains stable despite increased reports of isolated incidents."

Situation Report #20: "The Government reported that 211 live rescues were achieved by international and national S&R teams as of 9 February. A total of 139 live rescues were carried out by international teams and 72 by national teams." There is a decline in trauma injuries requiring treatment but the need for overall medical care is rising. The Ministry of Health's surveillance system reports acute respiratory infections as the main cause of morbidity.

*Jeff Benjamin*

**16 Feb Day 36 Situation Report #21** "The Office of the High Commissioner for Human Rights and the United Nations High Commissioner for Refugees are jointly urging countriesto suspend all involuntary returns to Haiti due to the continuing humanitarian crisis. They have called on all countries to continue granting interim protection measures on humanitarian grounds until such time as people can return safely and sustainably." "As of 15 February, the national Civil Protection Agency estimates that 217,366 people died from the 12 January earthquake.

An increase of 5,000 people since the last estimates were released on 6 February." Situation Report #21: "Provision of shelter and camp coordination continue to be challenging, including the need for debris removal and the identification of land for settlements. There is an urgent need to create adequate sanitation conditions for displaced populations, especially in congested settlement sites."

**19 Feb Day 39 Situation Report #22** "The security situation remains stable, and while some demonstrations have taken place in PAP over the last days, no major incidents have been reported." Situation Report #22:

"The Post-Disaster Needs Assessment (PDNA), to be carried out by the Government of Haiti and supported by development partners... was officially launched in PAP on 18 February. Focusing on key areas of the early recovery phase (sanitation, food security, water, debris management and removal and transitional shelter)...."

"There are currently 396 health NGOs registered in Haiti, however, many of them are due to depart the country in the coming weeks, without sufficient new capacity planned to arrive." "There is a risk of a large-scale outbreak of diarrhea, given the present overcrowding, poor sanitation and lack of effective waste disposal systems in spontaneous settlement sites."

**22 Feb Day 42 Situation Report #23** "Security in displacement sites, especially in large settlements, continues to be a concern and requires a more permanent police presence." "DPC estimates that 222,517 people died following the 12 January earthquake, an increase of 5,000 people since the last estimates were released on 15 February."

Situation Report #23: "The number of people who have left PAP for outlying departments has increased to 597,801 people from the previous figure of 511,405. An estimated 160,000 persons have come from PAP to the border area with the Dominican Republic." "There has been an increase in allegations of gender-based violence in general terms. Cases are being referred to health services."

**25 Feb Day 45 Situation Report #24:** "Together with the decongestion of spontaneous settlement sites, creating adequate sanitary conditions will be crucial in order to mitigate the risk of a large-scale outbreak of waterborne diseases in the coming weeks." "Through the ongoing vaccination campaign in temporary settlements, over 8,000 children under seven years of age have been vaccinated against diphtheria, tetanus and pertussis and over 5,000 against measles and rubella." 1 Mar Day 49 "The transition from US Military assets to commercial handling at the port and airport is complete. The humanitarian cargo village at the airport is closed and all offloading is performed by privately contracted entities." The death toll has risen to 222,570 people, an increase of 53. 1.3 million people live in spontaneous settlement sites. 604,215 people have left PAP. Situation Report #25: "Heavy rainfall in Nippes and Sud departments led to flooding on 27 February, killing at least 13 people and causing the temporary evacuation of 3,428 others." 4 Mar Day 52 Situation Report #26: The Government and humanitarian actors are coordinating to determine humanitarian needs in Nippes and Sud departments following floods on 27 February.

**9 Mar Day 57 Situation Report #27:** "With the early on- set of rains, shelter and sanitation remain the most urgent priorities; the distribution window for agricultural inputs has been reduced significantly by rain and resulting landslides in the earthquake-affected areas." "Government figures show a steady rise in reported cases of suspected malaria. This is to be expected during the current season and considering the conditions of people living in close quarters in the spontaneous settlements."

**11 Mar Day 59 Situation Report #28** "Preparation work is starting on two sites, Villages Des Oranges and Tabarre 2, identified by the Government for the relocation of displaced persons from other high-risk settlement sites." Situation Report #28: "Two months into the humanitarian response, more than 4.3 million people have received food assistance, 1.2 million people are receiving daily water distributions, and more than 300,000 children and adults have been vaccinated." "An estimated 494,600 children under five and 197,840 pregnant and lactating women have been affected by this disaster. All are considered at risk of malnutrition and need to be targeted in blanket supplementary feeding."

"Many trucks delivering water are not chlorinated. Reports from primary health providers show insufficient quantities of water for hygiene purposes. Many smaller settlements are underserved by humanitarian assistance."

**15 Mar Day 63 Situation Report #29** There is an increase in reports of Gender-Based Violence (GBV) cases; MINUSTAH, UNPOL and the Haitian National Police have joined forces to patrol, monitor and evaluate security issues related to GBV and Child Protection in IDP camps in PAP and Léogâne. "Two months after the earthquake, official figures from DPC states that an estimated 222,517 people died and another 310,928 were injured." Situation Report #29: "As of 15 March, 433 sites (including spontaneous and transitional) with a total population of 682,693 individuals or

132,383 families have been identified in the PAP area and some communes in Jacmei" There has been coordination of 314 health partners to aid government efforts. Eight cluster subgroups have been established: health care and mobile clinics, hospital and trauma care, health information management, reproductive health, mental health and psychological support, disabilities, medical supplies, early warning of communicable diseases and reproductive health."

**19 Mar Day 67 Situation Report #30**    "There are 460 sites with a total population of 1,170,000 individuals in PAP." Situation Report #30: "The continuing in- crease in both the number of camps and the size of existing camps is proving quite challenging for implementing agencies. Anecdotal evidence suggests that a percentage of these increases are persons not directly affected by the earthquake." "DPC reports 40,000 displaced persons from earthquake- affected areas residing with host families in the North department... hosting arrangements have placed considerable economic strain on households..."

302,000 children have been displaced to other departments, with an additional 720,000 children affected by the earth-quake but remaining in their home communities. Of this figure, 309,500 children are currently living in spontaneous temporary settlement sites, which lack basic social services."

**24 Mar Day 72 Situation Report #31**    There is an increasing number of reports detailing tensions between displaced persons located on private land and land- owners. Some cases have resulted in forceful evictions from the land. "The Post-Disaster Needs Assessment findings reveal that the total value of damage and losses caused by the earth- quake is estimated at US$7.8 billion (US$4.3 billion represents physical damage and US$3.5 billion are economic losses). The damage and losses are the equivalent of more than 120% of the 2009 gross domestic product (GDP)." Situation Report #31: "Following heavy rains in Haiti last week, the DPC states that no damage to infrastructure or loss of life has been reported." "While Transitional Shelter programs have started in parts of the affected area; obtaining agreement on land remains a key obstacle to speedy response." "Many patients trans-ported to the Dominican Republic for healthcare after the earthquake now need transportation back to Haiti. The ICRC and IOM will likely assist in coordinating repatriation. . . . Mental health problems have increased since the earthquake. With only 24 psychiatrists in the country, the lack of mental healthcare is more acute than ever. . . . Sanitation and hygiene remain top priority, particularly in the spontaneous settlement sites, where sanitation remains inadequate."

**31 Mar Day 79 Situation Report #32:** "A large portion of emergency shelters constructed will require strengthening for the rainy season....

Lack of certainty regarding land tenure, potential length of stay and ultimate ownership continues to be of concern throughout the affected areas: both for relocation of priority sites and for planning of transitional shelters." "From 28 February to 20 March, 17 malaria cases, 12 dengue fever cases and 4 tuberculosis cases have been recorded within the zone of intervention which has 25 first aid units and 3 hospitals. Over last week, 3 new cases of malaria have been detected in Fond Parisien and the cases of dengue continue to rise.

**11 Apr Day 90 Situation Report #33** "The International Donors' Conference Towards a New Future for Haiti, at the UN headquarters in New York, yielded more than US$9 billion for Haiti's reconstruction.... Of this amount, about US$5.3 billion was pledged for the next 18 months to begin Haiti's path to longterm recovery."

Situation Report #33: "Figures from the latest Displacement Tracking Matrix (DTM) identified 1,373 settlement sites in PAP, Jacmel, Léogâne, Petit and Grande Goâve, which was considerably higher than initial estimates. Of these identified sites, only 289 had Camp Management agencies present, thus registering an overall coverage rate of 21%. Some 411,090 households (2,090,877 individuals) are estimated to be displaced."

1. Violence. The impact of the earthquake on people was characterized by direct trauma caused by the collapse of structures. In subsequent days, injuries occurred in traffic accidents, demonstrations, robbery and assault during transport and delivery of aid, and in particular, there was an

alarming increase in rape and gender-based violence in camps and temporary settlements. During the 90 days of this study there was a noted fear of civil unrest, with demonstrations and mass protests, primarily controlled by the MINUSTAH.

2. Isolation and displacement. The impact of the earthquake on the physical structure of the Port-au-Prince airport and port, and the obstruction of roads by debris generated extreme hardships in terms of access and mobilization within the most affected areas, aggravated by the unusual increase in traffic, by air, land, and sea. Simultaneously, a significant number of the population (estimated at more than 600,000 people) left the affected areas to other regions within the country.

3. Mortality figures. During the first 10 days of the aftermath an increasing number of deaths were estimated, stabilizing at 112,000. On 2 February, with the decline of international aid, the media compared Haiti's earthquake to the 2004 Indian Ocean tsunami, which immediately generated a public statement by the Prime Minister, almost doubling the official figures. The Directorate of Civil Protection (DPC) held to the original figures indicating that they would review them, and two weeks later indicated that 222,570 deaths were recorded. Thus the Haiti figure outnumbers the death toll from the Indian Ocean tsunami (220,000 deaths). This situation is similar to what happened after Hurricane Mitch in 1998, when the international community focused on the tragedy caused by the Casitas Volcano flash floods in Nicaragua

with 1,212 deaths, diverting attention from the situation in Honduras. The reaction of the Honduras government was evident: the death toll rose suddenly from 334 to 6,600, a number that was repeated until it was finally accepted in the international data systems.

4.  Change in health care needs. In the first two weeks, trauma care demanded nearly all the attention of the few remaining health services and all the health teams deployed to Haiti. The provision of water services, energy, and waste collection in health centers was a challenge for health authorities. Following the initial period, there was a marked decrease in demand for earthquake-related trauma care, but an important increase in demand for general medical care. Two months after the earthquake, the health information system detected an increase in mental health problems, malaria, and dengue fever.

5.  Environmental health deterioration. The poor sanitation conditions prior to the event, together with the high concentration of people in camps, the difficulties in the provision of potable water, inadequate systems of excreta disposal and waste collection, disruption in the regular health services, the onset of the rainy season, and the remarkably difficult logistical conditions in Haiti demanded a massive mobilization to prevent outbreaks of communicable diseases by the health authorities and the international community. But there was a risk factor that did not get any attention: the arrival

to the island of thousands of individuals from different parts of the world who could introduce a communicable disease to the island. Nine months after the quake the first cases of cholera were detected. The disease was caused by Vibrio cholerae serogroup O1, serotype Ogawa, a strain found in South Asia.

# LIST OF ACRONYMS

AECID     Agencia Española de Cooperación Internacional para el Desarrollo

(Spanish Agency for International Development Cooperation)
CARICOM Caribbean Community

CCCM     Camp Coordination and Camp Management

CDC     Centers for Disease Control and Prevention (United States)

CDEMA Caribbean Disaster Emergency Management Agency

CERF     United Nations Central Emergency Response Fund

DANA     Damage Assessment and Needs Analysis

ERC     Emergency Relief Coordinator (United Nations)

EU     European Union

FAO     Food and Agricultural Organization of the United Nations

FFH     Foreign Field Hospital

FMT        Foreign Medical Team

Groupe URD Groupe Urgence-Réhabilitation-Développement

HHS        Health and Human Services (United States, Department of)

HQ         Headquarters

IASC       Inter-Agency Standing Committee

ICRC       International Committee of the Red Cross

IDP        Internally displaced person

IEC        INSARAG External Classification

IFRC       International Federation of Red Cross and Red Crescent
Societies

IHRC       Interim Haiti Recovery Commission

IHR        International Health Regulations

INSARAG    International Search and Rescue Advisory Group

IRA        Initial Rapid Assessment

LRRD    Linking Relief, Rehabilitation, and Development

LSS    Logistics Support System

MINUSTAH Mission des Nations Unies pour la Stabilisation en Haïti (United Nations Stabilization Mission in Haiti)

MOH    Ministry of Health (also MoH)

MSF    Médecins Sans Frontières (Doctors without Borders)

MSPP    Ministère de Santé Publique et Population

(Haitian Ministry of Health)

NGO    Nongovernmental organization

OAS    Organization of American States

OCHA    Office for the Coordination of Humanitarian Affairs (UN)

PAHO    Pan American Health Organization

PDNA    Post-Disaster Needs Assessment

PROMESS    Programme de Médicaments Essentiels

*Jeff Benjamin*

(Essential Medicines Program in Haiti)

RINAH    Rapid Initial Needs Assessment for Haiti

SOPs    Standard Operating Procedures

SUMA    Supply Management System

UN    United Nations

UNAIDS  United Nations Program on HIV/AIDS

UNDAC  United Nations Disaster Assessment and Coordination

UNDSS  United Nations Department of Safety and Security

UNICEF  United Nations Children's Fund

USAID  United States Agency for International Development

USGS    United States Geological Survey

WASH    Water, Sanitation, and Hygiene

WB        World Bank

WFP      World Food Programme (UN)

WHO     World Health Organization

# AUTHOR

# JEFF BENJAMIN

### Edited

### By

### Devika Matabadal

# #BELIEVE

Yeshua I will praise thee with my whole heart

Dedicated with love to my 3 sons

Dimarco Benjamin

Giovanni Benjamin

Juergen Benjamin

# HISTORY 1

Her name was Itao; she was the daughter of Tunga, chief of the Taino. Her breasts were full, her hips strong and wide and she was tall in comparison to other girls in the village. Two elders of the tribe braided her with long soft coconut palms as her hair glistened in the sun like long threads of gold. She sat playing with the black rock around her neck, given to her by her father.

Life was good in the village, chief Tunga had made peace with the other tribes, and Itao was set to marry Kupa, son of Aluwa. The men had gone fishing early that morning in the Ozama River. Slung across their shoulders as they walked through the village were fresh fish, green bananas and a young boar. The slow beat of the bamboo rods filled the air.

Later that evening, the men began to drink wine made from the root of the yucca plant. The women filled the pit with stones and cotton wood. The crackling fire spat out the earth like fireworks, as they wrapped the boar in young conuco leaves and placed it at the bottom of the pit. A top layer of stones and banza wood was placed over the boar and then the fish wrapped in the banana leaves as the final layer. At night fall the boar was taken out the pit and the feast laid out for the village. The men fought each other in tribal ritual customs; bloodied and bruised they drank wine until all was quiet.

The still of the morning was broken by the shrill cry of Sawkinay, she screamed as she ran through the village pointing to the horizon.

"The gods are coming ...The Gods are coming...The gods are coming"

There was fear in the village as they scanned the horizon.

Three great ships sat on the horizon, the Pinta the Nina and the Santa Maria.

Tunga shook his head in disbelief the gods had come in honor of Itao's marriage he told the village. They gathered gifts and prepared food for their arrival.

Christopher Columbus and his men saw the natives on the beach. "Savages" they whispered amongst themselves. They were well armed and they were sure the savages would be no match for them. They loaded their muskets and headed to shore. But Cristopher was amazed as they were presented with roasted fish and gifts.

The Indians called the Island Aiyti, land of big mountains. The Spaniards observed some of the villagers with gold ornaments and were eager to find out where they came from. They questioned where they found the gold and Tunga soon learned that these men were no gods but were ordinary men. They were greedy men from another land in search of gold. The villagers told Columbus there was a great

Chief on the other side of the Island who had lots of gold. Columbus was eager to meet this great Chief and soon he began to trade with all the Tribes, the Magua, Marien, Xaragua, Maguana and Higuey, that inhabited the island.

Columbus soon met Guacanagari, Chief of the Maguana, who told Columbus the Island of Baneque was rich in gold. Columbus became obsessed with the idea of finding the Island of Baneque. So he became a close friend to chief Guacanagari. He was eager to return to Spain for more men and supplies to find Baneque, the Island of gold and just before Christmas he set sail for Spain.

On the night of December 24th, the Santa Maria became stuck on a sandbar and was destroyed by a storm. Chief Guacanagari rescued Columbus and his men and assisted in bringing parts of the ship and its supplies to shore to build a small forth. Columbus returned to Spain leaving behind Luís de Torre, Diego de Araña and thirty nine of his other men.

His orders to the men were to collect as much gold as possible and await his return. Tunga had become increasingly disgusted with his guests hunger for gold and the village girls. Their diseases were killing his people, they were like parasites. Tunga called a meeting with Chief Guacanagari and his brother and they all agreed the men with the white skin was bad.

Although Chief Guarcanagari did not agree to Tunga's actions, he assured Tunga he would not intervene and that he would stay on his side of the island. When the moon was full, and the North Star was brightest in the sky, Tunga sat down with the village warriors and formulated his plan. They waited for when the moon was smallest in the sky, Itao and the village women made a great feast in honor of the men with the white skin. That night the stars lit up the night like fireworks. The Orionids meteor showers filled the sky. If the great turtle moved, this would be the sign the gods had approved. The Orionid meteor showers were on full display, with about twenty meteor showers per hour. The great Turtle was moving fast this year, this was a good sign. Chief Guarcanagari looked into the night sky and saw the movement of the Great Turtle and he knew this was good.

The guests were given much of the wine from the yucca plant and they drank to their hearts delight, feasting and enjoying the gifts of gold bestowed upon them. They groggily returned to their camp and went to bed. As they slept, the warriors moved stealthily in the night. They first barred the big wooden gates from the outside so no one could escape. They then blocked the doors of each home so no one could get out. Tunga had them soak the walls of the homes in coconut and palm oil and each warrior then lit a branch and placed it next to each wall and left the camp.

Bright red and orange flames leapt, as thick clouds of smoke rose into the air. The scent of hot roasted flesh filled their nostrils. The fire could be seen for miles. Chief Guarcanagari watched from the other side of the Island as the blaze engulfed the camp. Tunga knew the white beast would return, but he had prepared for their arrival. He moved his tribe deep into the mountains where the great river ran the fastest. When Columbus returned he was enraged, the entire settlement was gone. He could find no trace of any survivors. His men and the settlement were a pile of ash and burnt bones. As Columbus buried them, he vowed revenge on the natives.

Armed with seventeen ships and fifteen hundred men, Columbus searched for survivors but knew they had all perished. He embarked on his mission and moved swiftly with his men. He enslaved most of the tribal Indians, and those that resisted were killed. They laid claim to the entire Island on behalf of Spain and Queen Isabella and named it "Hispaniola". In the ensuing years disease wiped out most of the native Indians. This was due to the spread of cholera in Europe during the 1500's which was brought to the Island. This pandemic wiped out most of the tribes. The Cholera was unstoppable the continued migration of the Spaniards and seasonal warming of coastal waters made the infection rampant throughout the Island.

The Indians thought bathing in the sea would cleanse them from the foul disease brought by the white man, but they were wrong. Little did they know the transmission was occurring almost exclusively through their contaminated food and water. In addition they didn't know cholera was a saltwater organism, and its primary habitat was the marine ecosystem where it lived in association with plankton. They were doomed to die, as the hot season came around the disease became worse. The warm weather caused seasonal increases in the number of organisms associated with algal blooms. Tunga kept his distance as he watched from afar; he did not know why his people were dying but he knew there were two factors, the White Devil and their disease. His people died by the thousands, and when the outbreak ended, less than 1000 of his people remained.

Tunga kept moving his tribe to different mountains on the Island avoiding the white devil. His tribe was now 500. He cursed the day the Spaniards had landed on his shore. They were not gods; they were the dark ones, who came at night for the flesh of the young, and the blood of the old.

Soon more ships came, men calling themselves pirates traded with Tunga's people for gold, food, silver and cloth. For the first time Tunga and his men saw the people with dark skin. Their skin was black and their lips were thick. They worked on the pirate's ship, and some were bound by chains and whipped by the white devil when they were drunk. Tunga treated them well for they were men like him. They reminded him of his people when the white devil first came, how they were enslaved, and he knew the same faith had befallen the men of the dark skin.

Tunga was old now, many moons had passed. Kupa and Itao had made many sons and many daughters. His time was drawing near.

Soon some of the men with the dark skin began to ask to live with him. Tunga was fearful, he told them he would take care of their children but he was unwilling to fight or engage the white man. They agreed the time for change would come soon, when all men would be equal, if it was the will of the gods.

More of the men with the white skin came to Ayiti. Soon they were fighting amongst themselves for the Island. As the years passed, Tunga's tribe began to split after he died. Kupa and Itao moved north closer to the sea. Some members of the tribe moved and set up villages elsewhere, trading with English, Dutch, and French pirates who had established bases on the island's abandoned northern and western coasts.

When Akina was born, Kupa gave him the black rock of his ancestors. Akina was strong and a warrior. Akina was like Tunga, a visionary, a leader, and as the years passed he became more powerful and began leading his people.

By then, the French had taken control of the island, but the Frenchmen were just as uncivilized as the Spaniards. Akina's people were now trading with the newly established French West Indian Company. The French showed a small measure of respect to the indigenous tribes and in return the tribes maintained their distance from the cities and did not allow runaway slaves into their camps. The French West Indian Company encouraged Akina to have his people grow and cultivate tobacco, indigo, cotton and cacao on the fertile northern plain where they lived.

Akina's oldest son was Taqueo. Taqueo was out picking coconuts for the village, his body glistened with sweat. He was tall and lean, and his dark skin was burnt from the hot sun. Taqueo pulled his hair into a pony tail, picked up the string with the black rock, and placed it back around his neck. The rock had belonged to his father, his grandfather and who knows how many before him.

He was not a slave, he was a Taino and he was free. Oh! But how he longed to walk the streets of Saint Domingue - the city the white man had built. He stood on the hill side looking at the city from a distance, "one day" he said to himself "one day".

Then he lost his balance and fell. It felt like the earth was shaking. He shook his head in disbelief and stood up, I must have been in the sun to long, he thought. Then it happened again, this time he fell flat on his back. He grabbed his machete and began to run towards his village. He looked back at the sea, the water was moving backwards, and the waves were all going in the wrong direction. As he arrived in his village, he saw that the elders had made everyone pack their bags and make for the highest part of the mountain. They were not close to the water, but the elders spoke of gwo dlo (The big water).

From the highest peak of Morne La Selle they watched as the sea returned. It was the biggest wave Taqueo had ever seen, Gwo Dlo had come to cleanse the land, the old people said. When Gwo Dlo left there was nothing standing, no building, no roads, no homes, nothing. Taqueo changed his mind, he no longer longed for the thrill of the cities of the white men. His people, his life was perfect. After Gwo Dlo was gone, the white man brought more blacks as many had been killed. They worked them twice as hard now, and Saint-Domingue began to thrive once more, sugar and coffee were in abundance.

One day, whilst exploring to close to the city, Taqueo was startled by a woman on a horse. She was not black, but she was not white, she was the color of dried deer skin, pale with a hint of brown and green eyes.

"Hey what's your name?" she yelled.

But he knew better, and quickly began to make his way back into the hills.

"Poor soul" she said in French, "probably has no idea" she said aloud.

Taqueo wanted to scream back at her,

"Yes! I understand, I speak all three languages of the white man" but he moved swiftly back into the hills and as he looked back, two other riders joined the 'deer lady'.

Taqueo retuned daily in search of the 'deer lady' and soon weeks turned into months, and then his people were told there was a war between the French and the English. The war made Saint- Domingue that much more important, it had become the "Pearl of the Carribean". It was now 1767, and they were exporting 72 million pounds of raw sugar and 51 million pounds of refined sugar, one million pounds of indigo and two million pounds of cotton. It was now one of the most important French Colonies producing 40 percent of all the sugar and 60 percent of all coffee consumed in Europe.

Taqueo's people were smart, the coffee that grew wild in the hills, they harvested the beans and traded with the whites for the resources they needed. It was actually on one of these trips he saw the 'deer lady' with green eyes. She was making a receipt for his father.

"Vous ai-je vu auparavant"(Have I seen you before?) She said in French almost to herself.

"Non, vous ne l'avez pas" (No you have not he responded back in French)

She appeared stunned and their eyes locked for a brief moment.

His father nodded to her and they left.

The last thing he wanted was for his father to know he had been close to the City because he knew his father would be angry,

"never do we speak back to the whites" his father told him "never". "What possessed you Taqueo?" his father shouted, Taqueo did not respond. It was the way of the Taino. He nodded and continued the walk.

The next week he went back to the hill overlooking the City but she was not there. He continued to return every week for two months. Then one day as he was about to leave, he heard pounding hoofs. It was her again, and their eyes met.

"I knew it was you" she said him.

She had so many questions to ask him about his people, and his way of life. For months they met on the hill, day after day, they would sit and talk. She was what the French called Gens de couleur (people of color). Her father was the Chancellor of Saint-Domingue.

The City, she told him had the largest and wealthiest free population of color in the Caribbean, and the mixed-race communities in Saint-Domingue were not slaves. They worked, owned homes and were free. Her father had implemented a semi-official institution of placate. By this system, the children of whites and slaves were free people and could inherit property. They were a half breed a sort of class of "mulattos" with property and some with wealthy fathers. They occupied a middle status or stratosphere between African slaves and French men.

"Have you heard of Physics?" she asked him.

"No" He replied

"Well me, you, us, are like the air. Well mixed throughout the atmosphere here on this mountain top. All is not physically uniformed but each is vital to the survival of the Island. Like when it rains, or as we get higher it gets colder, the different variations in temperature and pressure with altitude, defines the atmospheric layers. In physics it is called stratosphere.

The boundaries between these layers are defined by abrupt changes in temperature, because temperature generally falls with increasing altitude and it gets higher with decreasing altitude" and then she kissed him.

They were careful, not all the French slave owners embraced her father's system, there were those that would kill him and have the old way return. Some of the slave owners enacted discriminatory laws. Statutes that forbade gens de couleur from taking up certain professions, marrying whites, wearing European clothing, carrying swords or firearms in public, or attending social functions where whites were present. However, these regulations only affected certain communities; it had become an Island divided by class and the color of your skin.

The population of the gen de couleur continued to grow. They purchased land, and many accumulated substantial holdings, some even became slave-owners. They had been seeing each other now for over a year. Then one day she came to him troubled, he looked into her eyes and he knew something was wrong. "Run she told him, run far from here. I am pregnant with our child and I don't know what will become of us."

"I will not run" he told her. "My name is Taqueo; I am the great great grandson of Tunga, Chief of the Taino." He wanted her to come and live with his people, but he knew she would not.

"Ms. Jacqueline DuPont what will you name our son" he asked smiling at her.

She was angry at him for not wanting to run, she was scared, but he made her laugh.

"Rene DuPont, because, you sir, do not have a last name"

she screamed half laughing half crying. He held her in his arms

"they will never catch me, and your father will never hurt you," he told her "and I like the name". She so wanted to believe him, but she knew differently.

They stopped seeing each other so frequently, and they started changing their locations. He also stopped going into town. Her class of people now owned one-third of the plantation property and one-quarter of the slaves on the Island. They were also the largest producers of coffee on the Island. The hillsides where they lived were the most fertile soil on the Island and the temperature was perfect for the growth of coffee which thrived under their care.

As the wealth on the Island grew, so did the amount of slaves. The numbers hovered close to 1,000,000 estimated African slaves, this accounted for a third of the entire Atlantic slave trade. They were receiving close to more than 40,000 slaves a year. But the brutality and inhumanity and inability to maintain slave numbers without constant resupply from Africa meant doom for the Island. The white population was 32,000, the slave population combined with the gens de couleur was closer yet to one and a quarter million (1,250,000).

Taqueo's father was becoming increasingly concerned that the hills were becoming infested with runaway slaves; he forbade them from joining his people. A fight with the French was not what he wanted.

The first time Taqueo saw his baby he was thrilled, he looked exactly like him, just lighter in complexion with green eyes. Their visit was brief, but he was so excited. This was his son, his child. Jacqueline explained to him the baby would have to be blessed in traditional customs. African tradition and culture remained strong amongst the slaves. The Island was now full of priest and priestesses who practiced the old African religion of Voodoo but now combined it with Catholic liturgy rituals, beliefs and practices of Guinea, Congo and Dahomey.

The Slave traders brought slaves from hundreds of different tribes, their languages often incomprehensible but their spiritual belief was pretty much a replica of each other.

In an act of true friendship she had confessed her relationship to Mr. Jacques Belluve, her childhood friend and a confidant. Jacques was fond of men and saw her pregnancy as a coup, a guise to continue his lifestyle, and so could Jacqueline. He told her his proposal and before anyone could question their rash decision they were married. Jacques asked Jacqueline's father for their son to carry his last name DuPont, so the name of the DuPont's could continue, her father was ecstatic.

Rene DuPont hung upside down over a wooden barrel of black water by his mother. Taqueo was in the hills watching. He now openly visited the home of Mr. Jacques Belluve. As the broker for the sale of coffee, it was Taqueo's job to bring the coffee to Mr. Belluve, and when the loads were heavy, which most of the times they were, he would stay the night in the room where the coffee was stored. This was the story which was told to those who asked.

Madame Laveau emerged from the shadows, took the child from the hands of the mother, and dropped the child into the black water letting out and eerie screech. Taqueo was stunned, he would not stand idly by as the crazy woman killed his son. But in the blink of an eye his son emerged from the black depths of the wooden drum screaming at the top of his lungs. Ms. Laveau held the child up to the sky and muttered some words to her god. His son was quickly wrapped in warm blankets and the ceremony began, Jacqueline then took the child inside.

A large circle was drawn in the dirt with an inner ring. Two young goats were brought to Ms. Laveau to be sacrificed; their necks were slit open, as some of the blood from each goat was placed in a calabash. The goats were held upside down and their blood made to fill the inner circle. Ms. Laveau stood in the inner circle as the group danced through the night. The beating of the drums and chanting continued for hours. Ms. Laveau then brought a black bottle with what appeared to be the root of a plant. The contents were poured into the calabash gourd mixed and each person was required to take a gulp of the potion. Taqueo was happy, watching from afar, that he was not part of the ritual.

One by one, minute by minute the drumming slowed, soon the dancers fell to the ground convulsing in spasms. The drums kept beating as they frothed at the mouth, but miraculously no one crossed the circle or fell into it. Ms. Laveau stood in the circle for what seemed to be hours.

Maybe he had fell asleep or passed out but it was morning and he was in the same spot from the night before. He stood up there was work to be done he had to get back to his village. He had a weird dream, he couldn't remember drinking the potion or meeting the people, his perch was from behind a rock at the side of the hill where the ritual was performed.

Taqueo dreamt the lady in the circle flew to him, took his arms, that of his son, his father, his grandfather and they were all standing in front of what appeared to be a burning tree. His great grandfather who was the father of Chief Tunga stood before them. He took the black rock from around his neck, placed it in the fire, and branded each of them on the back of their necks with the rock. The dream seemed so real. He hoped Jacqueline and Rene were fine. He got back to the tribe and spoke to his father about the dream. He then went to his hut and cleaned himself. As he poured the water over his head he screamed out in pain, the water touched the burnt scar on the back of his neck.

# HISTORY 2

Life was changing on the Island, the slaves who escaped formed communities of maroons and started raiding plantations on the Island. Jacqueline came to him with the news, but he already knew. That war was about to break out on the island and things were going to change. Some of the farmers had enacted the code noir, which accorded certain human rights to slaves and responsibilities to the master, who were obliged to feed, clothe and provide for the general well-being of his slaves. The code noir also sanctioned corporal punishment in its harshest forms. The purpose was to put down rebellions and instill fear in the hearts of men.

The retaliations for the raids were swift and brutal. They hung those captured with their heads downward; they tied them up in sacks and threw them in the Artibonite River, crucified them on planks, buried them alive, crushed them in mortars and made them consume feces. Some were beaten until their flesh was raw and then left in the open on ant hills, others tied to trees in the swamps to be devoured by wild beasts and insects. A favorite of the cane farmers whose farms were burnt was to take the captured slaves, prepare a boiling cauldron of cane syrup and boil them alive.

Taqueo watched as they captured six slaves, both men and women. They were placed inside barrels which were studded with spikes, and rolled them down the mountainside into the abyss smashing into the sea. They chased them with their dogs, man eating-dogs, who tore at their flesh and ate them to the bone.

Ms. Laveau's adopted son Makandal who arrived on the island from Guinea became the worst marauder. He paid savagery with savagery. He was a Voodoo Priest Houngan; he united many of the different maroon bands and the runaways.

Jacqueline felt unsafe, she had moved into the City with her father. Six years of continuous war had passed. Rene was growing into a fine boy. Taqueo had not seen him in years, he was now battled, scarred and wary. He had fathered three more children. Rene was his first born and he thought of him often.

For six years the war raged on. The marauders staged terrible raids evading capture by the French soldiers whilst killing over 10,000 people. Makandal preached and eye for and eye a tooth for a tooth. For every slave beaten or killed he promised the heads of ten whites would fall. One night Makandal went to the damn with his men to poison the drinking water of the plantation owners and he was captured. It was a victory for the French soldiers. They tied him to a stake in the middle of the public square of Cap-Francais and burnt him alive.

After the capture of Makandal, things settled down on the Island. Rene DuPont was becoming a young man, very French but different in every respect. He was tall and handsome, his hair was soft as silk, and he had the most piercing green eyes. His skin was tan, a golden hue like a cross between the old Taino Indians and white. He was a Prince in the City, and even the white slave masters noticed him. When he was twenty, a man came to their house late one night. His mother met the man in the dark and whispered. When she came back inside she was crying, he later learned that night that his real father, Taqueo had died. But Taqueo had left something he wanted him to have.

That night, he sat and spoke to his mother long into the night. She told him the reason he looked like a prince was because he was the true prince of Haiti. His father was the last of the great Chiefs that once ruled Haiti. His father was Taqueo, the man who delivered coffee to his step-father when he was a boy. Rene remembered Taqueo; he was smart and strong and was always kind to him, bringing him gifts when he was a young boy. He taught him to make boats from the tree of the sandbox, to float in the streams when it rained. He taught him to whistle and make kites out of brown parchment.

Rene went into his room and came out with the wooden knife he and his father had made when he was a boy. Taqueo carved it from a piece of wood they had found. How patiently his father sat that day and carved him his little wooden knife. Now he understood why the man who brought the coffee when he was a boy was so nice to him. His mother told him his father had died from yellow fever. His mother placed the black rock that belonged to his father around his neck. As he looked carefully at the rock, he observed that it was no rock but appeared to be a black gem-like crystal, emerald, diamond who knows but it was no ordinary rock. It had belonged to all the great kings of Haiti now it was his. That night he did not sleep. What did all this mean? Why him? Why now?

As Rene began to understand his role on the Island, he found ways to break the cycle of slavery. He used the new revolution taking place in France to open debates about how new revolutionary laws would apply to Saint-Domingue. But the old families were unwilling to grant the free men of color citizenship. Rene, along with other free men of color, led a revolt against the old establishment. They felt all men should be free but at the very least, the freed men of color were entitled too French citizenship as well.

Ten days before the fall of Bastille, in July 1789, the French National Assembly had voted to seat six delegates from Saint-Domingue. Rene DuPont and his group unsuccessfully petitioned the white planter delegates to support mulatto claims for full civil and political rights.

Through the efforts of a group he formed called Societe d Amis des Noirs, he petitioned the National Assembly, and in March 1790, the National Assembly granted full civic rights to the gen de couleur. Rene met with them in Saint Domingue to secure the promulgation and implementation of this decree. He went to Cap-Français and petitioned the royal governor, but the Comte de Peynier refused Rene's demands.

Rene was furious, but he knew time was all he had. He would have to wait until the time was right, the rest of his group was not quite so patient. They wanted recognition or war with the slave owners. Rene reminded them that they all had families and it was important to preserve the peace and let diplomacy run its course. Unknown to Rene, Ogé and Jean-Baptiste Chavennes, two of his closest friends and veterans of the Siege of Savannah during the American Revolution attempted to attack Cap-Français. The rest of the gen de couleur chose to side with Rene and refused to arm or free their slaves, Rene knew it was suicide. Ogé and Jean-Baptiste Chavennes attack was defeated by a force of white militia and black volunteers. Afterwards Ogé and Jean-Baptiste Chavennes fled to Hinche, the Spanish part of the island. They were however captured and returned to the French authorities, and both Ogé and Jean-Baptiste Chavennes were executed.

Rene was now married with children; he lived with his wife Antoinette and his mother Jacqueline. They were sleeping when they felt the first rumbling, then the house shook a second time

"head for the hills" he cried, "Antoinette get the girls!" as he quickly grabbed all their valuables. It was dark, he could not see but he followed his mother Jacqueline as she was familiar with the hills. They kept slipping and sliding; it was a massive shake, the land gave way beneath their feet. "Stay together" Jacqueline told him. They could hear voices in the dark, others were climbing the mountain.

After an hour they got to the lookout where she and his father would meet.

"This very spot is where your father survived his first earthquake" she told Rene, "it was fifty years ago."

Then they heard the screams and smelled the saltwater, the eerie sound of building and trees being washed away. They were safe, high and dry. Jacqueline and Antoinette unfolded the blankets and the children slept.

When dawn broke it was a mess, the water had not yet receded. The earthquake was strong it had destroyed and leveled all the buildings between Lake Miragoâne and Petit-Goâve. To the west of the Island everything was destroyed. The plain of the Cul-de-Sac, a rift valley under Port-au-Prince that extended eastwards into the Dominican Republic experienced extensive soil liquefaction, and a canyon had developed. The entire village of Croix des Bouquets had sunk and there were bodies floating in the water. The tsunami had come ashore along the Gulf of Gonâve as far in as 10 miles.

There was no time to fight each other, rebuilding the Island was hard work. Many of the slaves had escaped into the hills and a sickness had started. They claimed it was tainted meat from the traders, but those who didn't eat the meat also became sick. The heat, the stench of rotting corpse and strewn garbage filled the air. When his mother became ill he knew it was the end, she died 9 days later. They advised drinking rum in large quantities to stave of the delirium, but still they died. Then Antoinette got the sickness and she died.

He thought it was a matter of time but the girls survived. They were strong and smart and all he had left, he was lucky. When it was over the sickness had claimed 15,000 lives. The Island began to rebuild again, slowly Rene watched as the old way of life returned. Treatment of the slaves was even harsher now because the Island had to be rebuilt. That night, Rene rubbed the black diamond around his neck "what would my father have done?" he asked himself. Then he remembered a story Taqueo had told him as a boy. He was at the back of their house watching him unload coffee all by himself.

"Where are your friends?" Rene asked him. "Why does no one help you?"

"Ah but little Rene" he said in French "they do". "Who do you think picked all these coffee beans and how do you think they became dry and how did they get inside these bags? I have many friends and many people who work very hard. But my job is to protect my people and do all I can to make this a better place for my son who I love so dearly."

"Is your son a boy like me?" asked Rene. "Yes! A boy exactly like you!" replied Taqueo looking at Renee and smiling.

"Will you still let me ride your back like a horse until I'm old enough to get one and will your son be angry?"

"He will not be angry Rene, because you and he are one and the same and we don't ride horses. We ask their permission to carry us to our destination. We harm no living creature for pleasure but only out of the necessity of life, for this is our way, the way of my father and his father and me and now you." "When I grow up can I be like you and carry coffee and not harm animals?" asked Rene. "When you grow up, you will be smarter than me, stronger than me, and carry much more coffee than me little Rene."

"My daddy says when I grow up I will live in France" said Rene smiling at Taqueo. Taqueo replied sternly back to Rene "you were born on Ayiti were you not? This is your land is it not? Then here you must stay and become the best warrior for Ayiti, because this land belongs to you."

It was a cold rainy Monday August 22, 1791. Rene had Bosan ride to Alligator woods. Bosan arrived in Alligator woods around midnight. What he saw amazed him in the woods, gathered together were thousands of slaves. Dutty Boukman emerged from the shadows to receive the message; he nodded and smiled at Bosan. The he turned to the crowd and shouted "let the ceremony begin". The word from Rene was that the gens de couleur would support the revolution.

Dutty Boukman was from Xamayca, a British colonized Island. He was an enormous man, stood over six feet tall with big arms and the body of a warrior. He was also very loud and vociferous and the worst of all the appointed black slave commanders on the island. He worked them harder and treated them as bad as the white slave owners. But at night he was different, he herded in groups of slaves and taught them how to read and write. He also taught them Voodoo rituals. He was known as the most powerful Voodoo houngan on Xamayca with the ability to talk to the dead and bring spirits to life.

His British master soon learnt that he was not a commandeur, but a revolutionist who preached insurrection. He was tied to a tree and flogged, and his master told the slaves that Boukman would be taught a lesson and anyone who listened to him would be treated the same way. Left for dead tied to the tree.

His master awoke next morning to find Boukman working in the fields; his clothes tattered, but his body unmarked. The legend says that very day Boukman was sold to a passing French slave owner on his way to Saint Domingue. When asked if he could speak Boukman told his French owner. I can speak as well as read and write. It was then his new French owner decided his English nickname "Book Man" would be Boukman in French.

Their relationship did not last very long, Boukman escaped and began to organize all the escapees who lived in the mountains. He sent letters to all the Mambo's and all the other Houngans on the Island. He asked the gens de couleur for their support and when they did not respond he showed up at their homes. Boukman was somewhat of a bully, and if you didn't like the way he did things, then he threatened you spiritually or physically. The slaves loved him; the whites feared him, and the gens de couleur optimistically cautious.

As Rene returned home one evening, he was tying his horse when Boukman emerged from the shadows. "Mosuier Rene I have written you several letters and you have not responded what say you?"

"Coffee or tea?" replied Renee "my children may be asleep so please be quiet".

Boukman was taken aback and quickly said to Rene "my name is Boukman I am the Houngan who wrote to you".

"Yes!" replied Rene "and you came forty miles by foot to meet me and have been standing outside my farm on the hill since 4pm this evening. You must be hungry, would you like some dinner and did you say coffee or tea?"

"Coffee" said Boukman. "Mr. Boukman we do not know you, we have heard of you, but we do not know you and I speak for all the *gens de couleur.*"

"Many of us have immense wealth on this island and our families. You are a stranger in our midst. We have a lot materialistically to loose and little to gain. But believe it or not, that is not our main concern, though we hemorrhage internally for our brothers and sisters who are enslaved. Once we move forward on this, there is no turning back. Therefore it is important for us to trust who we are working with and victory has to be a must" said Rene.

Boukman knew Rene was no ordinary man he sensed it the minute they met.

"Who are you really Mr. DuPont? You represent gen de couleur but what do you want out of this?"

"Personally Mr. Boukman, I want nothing. I have all that I need right here on this farm, under this roof. But there are things on this Island that need to be healed, open wounds that are bleeding this tiny nation to death. I want these wounds healed and its people free, free from bloodshed, free from invaders, free so that my people can once more walk these lands and my children enjoy its prosperity and fruitfulness."

"But isn't that what we all want Mousier Rene? This too is my Island this too is mine."

Boukman was interrupted by Rene,

"No Boukman you are fighting for freedom and this is not your home. You were brought here against your will and if you could, you would gladly go back to your home. You want equality and the opportunity to be treated like a man. I am Taino; my father was the Chief of this Island and his father and his father before him. This is my home and I will die here just like I was born here, like my father and his father before him".

Rene took the black rock from his desk and placed it around his neck. He seldom wore it, now it was easily identifiable and its worth was said to be a King's ransom.

Boukman was stunned; the rumors existed even on Xaymaca. The one who possessed the eye of the Taino possessed the heart of its people. Deminán Caracaracol, the god from which all Taínos were descended it is believed had first possessed the black eye. The story goes, the Taíno were descended from the union of Deminán Caracaracol, and a female turtle. Who dove to the bottom of the ocean and returned with the eye of the world to lead the Taino people. The eye was safely guarded in a cave. But one day, there was a huge flood when a father murdered his son who was about to murder the father. The father put the son's bones into a calabash gourd and when the bones turned into a fish, the gourd broke. All the water of the world came pouring out and the eye was lost until the turtle brought the eye back to Deminán Caracaracol.

For the first time in his life Boukman was scared. He was not scared of the white man and he was not scared of gens de couleur or any slave. But tonight, he was scared of this man. He felt the power of the rock and he felt the power of Rene as he knew this was no ordinary man. Boukman hurriedly made his way out of the home of Rene. Letting him know on his way out, he would not attack until he had the blessings of the Taino people. Boukman told Rene he would not shed blood on this land until it was necessary as it was the way of the Taino.

Boukman was glad Rene had sent his blessings. Boukman painted his body in white chalk, Bois Caïman, the other houngan priest painted his body in red together with the mambo priestess, Cécile Fatiman, who painted her body black. Boukman prophesied that the slaves Jean François, Biassou, and Jeannot would be leaders of a resistance movement and they would free the slaves of Saint-Domingue.

Boukman called for the sacrifice of a black boar. As they began the rituals, Boukman began to ask for blessings. He called upon lwa, the various spirits of family members; the spirits of the major forces of the universe, good and evil. He called upon lwa to wreak havoc and destruction upon the earth. He called upon lwa to send messages by possessing the body of his people during the war. Boukman called upon the twins, a curious and rather mysterious set of forces of contradictories: good and evil, happy and sad to go forth and clear the path for victory and open their homes for death, so that the souls of the dead could welcome the living.

Boukman took heart of the boar, mixed it with the coup de poudre. Weak, drained, tired and delirious all three priests went into a trance. The others came forth drank the mixture and swore an oath to take revenge against their French oppressors. Then Boukman began to bow and pray to Deminán Caracaracol that he should cleanse the land of evil men. He prayed and made a pact with Deminán Caracaracol that if he blessed them with victory they would be indebted to him for cleansing the land of the Taino people.

The slaves had no idea who Deminán Caracaracol was and became very scared. Rumors spread that Boukman had made a pact with the devil to win their freedom. That week, 1800 plantations were burnt and 1000 slave masters killed. Boukman was happy things were going as planned. He commissioned the slaves to cast an iron boar to symbolize their sacrifices and struggle to commemorate the night the revolution began.

Rene was not fond of Boukman, and knew he could not lead a revolution or the slaves. He was inspirational, prone to rash decisions and volatile. He made a good captain, but he was not a leader. Renee needed to prep a leader, someone they could trust on all sides. But most of all, someone the slaves did not see as a master but as one of their own. He chose François Dominique Toussaint L'Ouverture. At the time François was a carriage driver, who was well respected; he had earned his freedom and was also someone the slaves looked up to. After earning his freedom, he rented a small farm where he lived with his family. Rene knew François could be trusted.

Francois was fifty years old, he was reasonable, a devout catholic who did not practice Voodoo. Having spent his life in slavery he was entering old age, but the revolution fired his passion and Rene knew if called he would answer the bell. Francois was well read; he would read books on Machiavelli and he loved his bible. His one weakness was his writing skills, but Rene would arrange so that most his ideas and thoughts could be dictated.

Rene prepared him for the next wave of the revolution, guiding Francois not to participate, condemn or take sides in the burning of plantations or the executions of the slave owners. That he should remain diplomatic and encourage the slaves to be organized. Rene told him the slaves must become militarily and politically organized and disciplined. He must become more political, stand his ground and resist outside pressures to return the Island to the old way. Francois was overjoyed, and embraced the opportunity to lead his people. He joined the revolution under the watchful eye of Rene. His first job in the revolution was to train a small military group that was assigned to him.

Three months into the war, Bosan returned with news to Rene. Boukman had been captured, and the slaves were in disarray. Rene knew it was time to act. Bosan told Rene the slaves who now occupied the eastern half of the Island were fighting several invading forces. The French were trying to reclaim the island, the Spanish who believed they were the rightful heir to the island and the English who saw every opportunity as a chance to gain more territory for the crown. Many of the slaves and new generals felt they should align themselves with the Spaniards on the Eastern part of the Island. But Rene had made it clear to Francois; the allegiance must be to France.

The French Legislative Assembly who had taken control of France sent Leger-Felicite Sonthonax to Saint Domingue as part of the Revolutionary Commission. Upon his arrival, he realized the only role France would play on the Island would be legislatively or as a colony of France. He sought dialogue with Francois on ways to stabilize the colony and enforce the social equality which was originally granted to free people of color by the National Convention of France.

Under the leadership of Francois Toussaint Louverture and his generals Jean-Jacques Dessalines and Henri Christophe, the Island seemed headed in the right direction. There were many battles, and it took a toll on Rene. He was weary, but he was continuously and increasingly maneuvering Francois and the Legislative Assembly to find common ground. His daughters were now grown, and when Francois successfully drove back the British in 1798 he became the de facto ruler of the Island.

Rene had problems of his own, his daughter Mychelle was with child. She was carrying the child of Jean-Jacque Dessalines, a known womanizer, and as Rene correctly predicted in his speech to the gens de couleur, a traitor.

Christophe was born on August 16th 1799, as he lay in his mother's arms Rene told the story of his father to both his daughters as they laid listening to him. It reminded him of the night the strange man came to his house and told his mother his father was dead. Why did he not tell the girls before- he had no idea. Their mother was white; they looked every bit French, but their blood ran a long line of Taino Indian blood, supposedly the very blood of Deminán Caracaracol. Josephina laughed as he told his story. She was his younger daughter and so much like him; sometimes he wished she was a boy.

"I know this story Papa" she said "and I know you are the heir to the Taino people".

Rene looked at her puzzled. "That's why the people called you the prince when you were younger. You wore the eye of Taino, you are the son of Taqueo, and your great great grandfather was Tunga. Even the whites know who you are Papa".

Rene was stunned; he turned to the girls and laughed. "And here I am all this time thinking I was called Prince because of my charm."

The very next day Josephina brought home a young French man who closely resembled Rene. "Papa this is my friend Felipe, his mother is Taino but his father is French."

Rene was intrigued, he liked Felipe. Soon Felipe was working with him in the business. When he and Josephina were married they named their first son Rene. His farm had come to life, little feet were everywhere.

It was now 3 years later, Francois was in control of all of Hispaniola after conquering Santo Domingo and proclaiming Abolition of slavery on the island. Peace had come to Ayiti, Rene was happy. Francois was careful not to proclaim full independence from France or seek revenge against the old slave masters. But France had a new leader, Napoleon Bonaparte, who despised the authoritarian rule of Francois. He had sent several decrees to Francois telling him to restore slavery in some form or fashion or face invasion. Francois responded by sending Napoleon Bonaparte cordial responses for dialogue and trade with the new colony. But Napoleon became incensed and sent a massive invasion force under his brother-in-law Charles Leclerc.

After he arrived, Leclerc joined forces with the whites on the Island and was able to gain back some territory for France.

When Dessalines called for a special meeting between Toussaint and Leclerc, Rene knew it was a trap and he warned Francois not to attend. But Francois felt it was in the best interest of all to negotiate a settlement and bring peace to the Island. Leclerc laid a trap and Francois was captured and taken back to France. Rene was devastated, he petitioned France to release Francois from Fort de Joux in the Jura Mountains, where the conditions were cold and harsh.

Soon after, Napoleon signed a law to maintain slavery where it had not yet disappeared, namely Martinique, Tobago and Saint Lucia. A confidential copy of this decree was sent to Leclerc, who was authorized to restore slavery in Saint-Domingue when the time was opportune. Napoleon also asked Leclerc to strip the *gens de couleur* of their newly won civil rights. Rene was aware of the document sent from France to Leclerc.

He reached out to the last of his people, some who still lived in the hills, the Taino Indians. He asked their participation in a coup d'état. Rene sent a message to be delivered to the free slaves. The message was to be delivered to each farm where there were slaves and to each free man of color. Rene had received a response from Napoleon when he petitioned for Francois to be moved from Fort De Joux. He had asked Napolen to treat Francois like he would had he captured Royalty, to treat him well and move him to better suited housing.

Napoleon declined writing back that Rene did not have the authority to ask for such a request when he was barely a free man himself.

Rene replicated Napoleon's seal in hot wax and sent several letters declaring the rights of the *gens de couleur* had been revoked and slavery under the code noir was to be enforced.

None of the original decrees from Napoleon made it to Leclerc. The day the ships landed they were burnt at the Port. There was now an all-out war; word had reached the slaves that their beloved Francois was dead. The Taino council asked for a meeting with Rene. When he arrived, an old Taino woman came out to meet him. She led him inside and placed him on a mat. She never said a word to him. She took the eye from around his neck and held his hand, he closed his eyes as she chanted and smoke filled the hut. It was hot, his eyes were burning, and his eyelids were heavy.

The next day, when he awoke, he was back on his farm. His daughters said he was brought home by two Taino men. He felt around his neck for the eye, it was still there. .

That night, he dreamt his ancestors said Deminán Caracaracol would cleanse the land of the invaders, he was standing in front of a burning tree with his father. As Rene got dressed that morning, he felt some soreness at the back of his neck. When he touched it, there was scar. For a while he was confused, but then he remembered how he got the scar. When the men were bringing him home they must have laid him on the eye which was caught on the back of his neck. The constant chaffing on the ride back to his farm must have bruised his neck. He refused to believe the dream was real.

This time, the war was the bloodiest Rene had ever seen. The war became a bloody struggle of atrocity and attrition. Britain declared war with France and Leclerc was replaced by Donatien Marie Joseph de Vimeur Vicomte de Rochambeau. Rochambeau was ruthless, and was sent to win the war at any cost. He sent word to Napoleon, in order to win the war he must kill 30, 000 Negroes. Napoleon gave him the go-ahead. He burnt alive 1000 prisoners in one day, hung 300, drowned 500, and tortured another 600 within the span of 48 hours. One night, at Port-Républican, he held a ball to which he invited the most prominent ladies from the *gens de couleur,* and at midnight, announced the death of their husbands.

But Dessalines, who had now taken charge, repaid his act of brutality with the same force. He captured 5 of his Generals and their wives and boiled them in cauldrons of molasses. Dessalines hung 500 captured French soldiers in one day and then as quickly as the atrocities started they stopped. Out of the sky came the rainy season and with it brought Yellow fever and Malaria, Cholera and Dysentery.

Within two months there was peace and the land was cleansed of the invaders. Over 20,000 soldiers were dead or lay dying. Leclerc returned from France to see what was taking place and within seven days he was dead.

There was no one left to fight Dessalines army. It is said 15 black soldiers died from the yellow fever. Rene was not a skeptic nor was he irrational. But he was a confused man. There were close to 20,000 dead Frenchmen. Napoleon had no choice but to abandon his dreams of restoring France's New World Empire.

Soon after, Jean Jacques Dessalines declared himself Haiti's new emperor. It was 1804; the war had lasted one year and on January 1, 1804 Dessalines declared independence from France. When he met with Rene, he thanked him for his support. Dessalines told Rene without the help of the Taino's and their gods he was not sure he would be standing as the first emperor of the Island. Out of respect for the Taino, he was reclaiming the name given by its original people Haiti (Land of Mountains) for the new nation. Dessalines also told Rene he would not spare the lives of the remaining French colonists and slave masters who fought to maintain slavery. He was not Francois. In a final act of retribution, Dessalines massacred close to 2,000 in Cap-Français, 900 in Port-au-Prince, and 400 at Jérémie. He then issued a proclamation declaring, "We have repaid these cannibals, war for war, crime for crime, outrage for outrage".

# HISTORY 3

Rene knew his time was drawing near, the wars had made him weary, and his soul was tired. Despite the Haitian victory, France refused to recognize the newly independent country's sovereignty until they were paid 150 million gold francs for ending slavery. Haiti refused to pay and France enlisted the help of the United States and Britain, who enforced an economic embargo which destroyed the Haitian economy. Rene was devastated; the Island had gained freedom only to be now stifled by economic slavery by the west. Rene petitioned France to lower the amount or cancel it all together. He sent a stinging letter to the French.

"What could have been the rational to impose a legal fine on a nation, unwilling to oppress their people? What was the incentive to impose such a harsh penalty on such a tiny struggling nation? Was this an act of war or institutional diffusion or some sort of political mobilization to keep the reigns of slavery intact? This debt would surely destroy the Island. For every Franc earned Haiti would be obliged to spend part servicing this debt. This economic bondage is sure to be a worst faith than walking the gallows. Based on France's claim to be repaid, 45% percent of Haiti's annual budget would be used to service said debt. The very idea that America and Britain would loan Haiti the funds to pay this debt is preposterous. It is well known Haiti's currency is soft and frequently fluctuates in value. As a result we would have to devote ever-increasing quantities of our currency to purchase the hard currency necessary to repay the same amount of debt. The difficulty in meeting this debt repayment obligations, provoked by these high interest rates would not only compound the repayment but destroy any chance of the debt ever being paid."

In addition, he addressed the French national assembly and sent letters to the United States Government and to the British and eventually France conceded and accepted 90 million gold Francs. Haiti did not have the money to pay France. The United States and Britain agreed to loan Haiti the funds but at an interest rate of almost double the original amount. Combined with the interest rate, Haiti would pay the total amount 170,000,000 Gold Francs. Rene saw this as a small victory. (The equivalent in today's money would be 22 Billion. Before Rene died, he gave specific instructions to Josephina, like his father gave to his mother. Little Rene is to have the eye; it must never leave our blood line.

President Dessalines was not a man of the people, he was concerned about power, and he had gained his position by betraying Francois. Dessalines named himself Governor-General-for-life of Haiti and proclaimed himself Emperor of Haiti. He was crowned Emperor Jacques I in a coronation ceremony in the city of Le Cap and on 20th, May 1805, his government released the Imperial Constitution, naming Jean-Jacques Dessalines emperor for life with the right to name his successor. After naming himself emperor for life Emperor Dessalines stayed aloof and never acknowledged his child with Rene's daughter. He was kind and cordial to the family but never engaging. Soon the people of Haiti became discontent and there were rumblings in different factions for his removal.

Two of his closest advisors hatched a plot to kill him. Disaffected with his style of leadership, Pétion and Christophe invited him to dinner at Rye l'Enterrement in Port-au-Prince on 17th October 1806. Emperor Dessalines arrived at the home of Pétion and thought he was amongst friends. He told his guards he would call them after dinner. His personal body guards stayed at Petion's house and sat in a chair overlooking the City. The saboteurs struck them on their head, whilst their backs were turned and they were killed instantly...

"What is this?" cried Dessalines.

But before he could mutter another word he was stabbed in the neck and chest. His body slumped to the floor. The conspirators quickly picked up his body and sent it with their men. Then they staged an ambush, shot four known adversaries of Dessalines and said they had been attacked.

Little Rene grew up knowing two Haities. The authoritarian State of Haiti in the north, and the Gen de couleur Republic of Haiti in the south. He had watched his grandfather run the country from the shadows. Rene Jr was different, he had decided from a child he would not be in the shadows but at the forefront. North Haiti was richer than the South, but they maintained a strict system of labor, almost the equivalent to slavery, just that their people were free and earned wages. They established a semi-feudal system, fumage, in which every able man was required to work in plantations to produce goods.

Little Rene joined the Parliament of Pétion and pushed him to parcel out the former colonial estates into smaller holdings. Their government was not rich, and it was continuously plagued by budgetary shortfalls, but the people were happy and enjoyed freedom of speech and a liberal way of life. In 1815, when Simon Bolivar was seeking Venezuelan independence, he came to Rene Jr and the gens de couleur and asked for asylum. Though there was much wrangling, they agreed that he could stay. Simon asked for a private meeting with Rene Jr. In the meeting he talked about the indigenous people and their fight for freedom. Their struggles to stay alive and not be wiped out which he knew would have resonated with Rene Jr. The preservation of their way of life and the oppression they faced. On his departure, Rene Jr convinced the Parliament to provide Simon with soldiers and substantial material support because of his respect and admiration for the indigenous people for whom he was fighting.

Pétion was growing weary of the Senate and their increasing meddling and oversight of all issues. He suspended the legislature and turned his post into the "President for Life". Rene Jr was incensed and told him that he could not proceed with his intent because it was not their agreement with the people. Pétion threw Rene Jr in jail and threatened to hang him for treason. The local Senate staged a protest and they too were threatened to be tried for treason. When Rene Jr was in jail he prayed, because he was Catholic, because it was how he knew to have faith, he prayed to his father and his ancestors to set him free. Two days later, Pétion developed yellow fever and died. His assistant Jean Pierre Boyer replaced him and released Rene Jr and reconvened the Senate.

The Eastern part of the island was in turmoil. General Juan Sánchez Ramírez's claimed Haiti was independent from France and owed no money. But by doing so, General Sanchez broke the Treaties of Bâle, and on July 9th 1809, Santo Domingo was born. They decided their part of the Island owed no money to France and would fall under the control of Spain.

In 1811, Christophe proclaimed himself King Henri I in the North and commissioned several extraordinary buildings. He even created a nobility class in the fashion of European monarchies. But by 1820, weakened by illness and with decreasing support for his authoritarian regime, he killed himself with a silver bullet rather than face a coup d'état. Immediately after, Rene Jr and the senators rode to the North and met with Christophe's wife. They were successful in reuniting Haiti through diplomacy.

Rene Jr was well schooled and well travelled. He had studied in France. Realizing America's role in burdening Haiti with an insurmountable debt during 1824 to 1826, while the island was under one government, Rene Jr promoted the largest single free-black immigration from the United States in which more than 6000 immigrants settled in different parts of the island.

Rene Jr was not pleased with President Boyer's actions as he was heading down the same part as Pétion. It was like they had traded in one dictator for another. He was acting independent of the senate and on Boyer's return from France he attempted to enforce the *Code Rural a type of slavery.* But the people of Haiti had no intentions of returning to the forced labor.

Then, as if to remind Haiti of their promises, an earthquake struck destroying the city and the Sans Souci Palace killing 10,000 people. Boyer tried again to establish a parliamentary rule under the Constitution of 1843. Revolts soon broke out and the country descended into near anarchy.

General Faustin Soulouque, a former slave, who had fought in the rebellion of 1791, became President. He was a man of the people and was adored by the former slaves. But Rene Jr watched as he too became power hungry. In 1849, taking advantage of his popularity, he proclaimed himself Emperor Faustin I. He united Haiti for about ten years and then in 1859 he was deposed by General Fabre Geffrard who liked to call himself the Duke of Tabara. Geffrard's military government held office until 1867 and he encouraged a successful policy of national reconciliation.

In 1860 the General asked Rene Jr what could be done to restore national pride so Haiti can be recognized throughout the world for what it truly was. Rene Jr along with the Haitian Parliament instituted a series of measures aimed at putting Haiti on the world stage. They reached an agreement with the Vatican reintroducing official Roman Catholic institutions. The Governments of Haiti lead a long period of democratic peace and development of the Island in which prosperity had returned. The debt to France was finally repaid in 1879 and Rene DuPont's family was now entrenched, prosperous and powerful. Rene Jr had left behind 12 children 5 girls and seven sons.

Rene Jr had invested heavily into monetary reform and cultural renaissance of Haiti. Rene's oldest son Louis led a growing chorus for the development and flowering of Haitian art. A historical museum and development of a Haitian intellectual culture was now the primary responsibility of the DuPont's. Major works of history were published in 1847 and 1865. Haitian intellectuals and famous artworks were put on display in Europe and the Americas.

Rene's last child, Isabel, became very active, socially and politically in Haiti. She engaged in a war of letters against a tide of sexism, racism and social Darwinism. She raised the question of women's rights on the Island. Why were they not allowed to be involved in politics and were not allowed to hold certain jobs? Isabel was not one to be confined by values or speech and she was definitely an exception to the rule during her time. During the opening of a new school in the Capital, she told the crowd.

"In general, women are considered unintelligent and untrustworthy, we are married at an early age so that our husbands can control us and so we can be good home makers and housewives, seen but not heard. This school represents a new horizon for those that wish not to accept this path."

Her brother Louis continued to lead progressive transitions in government which did much to improve the economy and stability of the Haitian nation and the condition of its people. Constitutional government restored the faith of the Haitian people in legal institutions. The development of industrial sugar and rum industries near Port au Prince brought economic stability and Haiti for a while became a model for economic growth in the Caribbean once more.

As the country's wealth grew, attacks on its stability rose. Revolutionary armies were formed by Cacos, which were peasant brigands from the mountains of the north along the porous Dominican border, who were enlisted by rival political factions with promises of money to be paid after a successful revolution and an opportunity to plunder.

The DuPont's started doing business with the Germans and influenced others to do the same. The Germans were hard working and honest and they did not plunder the Islands resources. The Germans were given

80% of the country's international commerce and were allowed to bring their engineering prowess to the Island. They operated utilities in Cap Haïtien and Port-au-Prince, serving the Plaine de Cul-du-Sac. They instituted railway and tram services, they installed giant cranes, boat building and repair services on the wharf. The DuPont's had made a wise decision, their wealth had grown enormously under the Germans. The Children of Louis, Isabel and their siblings all attended colleges and universities in Europe, diversifying their holdings.

The German community proved more willing to integrate into Haitian society than any other group of white foreigners, including the French. They married into the nation's most prominent mulatto families, bypassing the constitutional prohibition against foreign land-ownership. The German government also served as the principal financiers of the nation's banks, funding many major infrastructure developments, floating innumerable loans-at high interest rates-to competing political factions.

Isabela was not only a feminist; she was ambitious and knew what she wanted out of life. When Hans, a handsome young lawyer from the Island asked her hand in marriage, she smiled and said to him "thank you Hans, but I intend to marry your friend Johann Berenberg-Gossler who visited here last summer." Johann Berenberg-Gossler was from the house of Berenberg, the Berenberg–Gossler–Seyler banking dynasty. The family was a Hanseatic dynasty of merchants, bankers and senators in Hamburg, with branches in Livorno and other European cities and one of the world's oldest existing banking dynasties with a history spanning over 400 years.

When Johann's great grandfather, Johann Berenberg died without male heirs, the bank was passed on to Johann's grandmother, Elisabeth Berenberg. Elisabeth was a partner in her own right before passing control to Seyler and her son Johann Heinrich Gossler alone. The latter's grandson, Johann Gossler, was granted the name Berenberg-Gossler by the Senate of Hamburg and subsequently ennobled by Prussia and rose to Baronial rank. The Berenberg family belonged to the ruling class of the city republic known as Grand Burghers or Hanseaten, enjoying hereditary legal privileges. When the Berenberg's became aware of Haiti and its potential, they floated high interest loans to anyone who was involved in business on the Island. Johann Berenberg-Gossler visited as an emissary and to see his good friend Hans who was doing legal work for the bank on the Island. Johann was intrigued by the Island and by a young Isabel DuPont who was beautiful as she was fiery.

Isabel begged Louis to have the black eye. As the first born, he was given the eye. Secretly, Isabel coveted the eye. She was proud to wear the black diamond which was rare and enormous beyond comparison. One wealthy jeweler once said it was not worth a penny, it could not be really classified as a diamond because it was black and quite common on the African continent.

But try as he might, he could not find one similar or any diamond with its structure color and size. It was flawless and clear, the size of three fingers put together. In Europe it was said to be invaluable.

Louis relented, and the next summer Isabel took the eye with her on her trip to Germany. She arrived at the Port Of Hamburg with 10 female maid servants and 16 male servants. When Isabel returned to Haiti she was engaged to Johann Berenberg-Gossler. Louis had gone to University in the United States, his father was clueless. Haitians should be wary of the Germans not the United States, and in an effort to limit German influence; he courted a consortium of American investors who were backed by the American government who also felt threatened by the German influence in Haiti.

Isabel was incensed; she remembered their father Rene had warned them about the Americans. They were nation builders who would stop at nothing and no cost to achieve their goals. "They were worse than the French and the Brits combined" he said. They had killed over 10 million Native Indians; they stole their lands and put them on what they called "Reservations". The blacks in the South of the United States still lived under segregation laws. Louis was weak and though she loved her brother, he was like a straw in the wind.

When Louis asked for the return of the eye Isabel refused. Louis and Isabel became bitter towards each other. They continued to run the Banque National d'Haiti. Louis never really cared for his heritage.

He called a family meeting and told his siblings he was selling his shares of the family business to the Americans and they should do the same. Louis managed to convince three other siblings to sell their shares. This gave the American investors control of some of the businesses on the Island.

Two weeks after the sale, Isabel dreamt her father, he told her to leave the Island and to take the eye with her. The previous evening, she had attended a gala and wore the black diamond. Maybe it was the wine imported from Prussia, but again her father told her she had to leave. Isabel packed up and told Louis she was moving to Germany there were things that needed to be prepared for her wedding. She advised her siblings to leave Haiti for a while. Three of her sisters and two brothers went to Germany with her. Louis rejected Isabel's dream as utter foolishness and another attempt to flee with the black diamond. He called a family meeting where he announced that he had a deal with a jeweler to buy the black diamond. Isabel agreed and told the family that on her return the following summer, against the wishes of their father, she would agree to the sale.

Six months after their departure, February 25th 1915, the United States Government backed a coup d'état and installed Vilbrun Guillaume Sam as President of Haiti. A press release from the United States Government said Joseph Davilmar Theodore had resigned as President of Haiti and was seeking asylum in the Dominican Republic. President Vilbrun was promised autonomous control of the Island by the US Government. President Vilbrun immediately established a dictatorship. He rounded up the gens de couleur, all the wealthy foreigners and massacred 167 of them including Louis and his brothers. Isabel was devastated.

Things were going as planned for President Woodrow Wilson. The United States Government had been interested in Haiti for decades, but attempts to get involved on the Island were unsuccessful. Their first attempt was to establish naval base for the United States. Haiti's stability was of great interest to U.S. diplomatic and defense officials. They feared Haiti as an independent nation had become too strong.

In 1868, President Andrew Johnson suggested the annexation of the island of Hispaniola to secure a U.S. defensive and economic stake on the Island. But before the United States could act, Spain issued a statement that Hispaniola was still a territory of Spain.

Secretary of State, James Blaine, met with Rene and unsuccessfully sought a lease of Mole-Saint Nicolas, a city on Haiti's northern coast, for a naval base. But as the head of Haiti's gens de couleur, Rene flatly refused to negotiate or lease any land to the United States. The State Department report stated that Mr. DuPont was arrogant and unyielding.

Louis's death was a reawakening of Haitian pride of the suffrage of a nation. Isabel refused to allow her brother to be murdered by a government as ruthless as the United States. In May, Isabel met with German diplomats and declared herself the rightful head of the gens de couleur. An alliance was formed between Isabel and the Bundesnachrichtendienst (German secret service). They then met with officials from the Dominican Republic, military officials and senior advisors who all expressed their support for the operations.

On July 11th, Isabel met with the remaining gens de couleur in the mountains of the Dominican Republic. The military had assured the Germans of safe passage and safe harbor for Isabel. Isabel and the gens de couleur paid the Cacos the money owed to them by the previous President and bought their allegiance. Dressed in combat fatigues, looking like a young boy soldier, Isabel crossed into Haiti. Germany authorized the support to the Cacos by giving them "money, arms and equipment". They started targeted executions of President Vilbrun soldiers and extracting information through brutal measures. They found support among the people in the countryside and their numbers continued to grow. When Isabel had all the information she needed, she attacked President Vilbrun on July 27th 1915.

Unlike most women of her time, Isabel dressed in full military garb, rode into the City led by her band of rebels and attacked. President Vilbrun, being informed of the impending attack by the United States Government. President Vilbrun fled to the French embassy where he received asylum. Isabel was not to be deterred; she worked out an agreement with the French Ambassador who despised the Americans.

The Cacos broke into the embassy at night and found President Vilbrun. They dragged him out and beat him senseless, then threw his limp body over the embassy's iron fence to the waiting Isabel. They tied his body to the back of her horse and she rode through the Capital. President Vilbrun's body was ripped to pieces and paraded through the capital's neighborhoods. For the next two weeks anyone who had associated with the Americans or President Vilbrun was held accountable. The country was in chaos, for a time, Isabel seemed to rule the Island unofficially. News of the murder soon reached Washington. American Navy ships which had been anchored of the coast of Haiti headed back to the Capital.

President Woodrow Wilson was wary about the turn of events in Haiti and especially the possibility that Germany was poised to yield more power and have closer ties with Haiti. He ordered American troops to return and seize the capital. In the ensuing weeks a full scale invasion took place. President Wilson claimed Haiti was now under US control. The United States continued to occupy Haiti for the next twenty years. President Wilson stated a few years earlier in 1910, President William Howard Taft granted Haiti a large loan with hopes that Haiti could pay off its international debt thus lessening foreign influence. The attempt proved futile due to the enormity of the debt and the internal instability of the country. These events forced him as President to send U.S. Marines to Haiti, to provide stability and prevent anarchy.

Isabel made her escape through the Dominican Republic back to Germany, on the way back home; she recalled a famous speech from President Jean Jacques Dessalines with whom she was cousins "we have repaid these cannibals, war for war, crime for crime, outrage for outrage". Isabel felt empowered; justice had been served for the death of Louis and her brothers.

The United States Government implemented the Haitian-American Treaty of 1915. The articles of this agreement created a Haitian gendarmerie, essentially a military force made up of Americans and Haitians and controlled by the U.S. marines. The United States gained complete control over Haitian finances and the right to intervene in Haiti whenever the U.S. Government deemed necessary.

President Wilson forced the election of a new pro-American President, Philippe Sudré Dartiguenave by the Haitian legislature in August of 1915. However, the selection of the President did not represent the choice by the Haitian populace since they were not allowed to vote. The government of Haiti was now under the control of the U.S Congress. United States Marine Commanders served as Governors in the provinces. The gens de couleur negotiated a deal through Isabel where they were given authority with the U.S. government retaining the power of veto.

A new Haitian constitution was written by Assistant Secretary of the Navy Franklin D. Roosevelt. Roads were improved and expanded, but it was under what they called forced labor. The people were made to work under control of armed guards who were permitted to shoot anyone who fled from compulsory service. Workers who didn't participate were often imprisoned, beaten or starved. This was seen by the gens de couleur as slavery as even the poorest and former slaves from the rural classes filled these work gangs.

The constitution written by Assistant Secretary of the Navy Franklin D. Roosevelt restructured the education system. The previous system was aligned with the existing system of "Liberal Arts" education inherited from the French; this was replaced with an emphasis on vocational training. The constitution also removed the pre-existing class system with blacks at the low end and gen de couleur occupying the elite upper class. Roosevelt saw little difference between the two classes; you were either white or black to have access to privileges. The Americans treated both with equal contempt which further angered the mulatto elite who had previously enjoyed a higher standing in society. The whites received equal treatment to white Americans.

Isabel continued to fund the Cacos against the American invasion. The Cacos also now had a true General Charlemagne Masséna Péralte. He was from the North, the city of Hinche; his family had migrated from Hispaniola. It was now easy for the Germans to arm the Cacos. General Péralte had refused to work with the United States Marines whom he saw as occupiers, so he resigned from his position and returned home to protect his family's land. To resist the occupation, he was in frequent contact with Isabel but did not openly support the Cacos. After much feuding with the local officers stationed in Hinche, he was arrested for assaulting the home of one of the officers and sentenced to five years of forced labor. Isabel sensing the opportunity paid a group of Cacos to free Péralte. He escaped captivity and agreed to train the Cacos and escalate opposition to US occupation.

General Péralte fired up the people with his speeches.

"To those colonies and territories which as a consequence are free because of the blood we the slaves of Haiti have spilled on this land, I say fight. That we have ceased to be a sovereign nation under which all people of color are free. Sovereignty is a right we earned by spilling the blood of our children, fathers, brothers, mothers, daughters, a country formerly governed by the people, inhabited by these same peoples who can stand by themselves, prosperous and strong, godly and civilized. A nation built under the most strenuous conditions of the modern world. There should be applied, the principle that the well-being and development of such peoples form a sacred trust of civilization and that securities for the performance of this trust should be embodied in this covenant of thing called trust. But now, to be enslaved by the beast called the United States who roars like a Lion, sounds like a Lion but thieves like a dog in the night.

The mandate of our nation is to now fight fire with fire, bullets with bullets and we will roar like Lions and take their life in the night like the dogs they are."

The Cacos and the people of Haiti were ready for an all out war. They proved to be a formidable force causing President Wilson to call for more troops to battle the guerilla fighters. General Péralte declared a provisional government in the north of Haiti. Isabel was delighted they were gaining ground, taking back their country. Then she received word that he was killed. He was betrayed by one of his officers. Jean-Baptiste Conzé who was paid by the Americans and led disguised marines into the camp to kill him. Jean Baptiste Conze was called Judas and a manhunt ensued. He was soon captured and made and example by Cacos.

Assistant Secretary of the Navy, Roosevelt, after hearing of Péralte's capture, ordered troops to take a picture of Charlemagne Péralte's dead body tied to a door and distributed it throughout the country to demoralize the Haitian resistance. But the photo had the opposite effect. Péralte had fought for the independence of his nation from foreign invaders, he was killed at the age of 33 and was now seen as a martyr and a hero and Isabel and the Germans made sure of that.

World condemnation, internal investigation and accusations of money laundering were now plaguing the United States occupation. Forced slavery, brutality, murders and plundering of national resources left Haiti bankrupt. The Americans had abolished the prohibition on foreign ownership of land - the most essential component of the Haitian law. When the newly elected National Assembly refused to pass this document and drafted one of their own, preserving this prohibition, it was forcibly dissolved by the American Government. This constitution was then put to a vote for approval by the Haitian people. If you supported the constitution you were allowed to vote, if you disapproved you were turned away, because of this, the constitution was approved by less than 5% of the population. The US State Department authorized this plebiscite stating "The people casting ballots were 97% illiterate, ignorant in most cases of what they were voting for."

Isabel watched from afar as the Haitian people were used to prop up the United States Economy. Haiti's riches; cotton, sugar, coffee, cocoa, rum and gold were plundered to support the war. The United States slid into the Great Depression and the resources of the Haitian people became invaluable. Isabel knew Haiti would never be the same. Isabel now lived in the Dominican Republic; the war forced her to move closer to home. The US government paid little or nothing, decimated the prices of Haiti's exports and destroyed the tenuous gains of the previous decade.

A few years later December 1929, the marines in Les Cayes killed ten Haitian peasants during a march to protest local economic conditions under which they were working. President Hoover knew he had to address the issue, world condemnation was harsh. But the United States needed the resources of Haiti, they could ill afford to let go of the Island during the Depression. So he appointed two commissions to investigate the events on the Island. The report criticized the exclusion of Haitians from positions of authority in the government and constabulary, now known as the Garde d'Haïti. As time passed the struggle for Haiti to free itself from under the yolk of the Americas continued.

In 1930, Haiti elected a new President, Stenio Vincent, a long-time critic of the occupation. He asked for the US to withdraw its forces and President Roosevelt agreed, but under one condition. The US retains control of Haiti's external finances it's Banks, commerce and trade until after the Depression.

# CHAPTER 1

"This is Tom Day reporting live from Port au Prince Haiti where only minutes ago a catastrophic earthquake with a magnitude of 7.0 rocked this tiny Caribbean nation. The International Science Foundation has put the epicenter near the town of Léogâne, approximately 25 km (16 miles) west of Port-au-Prince, Haiti's capital. The earthquake occurred at 16:53 local time and as we continue to experience numerous aftershocks, the Haitian government is now estimating that millions have been affected. The local Red Cross officials are stating hundreds of thousands are either trapped dead or injured. They are calling for help from the international community. I can tell you there is nothing standing in the capital, which also includes the National Assembly building in Port-au-Prince. We now have official word, United Nations Mission's Chief, Hédi Annabi, has been killed in the earthquake along with the Archbishop of Port-au-Prince Joseph Serge Miot and opposition leader Micha Gaillard. Ladies and Gentlemen this is one of the saddest days in the history of this tiny nation. The devastation is beyond words."

**HAITI 2-Days before the Earthquake**

Marie was at work when her mother called. She was an only child and her father had died leaving her and her mother to fend for themselves. Sometimes she blamed him and sometimes she just missed him. He would have been so proud of her. Marie worked as a nurse at the State

University Hospital in Port au Prince. She was the charge nurse on her floor. Her cell phone was ringing… "Yes mummy" she answered, there was always something to pick up on the way home or to take care of. When she arrived home, her mother was up waiting on her coffee. Few people could drink coffee before they went to bed and when they woke up, her mother could do both. She claimed it was the Taino blood in her. Marie wasn't sure if her Mom made up the stories or if they were true. But she had pictures and a great family history.

Her parents weren't rich but they weren't poor. Both her parents worked when she was a child but they always took extravagant vacation trips which she enjoyed enormously. Her mother's family was rich, her cousins were rich, her uncles were rich but they weren't. She grew up in a house with one television; they had one car and one telephone. It was almost like her parents purposely did it that way. When she was old enough to drive, her parents traded in their car and gave her the new car so they still had one car which just made no sense. They both loved London, Germany and France and when she wanted to go to nursing school they chose England. They had never been to the United States and vowed they would never go. Her parents were strange. Their hatred for the United States ran deep. Americans were loud obnoxious free loaders. Europeans were civilized and well mannered. He father never met an American he liked and neither did her mother.

He mother had two sisters, Catherine who lived in the Domincan Republic and Antoinette who lived in Germany. Their family was large, humungous actually, with dozens of cousins, aunts and uncles, some of which she did not even know. But her mother did and so did her father. Her father's family was small; they were made up of farmers and government officials. Her mother was the matriarch of her family and everyone looked up to her, even her aunt in Germany. She rarely saw her mother angry, there was always a peaceful serenity about her and she spoke French, not Creole, she would say.

"I speak French".

She remembered playing with her cousin Cecile out in their yard and Cecile told her

"my mommy said your mommy is the richest woman in the world."

As a child hearing this she was stunned. She had one pair of gym shoes and one pair of church shoes; she had one watch and one Barbie. Impossible! Her cousins had a home in the Dominican Republic and one in Haiti; they also shared a flat in London during the summer. During vacations, they would stay with them or with their other cousins. Marie was not an unhappy child because she always got all that she wanted and most of all she was showered with love, but to say they were rich was preposterous.

After Cecile left she asked her Mommy.

"Mommy, Cecile said you are the richest woman in the world is that true?"

She could see the rage and fire inside her eyes,

"Don't you ever say that!" she snapped at her, "go into your room and stop this nonsense right now".

Her mother got on the phone and started speaking in German. Her mother only spoke in German when she was angry. Her father on the other hand spoke creole and mocked her mom. They were different, but yet so much alike.

His death devastated her mother, and although it was 6 years ago, it seemed like yesterday. She had been close to her mother, but her father's death brought them even closer. After he died, her mother opened up to her, she told her that they were not rich but comfortable. The legacy of the black diamond was fascinating, her history and her bloodline. It was a secret to be guarded for generations, the prosperity and financial commitments for future generations. It was the way of the DuPont's it was the way she would have to live her life.

Marie had one wish, and when she asked her mother she could see the displeasure, but her mother consented her to go. She wanted to see America; she wanted to travel to New York and L.A. She took

Cecile with her. They had a few Haitian friends who had migrated and some cousins who now lived in the United States.

New York was nice, it was gritty, real and the people didn't care who she was or where she came from. To New Yorkers it was all about money and whether you can get the job done. She liked the New Yorkers, they were like Haitians. As a matter of fact, there was a large contingent of Haitians in Brooklyn. Haitian food, clothes, radio stations and they all professed to know more about Haiti than the people who lived on the Island.

LA on the other hand, she despised it. It was all about being seen and who you knew or who you were with. Cecile was more into that stuff, but Marie realized money was relative to people in LA. They all talked about the cars and who lived in Malibu. It was a pity so many people could live such superficial lives, trapped in trying to outdo each other. Whenever she told someone in LA she was a nurse they all looked at her like she said she was dying of cancer. Her mother found her stories funny and Marie thought her parents were right about the Americans. Way to self absorbed.

They were watching a re-run of dancing with the stars, when she felt the first rumble and then came the second. Suddenly their house split in two and she was in the half that fell into their garden and her mother was in the half that fell towards the street.

"Mummy, Mummy"

tears running down her cheek. She was holding her mother's head in her hands. Her legs and body were trapped under the debris from the fallen house. Her mother's face still had that soft look to it.

"You must leave now Marie, go take the black case and go."

"Mommy I don't care about the case and I'm not leaving you."

"Marie you must go, this house won't stand much longer."

"I love you mommy."

"I love you too Marie, now go… run save yourself child."

Then came another aftershock and parts of the house began to crumble, Marie ran to her mother's bedroom and grabbed the case. Her mother's eyes were closed. She ran out the house screaming as the tears poured down her cheeks. Everywhere there was destruction. People were dazed and walking around, homes were crushed, mangled bodies.

"Help somebody help, help me please, help me get my mother, she is trapped. Somebody help me please, my mother is trapped in there, somebody help me."

Then there was a loud shattering boom and the house crumbled to the ground. Marie was screaming so loud she couldn't hear her own voice. Eventually her screams turned to sobs and she fainted.

She wasn't sure how long she was lying on the streets, but when she opened her eyes she found herself in the back of an American Humvee. "Ma'am, what's your name, are you ok? Do you speak English?" "Yes I speak English", replied Marie, "my mother is trapped in that house. Can you please help her?" "Ma'am tomorrow we will check the house, but right now we are going to take you to a clinic to have you checked out." Marie knew her mother was dead, and she began to cry again. The soldiers then took her to a makeshift clinic.

Dr. Dupre was astonished to see Marie. The Marines had taken her out and placed her on a cot and the only thing she remembered was being lifted onto a cot; nothing else. Her legs were heavy and her eyelids hurt. She wondered if she was still in the house or still in the street. Then the doors closed, her eyelids shut and she slept.

Marie finally opened her eyes. Through the fogginess she saw a doctor walk by. Thank god it was all a dream she thought to herself. She was back at the hospital. Then she began thinking that she must have passed out at work, earthquakes, soldiers, her mom dying it must have been a dream. Then she looked at her hands and her clothing, it was not a dream, she was bare-footed and in the same clothes. She sat up and looked around. She wasn't at the hospital; it was a camp, a refugee type camp. The ones you see in the movies.

The realization set in her mother was dead and she needed to call her aunt. She needed a telephone and then she remembered the case, the box, "where was it?" she asked herself. Dr. Dupre walked in; he was one of the doctors she worked with at the hospital.

"Marie, I'm glad you are awake, I was getting worried. You have been asleep for about 16 hours now, I knew you were ok, your vitals were good and I had you on a saline drip."

Marie looked at him and started to sob.

"It's going to be ok Marie, you were brought here by the American soldiers after your home was destroyed. I'm afraid your mother did not make it. I told the soldiers you were a friend, so they were kind enough to return to your home and collect whatever was still valuable and salvageable before the looters got to it. The boxes are behind my quarters. Pictures, your uniforms and work equipment, books jewelry and some money and documents found under your mother's bed. It's all safe."

"What about a black case I had in my possession?" Marie asked.

"It's safe Marie, it's with your possessions, and everything is safe."
Marie thanked him.

It was wrong of her to be so selfish she was fine physically. She saw
the numerous patients with broken limbs, bruised and bandaged.

Marie asked Dr. Dupre if the phones were working and he told her
yes. The local cell phone carrier was still up and running. He allowed
her to use his cell phone and she called her Aunt in Germany. She
told her about her mother and they both cried on the phone. Her aunt
wanted her to go over to her aunt in the Dominican Republic and then
fly to Germany. Marie told her no she was going to stay. She had to
bury her mother and take care of things. It was what her father would
have expected her to do. She told her aunt she was able to retrieve her
mother's valuable possessions. Her aunt asked if there was anything
she needed; Marie told her she was fine and that she would call her
after she made arrangements.

Marie went into Dr. Dupre's tent to retrieve her belongings. Everything
was there, she opened the black case and she saw the black diamond.
She removed it and placed it around her neck, it slid between her
bosoms, and it was cold. There was also the key to the vault which
had some of her parent's personal items. Marie realized she didn't
know where the vault was and she thought it might be in Germany
or London. She looked at her father's ring,

"what big hands he had" she thought.

She realized that she was slowly forgetting little things about him and tears began to fill her eyes again. They had brought her father's ring back as proof he was dead. She never quite understood why they killed her father; she never really quite understood why her mother let him stay. It was almost as if they both loved Haiti more than themselves.

Her Father was part of the United Nations committee to ensure fair elections. The opposition in Haiti had accused the government party of election fraud in the 2000 Haitian Elections. Her father was convinced there were no irregularities that occurred in the election and although there was a post-election vote count, there were still no irregularities found. Her dad told them it wasn't the votes that were fraudulent, it was the process. The poor was either threatened or bribed, it was the process that was threatening to undo the democratic work of the citizens of Haiti.

Aristide's Government was delaying the distribution of voter identification cards. Aristide's supporters claim that an opposition boycott of the election would be a ploy in order to discredit it and that they did not have anywhere near majority support. The European nations had suspended government-to-government assistance to Haiti and Haiti had received no help from the World Bank and the Inter

American Development Bank in years. The U.S. Congress banned any U.S. assistance from being channeled through Aristide's Government.

Her mother was wary of her father's involvement in the elections. She liked it when he worked with UNICEF, but she understood his need to stand up for the Haitian people. Her mother told her as a child she had watched her mother leave for months at a time fighting for the Haitian people.

Aristide requested that France repay billions, which he said was the equivalent in today's money for the 90 million gold francs. Which Haiti was forced to pay Paris in ransom for winning its freedom,as the hemisphere's first independent black nation 200 years ago. And Haiti wanted their money back. Her mother and father laughed at Aristide. They told her that France had requested 150 million gold francs and that it was her great great grandfather, Rene DuPont, who negotiated down the amount to 90 million Francs. She told him it was rumored that Haiti had promised him a million gold Francs if he came back with a negotiated settlement of 100million Francs.

"So did he get the one million gold Francs?" asked Marie.

"Obviously not Marie" said her Dad.

"We would at least have had two cars" her dad joked. Their one car was a running joke between her and her dad.

She knew their home was happy, but the streets of Haiti were riotous. She heard the rumors at the school. Her father was waiting on word from the United Nations Council of which France was a permanent member. They were supposed to send troops based on an appeal from Caricom for international peacekeeping forces to be sent into its member state Haiti for the elections. Her father received a telephone call that evening and told them no troops would be coming. Apparently, the decision was reached at the Ottawa Initiative conference hosted by Canada that took place in Montreal, Quebec months before. The conference was held to decide the future of Haiti's government. The conference was attended by Canadian, French, and U.S. and Latin American officials, no Caribbean country or Caricom members were invited.

It was agreed that a regime change in Haiti was necessary and they would arrange with the Americans of the possibility of Aristides's departure and the setting up of a potential trusteeship over Haiti. Arming the militia to oust Aristide would be the first step.

Her father told them, starting the next day, the first wave of protest would start. Her mother said they should leave and her father agreed. They would go to the Dominican Republic for a few months or even to Germany. Whilst they packed her father sat in his chair in his office.

"Papa why aren't you packing?" she asked.

"Because I packed yesterday" he replied.

She went to her mom "why isn't Papa packing?"

she asked her mother. "Because he is not coming, he never was, but I have to make sure you are safe, so we have to go" replied her mom. We shouldn't leave him she told her mother. She was panicking and it felt bad, something was wrong, he had to come because bad men ruled Haiti and people were killed every day, he must come with them.

She went to him and he hugged her, and she cried.

Why, she didn't know, but yet she knew. Her mother was so silent she never spoke a word. They drove to the border and her aunt met them. She hugged her father and cried and her mother began to cry. They held hands and walked away from her and kissed. Oh my god, she realized now, it was everyone saying final goodbyes. How could she be so naïve? He held her so close and told her he would see her soon to take care of her mother. Marie felt relieved when he had said that. He would see her soon. But yet the drive was quiet. Still uneasy she couldn't help the feeling that something was wrong. But again she found comfort in his words.

"I love you Marie, be brave, be strong, remember I'm always with you and I will be seeing you soon."

The next day, the news in the Dominican Republic said a student protest against President Aristide led to a clash with police that left two dead. She spoke to her father from time to time and she was comforted all was fine. President Aristide's popularity was on the rise. He was enjoying support by the majority of Haitians. He had pushed with mixed success, a populist agenda of higher minimum wages, school construction, literacy programs, higher taxes on the rich and other policies. These policies angered the opposition movement which was run largely by the mulatto elite or formerly gen de coleur that had traditionally controlled Haiti's economy. Aristide's "us against the world" strategy was working. He blamed the French and the Americans for plundering the Haitian economy. Her father said Aristide was 100% correct but two wrongs don't make a right. His role in the drug trade financed by Colombia's Cali cartel had made him so rich that his fortune sat at around (200,000,000) Two hundred million US dollars. President Aristide had become uncontrollable, dealing with the Colombians and exposing the CIA drug traffic dealings. He told the UN that each year Haiti is the transit point for nearly 50 tons of cocaine worth more than a billion dollars, providing Haiti's military rulers with $200 million in profits.

President Bush and the French Government needed President Aristide gone. He was taking dirty money whilst exposing those who did exactly what he was doing. The International Republican Institute, a nonprofit political group, backed by powerful Republicans close to President Bush administration funded the opposition to remove President Aristide. They trained President Aristide's political opponents, uniting them into a single bloc and encouraged them to reject internationally sanctioned power-sharing agreements in order to heighten Haiti's political crisis. The groups started protesting, espousing change in Haiti, "fundamental change" they called it. Then they started their march, armed with American made M16's, they began in the North moving South.

Her father called and told her mother it had started. She wasn't sure if he was on any side, so she asked her mother. She told her he is on the side of Haiti; he is there to protect our home and his family, his brothers, sisters all who would die for Haiti. The rebels included former members of the dissolved Haitian army, drug dealers and members of the former paramilitary organization who was universally recognized as having operated terrorist/execution squads during the previous rebellions. The driving force behind these rebels was Jean Tatoune, a former member of the Front Revolutionnaire pour l'Avancement el le Progres d'Haiti (FRAPH), and Jodel Chamblain, the co-founder of FRAPH. Both men were convicted human rights violators. The other rebel leader was Guy Phillipe, a well-known drug dealer who had been implicated in masterminding another coup attempt against the previous Haitian President (President Preval). The movement of the rebel army towards the South was rapid; it eviscerated the local police force.

President Aristide had accepted the proposals of the international community and had entreated the opposition to agree to the proposed political solution in order to avoid the return of power to the forces that in the past had terrorized the Haitian people. The rebel army backed by the US and French government killed, mutilated and maimed civilians in the North. They threatened to enter Port-au-Prince and destroy the City. They also threatened to kill the President and his family. Marie's father had moved her grandmother into their house as he knew she would not leave Haiti.

They continued to call for President Aristide's resignation, rejecting the international proposals. Two days later, the Steele Foundation, a U.S. company, which had provided President Aristide with security under contract and by agreement with the Pentagon, informed him that the U.S. government had forbade the company from bringing in additional security forces to protect him. The same day, U.S. diplomats told the President that if he remained in Port-au-Prince the U.S. would not provide any assistance when the insurgents attacked and that they expected the President, his wife and supporters would be killed.

The rebels had started fighting in the Capital. That was the last night they heard from her father. The next day, Amiot Metayer, a known gang leader also known as (The Cannibal Army an anti US brigade) from Gonaives, was found dead. His eyes shot out and his heart cut out. His brother, Buteur Metayer, swore vengeance against those he felt responsible for Amiot's death—namely President Jean-Bertrand Aristide. Buteur took charge of the Cannibal Army and promptly renamed it the 'National Revolutionary Front for the Liberation of Haiti'. They now controlled Gonaives and then they moved to Cap-Haitien which they overtook in two days.

There was a full blown war between two rival factions both wanting control of Haiti. The US government backed forces and the anti US forces. Haitians were fleeing the country on boats seeking to get to the United States for asylum.

When Marie returned, their neighbors told her that their house had been targeted. US backed rebels knew her father was an outspoken critic of the United States Government so they shot him and killed her grandmother. Tonton buried their bodies in their garden but kept his ring for her mother.

The same night her father was shot U.S. Depute Charge de Mission (DCM) in Haiti, Luis Moreno, accompanied by a contingent of U.S. marines met with President Aristide. Moreno told him that only if he left Haiti would the U.S. provide an aircraft for him to leave, but that assistance was contingent on Aristide signing a letter in their possession.

President Aristide protested, he had not read the letter and he was not being given any assurances where he was being taken. The next morning of February 29, the President and some family members were taken by Moreno and the marines to an airplane rented by the U.S. State Department. Moreno told the President that he must sign the letter before he boarded the plane. President Aristide still had doubts and was still not sure that he wanted to leave. Moreno told President Aristide it was a letter of resignation and should agree to ask no questions about where he was being taken. If not, the President and his wife would be left at the airport and they would be killed. Fearing for his family, President Aristide agreed and boarded the plane. He was denied access to a phone for nearly 24 hours and he knew nothing of his destination until he and his family were deposited in the Central African Republic.

The Caricom States held a meeting and issued the following statement: There are several tragedies in this surrealistic episode. The first is the apparent incapacity of the U.S. government to speak honestly about such matters as toppling governments. Instead, it brushes aside crucial questions: Did the U.S. summarily deny military protection to President Aristide, and if so, why and when? Did the U.S. supply weapons to the rebels who showed up in the Capital with sophisticated equipment that was last year reportedly taken by the U.S. military to the Dominican Republic, which is next door to Haiti? Why did the U.S. cynically abandon the call of European and Caribbean leaders for a political compromise, a compromise that Aristide had already accepted? Most importantly, did the U.S. in fact bankroll a coup in Haiti, a scenario that seems likely based on present evidence?

One hour after the departure of President Aristide, US ships anchored off the coast of the Dominican Republic dropped of marines to keep the peace in Port au Prince. Vice President Dick Cheney of the United States quickly issued a press release denying that the United States arrested or forcibly ousted President Aristide by saying that President Aristide, who had "worn out his welcome with the Haitian people," had "left on his own free will." Shortly after Boniface Alexandre was named acting president of Haiti, all 3,000 people held in the national penitentiary were freed after he was named acting President.

Marie watched the news on television. The Santa Domingo newspaper Al momento reported a security vacuum throughout the country and the BBC reported that rioters in Port-au-Prince looted stores, ransacked police stations and set fire to gas stations. There have been many brutal reprisal attacks on political opponents, extra-judicial arrests and killings, lack of effective civil authority and disruption of humanitarian aid efforts. Serious human rights abuses, political violence and social turbulence have escalated to the level of a humanitarian crisis. People were being shot dead in the streets by gangs of criminal thugs; it was unconscionable for the United States to have been part of these atrocities. The BBC reported Haiti remained unstable and insecure. The international community must take rapid steps to take the country back from armed criminals and thugs who are now in control of the country.

Many international politicians, including members of the U.S. congress expressed concern that the United States had interfered with Haiti's democratic process by removing Aristide with excessive force.

US congresswoman Maxine Waters, D-California confirmed that Mildred Aristide called her at her home at 6:30 am to inform her that the coup d'etat has been completed and Jean-Bertrand Aristide said that the U.S. Embassy's Chief of staff came to his house to say he would be killed, a lot of Haitians would be killed if he refused to resign immediately and said he "has to go now". US congressman Charles Rangel, D-New York expressed similar words, saying Aristide had told him he was disappointed that the international community had let him down and that he resigned under pressure – As a matter of fact, he was very apprehensive for his life. They made it clear that he had to go now or he would be killed.

When asked for his response to these statements, General Colin Powel said

"it might have been better for members of Congress who have heard these stories to ask us about the stories before going public with them so we don't make a difficult situation that much more difficult" and he alleged that Aristide "did not democratically govern or govern well"

Jamaican Prime Minister P.J. Patterson released a statement saying "we are bound to question whether his resignation was truly voluntary, as it comes after the capture of sections of Haiti by armed insurgents and the failure of the international community to provide the requisite support. The removal of President Aristide in these circumstances sets a dangerous precedent for democratically elected governments anywhere and everywhere as it promotes the removal of duly elected persons from office by the power of rebel forces."

As they ate breakfast that morning, Marie's mother looked at her and asked

"do you know the story of the eye of Haiti?" "No" said Marie …. "Why?" "Because you are descended from the Taiano people and Deminán Caracaracol, the god from whom all Taínos were descended, it is believed had first possessed the black eye which you have around your neck."

As Marie sat listening to the story one thought kept recurring in her mind. How drunk were the Taino's when they first told this story and was her mother drinking now. She laughed and hugged her mother after the story. She remembered saying

"it doesn't matter mom where it came from fact is it belonged to you and your mother and our family and it's blessed with your love."

It was now so many years later, both her parents were dead and here she was going through their things. She was wearing the black diamond around her neck which belonged to some turtle and her father's ring. She wanted a trade, the turtle could have his diamond back and she would give the ring up to have her daddy back.

Dr. Dupre poked his head in the tent,

"everything ok Marie?"

"Yes Dr. Dupre" she replied.

"I was hoping you would stick around and help".

"I will be back" replied Marie.

"I have to take care of my Mom's burial and then I'll be back."

She had her aunt send help from the Dominican Republic. Her mother's body was removed and taken to the morgue in Santo Domingo by Tonton. They cremated her so her ashes could be returned to Haiti. Marie then flew to London to Lloyds TSB Bank, her aunt had told her all the answers she needed were there.

She arrived for her appointment and was led to the safety deposit box. A special room was assigned to her to go over the documents. When she opened the box there were two letters, one from her father and one from her mother, each in their own handwriting. Their letters were vaguely similar. It spoke in past tense about them being dead and her being on her own. They were so proud of her, the type of woman she had become. Her father was silly even in death. He told her to get married because her eggs would soon be dried up.

She broke out laughing in the room. Just like my dad she thought! He asked her to never stop being a daddy's girl and again the tears trickled down her cheeks.

There was a knock on the door, she was brought a pitcher of water and a glass and then the attendant left. Her mother's letter was more business-like. Above all, she left detailed instructions. It was moments like these she felt she was more like her mom. Because it was how she was, it was how she would prepare if she had a child. Before she left, the bank manager came to her and expressed his condolences. He told Marie he hoped she would continue to use their services and if she needed anything he was there to assist her. Marie felt quite uncomfortable since all they had with the bank was a safety deposit box.

Her next stop was an attorney her mother said would be expecting her. She arrived at the address on the business card left in the safety deposit box. The clerk was cordial and escorted her to the office where she sat and waited. An old grey haired attorney walked in, "Marie how are you?" She was shocked! It was her mother's friend whom she called Uncle Tom. "I'm terribly sorry about your mother", Marie nodded. Tom came out with a thick file and started going over her mother's assets. It was overwhelming to say the least; they had gold Francs, millions of dollars' worth. Her mother's net worth was (900,000,000) Nine hundred million dollars. Four hundred was in liquid assets, one hundred million was deposited in a trust at Lloyds TSB Bank of London.

Marie returned to Haiti with a sense of purpose, she now understood why her parents had lived the lifestyle they did. No one knew their worth; they were never a threat to Haiti but part of Haiti.

# CHAPTER 2

## INTERIOR-HOSPITAL OPERATING ROOM

Dr. Jason Bramer "I want the incision to be about 2mm lower."

Dr. David Coburn "To the left or right?"

Dr. Jason Bramer "To the right."

Dr. David Coburn "nurse increase the dopamine, give me to more mics".

Dr. Jason Bramer "Nice and easy does it."

Dr. David Coburn "Jason there seems to be just a little more blockage than was initially shown."

Dr. Jason Bramer "Yes! yes I see it. I'll open it up just enough so the stint can stabilize it".

Dr. David Coburn "Be careful Jason, it's more centralized than we thought."

Dr. Jason Bramer "I got it Dave."

Dr. David Coburn "Looking pretty good ...Nurse suction."

Dr. Jason Bramer "Close him up."

Dr. David Coburn "So what's this rumor I hear about you going to Haiti, is it true?"

Dr. Jason Bramer "God is nothing sacred around here....Yes David, Yes" (smiling) walking away.

He was a young, handsome, cocky doctor, and he was a millionaire. He had made his money from the collapse of the subprime mortgage market. He was a Doctor because he liked the prestige that came with the title. He watched the chain reaction of economic and financial adversity that had spread to the global financial markets, creating depression-like conditions in the housing market and pushing the U.S. economy to the brink of recession.

In response, Congress and the executive branch had proposed new federal spending and credit programs that greatly expanded the role of government in the economy. Was he this smart or was the Government that stupid? Everyone was making quick money off the Government flipping houses. Some selling and buying, walking away when deals went bad, pocketing wads of cash.

He was a California boy, fast cars beautiful women. He was going to invest in real estate. But first he needed a crash course in the market.

He signed up for a four week course, but by week 3 he was ready. He had taken a leave of absence from the Hospital. His mother told him he was crazy. His father told him he was a genius.

The lending industry had defined subprime mortgages, in terms of the credit bureau risk score (FICO) of the borrower. Other credit imperfections caused borrowers to be classified as subprime for a particular loan. This was available to poorer families. For example, the addition of the mortgage loan might increase the borrower's debt-to-income level above traditionally prudent thresholds.

Home owners were looking for various ways to find capital to buy homes. They were increasingly seeking alternative mortgage products. This was where he would make his money. He would finance interest only mortgages (I-O). During the introductory period. After the introductory period, loan payments would reset to a higher amount to cover the loan's principal. The Principal would be financed by a third party lender.

He would package the loan into a (NegAms) Negative amortizing mortgages. This allowed the homeowner to pay less than current interest due, which resulted in a higher loan balance and higher future payments.

He was all about the money, he would structure the subprime mortgages to include mortgages with very low or no down payments. The second mortgage would serve as the "down payments" for first mortgages to eliminate the need for a cash down payment and/or a monthly premium for private mortgage insurance.

His target was minority communities; he needed to get into the black communities. He took two loans from two different banks. His mother had warned him he would not be moving back home and he should concentrate on his job as a Physician. "But why?" he asked her.

Being a doctor hadn't cropped up to all that they said it would be. It was long hours and hard work. And the money was good, not great. The RN's who worked at the hospital all had a signs on their foreheads that read I want to marry a Doctor. It was like the book "Inglorious Bastards". Even when they took off their too tight uniforms, they still had "I want a Doctor for a husband" stamped on their forehead. As a rule he tried his best not to date nurses.

Soon he had four offices up and running in mostly black low income neighborhoods. He was offering them the American dream. Jason soon started snapping up foreclosed homes and reselling it to the same families. He was raking in over 15 million clear after profits per year. His mother was not happy with his business. She felt he was preying on the poor.

"Would these people ever be able to pay back these loans?" she asked him one night at dinner. "Probably not" he answered "but Mom, I'm sure you and Dad liked your anniversary gift I bought you in Orlando, five bedrooms and an ocean view."

"Actually I don't Jason, Mark showed me the pictures and it's an absolute hideous monstrosity."

Jason's net worth was well over fifty million. His argument was that the economy also benefited from the building and financing boom that took the homeownership rate to record levels. Generous federal subsidies propelled the market to unsustainable levels and an all-time record of almost 2.4 million new homes coming on the market yearly. As a consequence, construction workers, mortgage brokers, real estate agents, landscapers, surveyors, appraisers, manufacturers, suppliers of building materials and many other professions and businesses saw record levels of activity and incomes.

He was helping build America he told her. He was doing well, working one to two days at the hospital and reaping the fruits of his labor, as he called it. Then some early defaults in some subprime mortgages began to emerge, revealing a pattern of fraud in some of his transactions. As the problems worsened, housing starts and new home sales fell sharply. Additional defaults in which some borrowers had assumed that perpetual home price increases would allow them to refinance their way out of onerous loan terms, including the scheduled "resets" to higher monthly mortgage payments.

A growing number of borrowers who had used subprime mortgages and/or seconds to buy at the peak of the market with 100 percent financing found themselves carrying debt loads that exceeded the values of their homes, making refinancing impossible. The feds started asking questions. Jason realized that it was time to leave real estate. He closed his offices, leaving many poor low income families he had refinanced in chaos. Selling their homes was largely impossible because the proceeds would fall short of outstanding debt, forcing them to cover the differences out of other financial resources, which they did not have. The banks started to call them as they were the primary holders of their mortgage. Jason was just making money on the initial transactions so it was easy to walk away. He moved into the house he had bought for his parents in Orlando and took up a job at one of the local hospitals.

He was out on a date with Jenny when she saw her friend Lisa. Jenny introduced him to Lisa and he immediately knew he wanted her. They were going to the club and he asked Lisa to join them. She did, she called up her boyfriend and they joined them at the Green Lizard. He openly flirted all night with Lisa. It made everyone so uncomfortable and when Jenny brought it up on the way home he told her the only reason she felt that way was because she was insecure about her breasts and should consider having a boob job done.

Jason had never dated a black girl before, and he wanted Lisa. At first she rebuffed his advances then one evening he saw her furiously texting on her break. Might be an opportunity he thought as it seemed she was fighting with her boyfriend. She agreed to have a drink with him after work.

He was excited, black girls were an enigma. By the third date they were having sex. He loved it and she was beautiful. Now he knew what all his friends were talking about. He wanted to see if all the stereotypes about black girls were true. He invited her to a pool party and sure enough she didn't swim and would not get her hair wet. Then he took her to a restaurant and purposely made an excuse to go to the bathroom, he gave her his wallet to pay the bill and tip the waiter. His myth got blown out the water, she tipped more than he would have tipped and she paid the bill from her money. For the first time it made him feel a bit uneasy. He really wasn't going to stay with her; he just wanted to have sex. Is this what his mother talked about? He realized how inappropriate or how what he was doing could be considered racists or stereotyping and he was no racist. Not that he wasn't an asshole, he accepted that long time ago. Take me as I am or get out of my life was his motto,

"you can be unhappy in a Mercedes or be unhappy riding in a Honda your call", he told one of his dates. He told Lisa he had to visit his parents and broke it off.

He was home on his day off making his holiday list when he received a call to come into the hospital. There was an Earthquake in Haiti and thousands were dead. His hospital was putting together a team to spend 3 months in Haiti. As they were having the meeting, CNN broke on with a news flash.

Haiti Exterior - Prime Minister Jean Max Bellerive surrounded by local Politicians and his Chief Army Commander, President Rene Preval and His wife Elisabeth Delatour Preval, Minister of Education Joel Jean Pierre.

(Press Conference) President Rene Preval

"First I want to thank the Haitian People for being so calm and helpful in this time of our nation's tragedy. We want to assure the rest of the world we are here working for our people and our nation and we are in full control of the relief efforts. We estimate there are hundreds of thousands injured and dead, with millions homeless. The head of the Haitian Red Cross, Mr. Guiteau Jean Pierre is monitoring the situation very closely and will report back to us in the upcoming hours. We need massive amounts of relief and help from the international community. In the upcoming days we will work closely with the US government and the United Nations to assist in getting supplies and medical help to those who most urgently need it. Thank you that is all for now."

"The images were surreal; wow its bad" said Jason

"yes said some of the other Doctors". They had pulled the disaster list, those who had voluntarily signed up were the first ones called.

"Jason your name is on the list, that's why you were called" said the Administrative Director of the hospital.

"No way" said Jason "I signed up for disasters states side, I'm not doing that, I'm sorry, don't we have like Haitian doctors or something that want to go help their people?"

"We do Jason, 90% have already volunteered and are on their way to Haiti for personal reasons. We are a non-for profit Hospital that works with UNICEF, therefore we have commitments we must keep".

"Fine, I'll figure it out" replied Jason and left. As he walked out he called Paul, "Hey Paul I have a favor to ask, would you like to go to Haiti for 3 months for me, I'll write you a check for fifty large if you do?"

"I would love to Jason, but Brenda is pregnant, but to think, fifty large because you don't want to help these people? Jason you have issues man."

Jason called his father, he told him about the request, his father told him he was proud of him for volunteering and so did his mom. They never gave him an opportunity to let them know he didn't want to go to some mosquito infested poor nation with an identity issue, ravaged by disease, guns, drugs and gangs. There wasn't a whole lot he could do and his reputation was at stake. To save face, he called Paul and told him he got someone to take care of the issue with his parents so he could go. That was the only reason he didn't want to go but he was fine now.

He went out and got drunk the night before, he got to the airport just in time to board the aircraft. He hoped at the very least, they would be put up in a motel. There was a bright side to this whole trip, Island girls and maybe he could get a little beach and some sun in. He knew he would be good with the locals on the island, he had black friends and he dated black girls. He would blend in quite nicely. His only concern was food and water, the whole third world thing wasn't in his schedule. It was a short flight, just about two hours. When the plane landed, he realized it was worse than how it looked. They were hoarded into little open back vans which they called a "Tap Tap" bus.

There were no motels, they were given sleeping bags and assigned to clinics. Then he saw how violent it really was as gangs roamed the streets openly carrying weapons. They were militia type and as the bus stopped he saw looters and persons openly taking goods out of stores. There were those who seemed to have lost all hope and others who stood around, dazed and confused. A young boy was struggling to carry what seemed to be a bag of rice or flour. One of the Militia men tried to take it away from him and a standoff ensued. The boy was not giving it up and the Militia officer pointed his gun at the face of the young man. He still refused to give up the bag or take it down from his head…

Two shots exploded from the muzzle of the rifle, the bag fell and split open, the young man lay dead. The Militia man picked up the bag and took it to a waiting vehicle. Jason saw the Militia man look over and make eye contact with him; he dived to the floor of the tap tap bus and closed his eyes. Jason could feel the warmth of the water running down his pants leg and soaking into his shoes. The tap tap driver looked through his little back window and told him to stay calm. "Relax man...dem only shoot each other...you safe". When they arrived at the clinic the tap tap driver asked him.

"What's that smell?" asked the driver. "Peeing up in my bus? Now the whole bus will smell like pee for my next trip. Come look, we reach. This is the relief camp where you will stay...out out" Jason told him he was sorry for the little accident (handing driver 10US).

"You better put another 10 with that because I'll have to get inside this bus and wash and clean it". Jason gave him the extra 10 and apologetically mumbled sorry again. Dr. Dupre went out to meet Jason; he was excited to have help at the clinic.

"Dr. Bramer, welcome and thank you for volunteering your services. I am Dr. Claude Dupre". "Thank you Dr. Dupre, but call me Jason, there is no need under these circumstances". "Welcome, welcome" said Dr. Dupre. "I was informed by the bus driver you had a little accident. Let me show you to your tent where you can freshen up". The embarrassment was overwhelming, "thank you" said Jason.

Word had already spread through the camp the American doctor had peed on himself on the way to the clinic after seeing a man get shot. At dinner that evening, he was introduced to everyone. Ellen, who handled all the foreign aid, Jacqueline Santiago, who works to control and coordinate the flow of aid to all the camps and Marie, the resident nurse who volunteers on a full time basis, Dominique and Isabella rounded up the immediate staff.

# CHAPTER 3

Marie refused to be a victim of the Earthquake, she was a DuPont. The DuPont women had time and time again risen when all the chips were down. She went back to Lloyd's and secured a donation for Haiti and did the same for everyone who had done business with the DuPont's throughout the years. Her uncle in London had strategized a plan where she could use funds under a pseudonym so it would not be detected. If she solicited donations she could openly have the funds accounted for and use her personal funds to enhance the projects. She would be safe, the money would be accounted for, and it could be held in a local bank as public funds.

She travelled to Germany and asked her to cousins to come to Haiti with her. Gotlieb was an engineer and Marko was in the German military. They agreed to go back to Haiti with her and help. When she got back to the Dominican Republic she had a convoy of 8 trucks and several family members and friends ready to go back to Haiti.

As they drove through the barren windswept mountains, she saw old ladies and families singing hymns going about the restorative process of putting their lives back together.

"Let's stop and give them money" she said to her Aunt. "That is not how the DuPont's go about rebuilding" her aunt told her. These are proud people, look around see what are their needs, food, seeds, livestock, these are the things they need and will appreciate, and this is how your great grandfather restored this Island."

The locals told them there was a disaster recovery center in Fond Parisien. Marie stopped and made contact with the director who sent her to the field hospital which was run by the Harvard Humanitarian Initiative and the Love a Child Foundation. It was one of the best facilities of its kind in Haiti, but currently they were overwhelmed. Marie was working on her list when she met with them. The center was amazing; they had taken in so many displaced children and the children were receiving a level of care even Marie couldn't believe was possible. They had advanced prosthetic limbs, an operating theatre, and doctors from across the world, each, expert in their own respective field. Marie spoke to Professor Gregg Greenough who told her the outlook for the facility was dire. Despite promises of funding and visits from various officials, no money had emerged or seemed forthcoming.

He was afraid to tell the children, his patients, they may soon have to leave. He couldn't meet payroll and reality is he wouldn't be able to keep the volunteers. "These are highly specialized professionals, they will stay voluntarily for a while but we will eventually have to close and these patients will have nowhere to go. There is no other outlet for them". Marie looked at him and smiled, Professor Gregg Greenough was utterly confused, why was this woman smiling at such grave news,

"I feel sick to my stomach" he told her "really sick".

Marie watched another site close by, where a group of children who seemed orphaned by the earthquake were setting up camp in a field next to a stream, using tents donated from the US marines. She told Professor Gregg Greenough she would provide all he needed if he promised to take in the orphans setting up tent downstream and any others who came by. She told him he would have the help he needed within forty eight hours.

Professor Gregg Greenough was not quite convinced about this Haitian woman whom he had never heard of before, who was promising miracles from the sky. He promised he would take in the children downstream, but he had no hope she would return because he had been given so many reassurances and promises never to see them materialize or the donors return. Marie asked him for the Bank account where the trust that funded the clinic was setup.

Professor Greenough was very deliberate and cautious. He did not give Marie the bank information but a liaison for the clinic that could assist.

As they drove down to Port au Prince, Marie called Lloyds and gave them the information for the liaison for the clinic. They were approved to transfer fifty thousand pounds from the Haiti relief account directly to the clinic and another fifty thousand within thirty days. Marie then called Professor Greenough to let him know that the funds would be available within the next twenty four hours. Professor Greenough was astonished when he received the call.

Marie's next stop was to see Pastor Jean Guillaume who had taken in so many orphans into his home in Port-au-Prince. He had sent out a plea for help, two of the trucks from the Dominican Republic were for him. He was pleasantly surprised to see the convoy. He knew Marie; he had worked with her father through Unicef. He had heard of her mother's death but had not seen her since. He offered his

condolences Marie asked Pastor Guillaume to update her as she had been away for a month raising funds and trying to get international help. He told her it had been rough but he, like many others, was determined to get by regardless and wanted to remove the children from the capital as soon as possible.

"The city, with its makeshifts camps and lack of security had become a dangerous place for the children. There were very mean men in the City, going around sexually abusing children in the camps everywhere in Port-au-Prince. That's why we came here with them to be away from that."

Marie was sick to her stomach when Pastor Guillaume had told her about the 200 girls and boys living with him. He would now need to build some type of temporary shelter and school house, but without money, the children's future remains bleak in the tents. The rainy season would soon be upon them, he reminded her, and when it comes there will be more than a million people sleeping on basketball courts and in riverbeds and hospital car parks, beneath hastily constructed shelters and donated tents. He told her water distribution was a good, aid agencies had shipped massive quantities of bottled water and water purification tablets.

Many people, however, have complained that they had not received any help. The government he told her was still in the rapid response phase, which was expected to last about two months. They had not said what the follow up plan would be, but there was a need for longer-term activities such as providing reliable water supplies for rebuilt homes and new settlements. There remained an acute shortage of drinking water in the countryside and other hillside areas affected by the earthquake.

Marie knew this would have been a major problem. The water supply system before the Earthquake only provided 40% of the population of Port-au-Prince with clean water.

When her father worked with UNICEF, they had set up the main public institution for water distribution, the National Directorate for Water Supply and Sanitation in the Ministry of Public Works. They called it DINEPA after its French acronym (Direction Nationale d'Eau Potable et d'Assainissement). The directorate was in charge of implementing the sector policy, coordinating donor assistance and regulating service providers. The way it was supposed to work was the Regional service providers under the authority of the DINEPA or OREPA provided water supply to urban areas. Local Municipalities were supposed to become responsible for water supply and sanitation in the long run as per the framework of the law, but somehow that never happened.

Private operators called "professional operators" were given license and allowed to operate water systems according to their own rules.

Hundreds of water committees, called CAEPAs (*Comités d'Aprovisionnement en Eau Potable et d'Assainissement*) or simply *Comités d'Eau*, were now in charge of the water systems.

Her next stop was back to Camp de la Selle where Dr. Dupre was in charge. He was happy to see Marie.

"I though you forgot about us" he told her.

She had brought back supplies and medical equipment she knew they needed, that night at camp de la selle. Dr. Dupre told her the most urgent need was to care for the amputees in the camp as infection was his main concern. They needed physical rehabilitation as well as mental health services. That means more nursing and mental health personnel and more physical therapists, and of course the right equipment. None of which they had. His fear was many of the amputees would languish or even die without proper rehabilitation.

When the emergency phase of the disaster winds down, there will be a pressing need for mobile and community-based clinics to provide such services as maternity care, post-operative care and treatment for chronic health problems. There were no such services before and now with the Earthquake it would be near impossible. He told Marie forty three of the fifty nine hospitals were not functioning. Camp de la selle was the largest and he had no way of establishing a surveillance network to detect outbreaks of communicable diseases.

As far as he was aware thousands were stranded in makeshift shelters in Port-au-Prince and more and more people were taking advantage of the government's offer of free transportation to cities in the north and south-west which were not affected. He told Marie 30,000 tents were on their way to Haiti, but the supply was unlikely to address the extensive shelter needs. The UN had told him that 100,000 family-sized tents were needed to house about 500,000 people. Marie knew that wasn't enough, the United States Marines had counted over one million Haitians requiring shelter.

After a week of assessing how to proceed and visiting different camps, Marie's aunt and her cousins returned to their homes. Marie needed them to go back and source the equipment and items they had raised funds to purchase. Marie matched dollar for dollar every dime donated. Meanwhile she had begun work on the sites identified for the establishment for organized tent settlements. They had estimated that each settlement would be able to accommodate up to 10,000 people. The process was being held up due to the slow access of water and sanitation facilities and because of this, the tents could not be set up and displaced people started to congregate looking for somewhere to sleep. Marie was very frustrated.

She placed a call to Germany and they assured her within a couple weeks mobile water treatment plants would arrive from Germany via Santo Domingo in the Dominican Republic. The tent settlements would be up and running. The volunteers were very happy, especially because the rainy season was expected to start soon. Marie soon realized the money she had was a needle in a haystack. The estimate was in the billions of dollars to build new homes, government buildings in Port-au-Prince and the surrounding area, which were densely-populated before the earthquake. Gotlieb, her cousin who had spent the week with her sent her a comprehensive report. Many of the buildings that collapsed were poorly designed and built mostly with concrete and often without steel reinforcement and foundations. There was a clear need for higher technical standards to be used during reconstructions.

The Government, along with many planning and architectural experts were also calling for drastic changes to help Haiti build for the future. This included reducing Port-au-Prince's population density and replacing slums on unstable hillsides with homes that were safe, affordable and sustainable.

Marie was confused; she was an 80's child. She grew up in the age of cell phones and laptops. She may have only had one of everything but guess what? She had one. Her parents were supposed to be here. She was too young to be dealing with these things. Not solving world problems and saving children. That night she prayed, she prayed for help, for guidance, she prayed for Haiti, she prayed for her parents, she prayed to the black rock. The next morning she went back to her mother's house and buried her ashes in the garden next to her father. As soon as thinks settled down she was going to rebuild their home. It was her home and it meant so much to her.

She listened to President Preval talking about the lack of investment in Haiti's rural economy. Over the past three decades it has led to an average of 75,000 people moving to the capital, Port-au-Prince, every year. Since 1982, the city's population has grown from 750,000 to more than 2.5 million. He was essentially blaming the people. When they knew the Government was to blame.

They never planned for the rapid expansion which resulted in overcrowding, inadequate infrastructure and the proliferation of slums containing scores of poorly-built homes, many of which were destroyed by the earthquake. Key official buildings like the presidential palace, parliament building, police headquarters and 13 of the government's 15 ministries were also destroyed. Port-au-Prince's main port was also badly damaged and other ports in the area could only accept smaller vessels. One of the two piers in the capital's docks was recently reopened by the US Navy, allowing bulkier shipments to be delivered by sea.

They were so full of crap, Politicians everywhere were the same. Listening to the President speak only angered Marie. Transportation by road continued to be hampered by piles of rubble, she and her team had cleared parts of the road on the way in and the volume of people trying to leave the capital were in the thousands. The Politicians were saying one thing and obviously doing another, but then again this was the Haiti she had come to know. There was nothing new here nothing to see nothing to expose. The UN Development Program (UNDP) has begun employing local people to clear roads.

It was all nonsense and she was tired and really did not want to be bothered with the politics. She asked Dr. Dupre about their clinic and how were they going to move forward.

"Well Marie, telephones and internet connections are still down. Our situation has improved since you were here last. We were given emergency radios and some phones with limited internet capacity, but the local cell phone company has been pretty reliable."

Marie decided to stay and help Dr. Dupre. She told him she was committed to staying until they had everything under control. Marie had asked Mr. Diouf from the local farmers Corp to meet with her. The famers had to get immediate support before the spring planting season begun in March. The season which lasts until May accounted for 60% of Haiti's national agricultural production. If they were unable to get the necessary supplies before the season started there would be a food shortage or worst yet famine. She told him she knew people willing to help and they would get in touch with him. She had to get back to Camp de la Selle. She needed to stay focused and channel her energies spreading herself to thin could be disastrous.

That evening, they would be having a small dinner and with the new doctor who had arrived to help them. She had donated new tents and cots and had gotten two trailers to be delivered to secure the medicine and items that could be stolen. The smaller trailer she would use as her home.

# CHAPTER 4

The dinner was nice; the cooks had made Traditional Haitian dishes which consisted of Joumou (Pumpkin soup), Grillot (fried marinated pork), Lambi (conch meat) Stewed goat, Plantains and Rice and Beans. Jason was intrigued, but did not quite like the spicy food. He ate the soup, rice, plantains and conch meat; the goat needed an acquired taste and pork was a no no. Jason thought Marie was hot as hell, and having been with a black girl before, he knew this would be easy especially coming from a third world country.

That evening, they all mingled and got to know each other. It was a well needed respite. The same food they served themselves they gave to their patients. All the girls fawned over Jason with his blond hair and good looks, he felt like a king. Then he saw the "Tap Tap" driver had been invited and was talking with Marie.

"Marie you should see that grown man cry like a little baby, peed on himself and hiding under the seat in my bus."

They both broke out laughing. Soon Dr. Dupre joined their group and he too stared laughing. "Jason join us" said Dr, Dupre beckoning Jason over.

The "tap tap" driver was some-what like the local comedian. He was telling jokes, and had everyone in an uproar.

"This one for you Jason" said the "tap tap" driver.

"A British doctor, a Haitian doctor and an American doctor were chatting. The British doctor said, "Medicine in my country is so advanced that we can take a kidney out of one man put it in another and have him looking for work in six weeks". Then the Haitian doctor bragged, "That's nothing, we can take a lung out of one person, put it in another and have him looking for work in four weeks". The American doctor, not to be outdone, says, "You guys are way behind. We took a man with no brain out of Texas put him in the White House and almost immediately afterwards half the country was looking for work."

Jason was laughing so hard his heard hurt. The "Tap Tap" driver was really funny. Jason and everyone else were having a good time. Most of the people had nothing to laugh about for weeks, and when the driver was leaving he hugged Marie. She tried to slip him some money and he pulled his hand away.

He looked her in the eyes and said "you not too big for me to put you over my lap and spank you eh" she laughed. Jose, the "tap tap" driver, was her father's childhood friend. It was he who had found her father's body cremated and buried him in their back yard. He had also gathered up all Marie's things and was standing guard at the house when the marines came back. Jose was also responsible for putting her mother's body in the back of his Tap Tap bus and taking it to the morgue. But now he was her surrogate father, but so was probably half of Haiti.

"Be careful of that one" said Jose, rolling his eyes to Jason. "He is no good, just an American playboy. I saw him watching you when you were eating, no good I tell you no good".

"Ok Tonton" she said.

Jason came running up, "hey where are you are going one last joke before you leave".

"Oh you like jokes?" said Jose. "Long time ago, an American doctor came to Haiti and he found a sweet Haitian girl. He found she was so sweet he decided to give her a little 9 month present before he left. When he was boarding the plane, his eyes started to bleed by the time the plane landed he was dead".

"Ok that wasn't very funny" said Jason. "No it wasn't" said Jose "but its true" and he turned and walked away.

"Man that dude is weird" said Jason looking at Marie, "one minute he's cool as heck and next he's acting like some creepy weirdo douchebag".

"That creepy weirdo douchebag is my Uncle" said Marie walking away. Jason reached for Marie's hand "I'm sorry" he said. Marie pulled her hand away "no you're not and please don't take my hand in that manner again Doctor".

152

Rough night, rough crowd thought Jason as he lay in his tent. What was up with this Marie girl anyways he thought, she is a nurse but she gets a trailer? Shouldn't the Doctors be sleeping in the trailers? He was going to make some inquiries about it because he needed a trailer, the tent thing was not happening.

The next morning when he awoke, Dr. Dupre was addressing all the medical personnel as well as a small group of camp workers. "We are seeing way too many people with diarrhea and vomiting. There must be an infection outbreak somewhere or they are drinking from a contaminated source. Please monitor them very closely".

Jason was thinking half out aloud when he said "shouldn't these people know better than to drink dirty water?" The steely gaze of death looked back at him, horror on the face of some of the workers. Jason wasn't sure; did he actually say those words? After realizing that he did he quietly sat down.

Dr. Dupre said to him "Jason lets be more conscientious of the terms we use and show a little more respect for those who are less educated in the field of medicine."

The first word that came to his mind was #1. OMG no, I didn't, and #2. there goes Marie. Well he might as well do some work he thought, because he sure wasn't going to get anything more on this trip. Hell he might even be lucky to get out of Haiti with all my limbs intact the rate this was going, he thought to himself. Marie just had to get her two cents in; actually she wanted to get a whole lot more in but was just too polite.

"Excuse me ... And you are? Actually it doesn't matter who you are, these people as you call them, are just trying to stay alive."

"I didn't mean it like that I just meant, well you know."

"Actually I don't know Jason, and quite frankly at this point I don't care to know. We have to be present for the medical conference today as per Dr. Dupre's instructions, if you still wish to join us great if not great also."

Marie, Ellen and Jason headed down to the conference; they were picked up by Jose. No one was talking to him at this point, and he was ready to fly back to Florida, he kept thinking on the drive of the possibilities. When they got to Port au Prince the security was intense. US marines checked everyone. They were given security passes and taken to an enormous tent with about 50 persons sitting, it was hot and sticky but there was plenty of water. Foreign journalists, Americans, there were people everywhere. Then Jason and Marie found out the President of the United States of America, Barack Obama, would be giving a live speech on Haiti from the White House lawn.

Marie found it very exciting, she was glad she had dressed
appropriately and Jason was actually behaving himself, he hadn't
made any foolish remarks since they arrived, he was quite courteous.
Maybe it was because he was around his people and maybe he just
thought less of Haitians. Well as her father would say 2dozens-
Doesn't care and doesn't wanna know.

She remembered the first time he said it, she was like "what Papa?"
and then he said it again even her mother started laughing. Jose did
remind her very much of her father, there was a story about why
Jose called her his niece and why he had always been there for her
family. If he had known they were going after her father he would
have been there too. But then he would not have been able to be here
for her now. Life she was learning had its own way of working itself
out. She found she was no longer excited to hear what was in store
for the camps and hospitals but she was excited to hear President
Obama speak.

President Preval addressed the packed assembly letting them know
the citizens needed more aid. There was an urgent need for more
food and aid in the outlying provinces. He was concerned that there
might be an outbreak of Cholera and if it was indeed Cholera it was
going to be a big problem and would compound relief efforts. The US
marines, in response, said they could provide more aid, but President
Preval would have to relinquish control of the airport to the armed

forces and let them handle the flow of aid, as this is what they were trained to do.

The meeting was long and boring, Marie was restless. The President agreed to give the United States control of the airport. The US would work with Russia on approval for the Russians to fly in their Antonov An-225, which was designed to airlift the Buran space shuttle for the Soviet space program. It was one of the biggest in the world and would be able to fly in a mobile Air Traffic control tower.

Jason looked over at Marie. He was confused as there was no mention of medical supplies or updates, just political rhetoric. But they were both glad for the break during the speech.

"Jason why did you really volunteer to come to Haiti?" asked Marie.

"I didn't Marie. I was chosen, quite honestly. I would have preferred to stay and not come."

"You are a bit of a jerk actually, you are an ass, you don't think before you talk and you are quite full of yourself."

"Wow that's a mouthful but ok. We both have to work together so it is what it is"

"Yes!" said Marie, walking away.

They both got back to their seats in time to hear the US President deliver his speech

**President Obama**
**Remarks by the President on Recovery Efforts in Haiti**
**Diplomatic Reception Room**

10:10 A.M. EST

THE PRESIDENT: "Good morning everybody. I've directed my administration to launch a swift, coordinated and aggressive effort to save lives and support the recovery in Haiti. The losses that have been suffered in Haiti are nothing less than devastating, and responding to a disaster of this magnitude will require every element of our national capacity -- our diplomacy and development assistance; the power of our military and most importantly the compassion of our country. This morning, I'm joined by several members of my national security team who are leading this coordinated response.

I've made it clear to each of these leaders that Haiti must be a top priority for their departments and agencies right now. This is one of those moments that calls out for American leadership. For the sake of our citizens who are in Haiti, for the sake of the Haitian people who have suffered so much and for the sake of our common humanity, we stand in solidarity with our neighbors to the south, knowing that but for the grace of God, there we go.

This morning, I can report that the first waves of our rescue and relief workers are on the ground and at work. A survey team worked overnight to identify priority areas for assistance and shared the results of that review throughout the United States government and with international partners who are also sending support. Search and rescue teams are actively working to save lives. Our military has secured the airport and prepared it to receive the heavy equipment and resources that are on the way and to receive them around the clock, 24 hours a day. An airlift has been set up to deliver high-priority items like water and medicine. And we're coordinating closely with the Haitian government, the United Nations, and other countries that are also on the ground.

We have no higher priority than the safety of American citizens and we've airlifted injured Americans out of Haiti. We're running additional evacuations and will continue to do so in the days ahead. I know that many Americans, especially Haitian Americans, are desperate for information about their family and friends. And the State Department has set up a phone number and e-mail address that you can find at www.state.gov to inquire about your loved ones. And you should know that we will not rest until we account for our fellow Americans in harm's way.

None of this will seem quick enough if you have a loved one who's trapped, if you're sleeping on the streets, if you can't feed your children. But it's important that everybody in Haiti understand at this very moment, one of the largest relief efforts in our recent history is moving towards Haiti. More American search and rescue teams are coming. There will also be more food, more water, doctors, nurses, paramedics. More people, equipment and capabilities that can make the difference between life and death.

The United States armed forces are also on their way to support this effort. Several Coast Guard cutters are already there providing everything from basic services like water, to vital technical support for this massive logistical operation. Elements of the Army's 82nd Airborne Division will arrive today. We're also deploying a Marine Expeditionary Unit, the aircraft carrier USS Carl Vinson, and the Navy's hospital ship, the Comfort.

And today, I'm also announcing an immediate investment of $100 million to support our relief efforts. This will mean more of the life-saving equipment, food, water and medicine that will be needed. This investment will grow over the coming year as we embark on the long-term recovery from this unimaginable tragedy.

Finally, I want to speak directly to the people of Haiti. Few in the world have endured the hardships that you have known. Long before this tragedy, daily life itself was often a bitter struggle and after suffering so much for so long, to face this new horror must cause some to look up and ask, have we somehow been forsaken?

To the people of Haiti, we say clearly and with conviction, you will not be forsaken; you will not be forgotten. In this, your hour of greatest need, America stands with you. The world stands with you. We know that you are a strong and resilient people. You have endured a history of slavery and struggle, of natural disaster and recovery. And through it all, your spirit has been unbroken and your faith has been unwavering. So today, you must know that help is arriving -- much, much more help is on the way.

Thank you very much, everybody."

END
10:16 A.M. EST

What an amazing speech thought Marie. She was glad they had decided to attend the conference. Now they knew there was a possibility of a Cholera outbreak that changed the dynamics on care, she looked at Jason. He was aware she was looking at him, but could not read her face. All the great smart Americans and they sent us this klutz she though looking at Jason and smiling. Jason smiled back, maybe there was hope he thought. She must be thinking wonderful thoughts about me. They all got back into Toton's bus for the drive home.

"I have a joke for you guys. Since everybody had such a great time at the meeting."

Tonton was like a breadth of fresh air. They were exhausted from the meeting and Jason was turning out to be the worst human being on the planet. The audacity, the nerve of this young man to tell her he didn't want to come and help. Who says that? What type of human being turns their back on another? So many thoughts were going through her head, it was sad to say, but people like this really offers no real contribution to the world. Haiti was small, and yes there had been many conflicts, but generally the people were decent. Her mother always said, "Marie you have to find the goodness in people, look for the positives not the negatives." Well there was one positive, he was a doctor.

Her thoughts were broken up by Tonton's joke.

"Ok, three men were standing in line to get into heaven one day. Apparently it had been a pretty busy day, so Peter told the first one, "Heaven's getting pretty close to full today and I've been asked to admit only people who have had particularly horrible deaths. So what's your story?" The first man replies: "Well, for a while I've suspected my wife has been cheating on me, so today I came home early to try to catch her red-handed. As I came into my 5th floor apartment I could tell something was wrong, but all my searching around didn't reveal where this guy was hiding. Finally, I went out to the balcony, and sure enough, the man was hanging off the railing. I got really mad, so I started beating on the man, but the man wouldn't fall. So I got ah hammer and ah started to hammer he fingers. So he let go and fell -- but he fell into the bushes, stunned but not dead. So I ran into the kitchen, grabbed the fridge and threw it over the edge, killing him instantly. St. Peter all the stress and anger got to me, and I had a heart attack".

"That sounds like a pretty bad day" said St. Peter, and let the man in. The second man comes up and St. Peter explains to him about heaven being full, and again asks for his story. "It's been a very strange day. You see, I live on the 6th floor of my apartment building and every morning I do my exercises out on my balcony. Well, this morning I must have slipped or something, because I fell over the edge. But I got lucky and caught the railing of the balcony on the floor below me. I knew I couldn't hang on for very long and then suddenly, this man bursts out onto the balcony. I thought for sure I was saved, then he started beating on me and kicking me. I held on the best I could until he ran into the apartment and grabbed a hammer and started pounding on my hands.

Finally I just let go, but again I got lucky and fell into the bushes below, stunned but I was alright. Just when I was thinking I was going to be okay, this refrigerator comes falling out of the sky and kills me, now I'm here". "My son" said St. Peter "that I concede that is a pretty horrible death". The third man came to the front of the line and again

St. Peter explained that heaven was full and asked for his story. "See what had happened was I'm hiding inside this refrigerator right..."

They all broke out laughing... leave it to Tonton to make everyone laugh.

Jacqueline was sitting next to Jason. Marie couldn't tell what they were talking about but it sure didn't look like work.

# CHAPTER 5

Jaqueline Santiago was walking out of Jason's tent and Marie saw her. It had been a long week. They were receiving more and more patients showing signs of Cholera. Then Jason came out of his tent "well don't you look the picture of the quintessential Doctor, if I may dare say so" said Jacqueline.

"Dr. Bramer, you won't need that coat here, you will find it more effective to work in regular clothes and use disposal gowns...if needed" said Marie as she walked away.

"What's eating this woman?" asked Jason, "she walks around like she owns the place and is always mouthing off about something SMH".

"Jason, it's more than you know and more than you can imagine" said Jacqueline. "I'm not supposed to tell you this, but just so you know, Marie lost her mother in the earthquake, but rather than feel sorry for herself, or mourn, she decided to help others. She has sacrificed everything getting donations and with the help of her family has raised millions. Marie has a heart of gold."

Wow! He just couldn't get it right in this country; nothing ever seemed to be what it looked like. "So cut her some slack, ok?"

"Damn that must be tough" replied Jason.

"You have no idea Dr. Bramer, you have no idea".

They heard a disturbance outside the tent. Shouting, screaming, a young girl was trying to run into the camp but was being dragged by a group of thugs. Her clothes was ripped, her breasts exposed her lip was bloody. "Please help me, please somebody" she screamed as she was being led away. Marie bolted to her and ripped her from the arms of the would-be kidnapper. She took off running inside the camp. The attackers then grabbed Marie by her hair "do you want to take her place" one of the guys asked whilst bending her arm behind her back.

Dr. Dupre soon got on the phone and called for the marines telling them the clinic was under attack.

Jason walked over "let her go now" he told the thugs.

"Or what?" asked one of the attackers. He then pulled out a gun and pointed it at Jason, he ripped the diamond off Marie's neck, "what's this?" he asked. Holding it out in the sunlight, Marie tried to fight back, but he was too strong and there were so many of them.

Jason had moved within 3 feet of the thugs, and in one swift movement he grabbed the necklace and pushed the thug away. Marie came flailing in his arms. She grabbed the necklace and ran back to her trailer. Jason never saw it coming, the gun hit him at the side of his head and suddenly everything went black. The darkness soon lit up with little twinkling lights, he was blinded for what seems like twenty seconds. Then he got hit again. He was trying to fight back, but there was so many of them. His eyes were running water, he was gagging, he felt being kicked repeatedly in the stomach, his back and head. The he heard 3 gun shots one after the other repeatedly. He looked up and saw that Marie had come back. She had a P226 German 9mm hand gun, which belonged to her father.

"The next bullet goes through your eyes" she said in Creole. Jason had never heard her speak Creole before and he had no idea what she was saying, but he knew she meant business. He got up off his knees with the help of Dr. Dupre. His shirt was bloody and he had a nasty gash on his forehead.

"Give us back the girl and we will leave" said the thug.

Marie leveled the gun cocked and said to him

"Say gives me the girl one more time, say it."

The thug didn't, he was quiet. In this instant, in that very moment he knew he was choosing life or death, and he chose life.

Marie was ready to shoot him at point blank range and not even think twice about it. Her eyes spoke volumes, her body was tight, her mouth was dry, her eyes focused. She had never taken another person's life before but if ever there was a time now was the time.

Then the sound of the marines coming broke the tension, and the thugs began to walk away.

"We are coming back" he told Marie as they walked away.

"I want you to come back" Marie told him.

The marines jumped out of their truck and followed them. They were not supposed to engage or threaten civilians. Only if civilians were engaged in the acts of violence or openly breaking the law. The first lieutenant was the officer who had rescued Marie, he walked up to the thug and hit the leader with his gun butt. He fell forward and blood began to ooze from the back of his head. The rest of the marines had their guns drawn and aimed at the group. The first lieutenant stepped on his hand, as he removed the gun the attacker had stuck in his waistband.

"Any one has issues speak now?" he asked, hitting him with his gun butt again.

"If you come back here, I will personally hunt you down and kill every last one of you" he told them "and if just by chance I see, smell or even hear you're around here I'll shoot you on sight."

Mam can you repeat that in creole for me said the first lieutenant looking at Marie. Marie repeated the words of the officer in creole. The thugs picked up their leader and walked away.

Marie and Jacqueline rushed to Jason.

"I'm fine, really I am" he kept insisting.

The marines said they would stay the night.

"Good lord Jason what were you thinking? You could have been killed" said Jacqueline. "That would have created an international crisis."

"Jacqueline I am a lot of things, but a coward I'm not and any man who hits a woman is a coward and man who rapes a woman needs to be in jail and any man who molests children needs to be shot. These thugs, murders and rapists needed to be shot and I'm glad Marie was ready to shoot them."

"Thank you Jason" said Marie, blinking back the tears.

"You're welcome Marie, but I'm not sure you needed my help. You are a pretty bad ass, what else you got in the Trailer? Hold on, don't tell me, I don't think I want to know". "Ouch!" said Jason as Dr. Dupre stitched him up.

"And to think Tonton said you were chicken shit" said Marie smiling.

"Hey I may have peed my pants but I still have a little pride and chivalry left" said Jason laughing and grimacing at the same time.

"I have been taking care of the young girl who was raped" said Ellen. "She is in shock and very worried. There were two of them; it was her and her sister. Her sister was taken and she is scared after what has happened they will kill her".

Marie was silent; she left the group and walked over to the marines. They chatted for a few minutes and then she came back.

"What was that all about?" asked Jason "nothing" replied Marie.

"That looked like a lot of nothing to me" said Jason.

Marie smiled "listen up Mr. Chivalry, you need to get healed and think about going back home, it's dangerous here.

Don't you have a wife, girlfriend, parents to go back to? This is our home and our fight. I would never forgive myself if something happened to you".

"Marie two days before I came here I almost got hit by a bus".

"That is such a random statement" said Marie.

"And two days before you got here I was buying coffee for my mother."

"I'm sorry Marie. I heard, but the point I was making was, I could die any day, any time anywhere. Fighting, well in my case getting my butt kicked never felt so good. If I died today, I died because I believed in something; I died trying to save a child's life. If I had gotten hit by the bus, it would have been because I was trying to cross the road drunk. And yes I didn't want to come here originally but that was only because I was being selfish. Marie I know what you were talking about with those marines, and I am coming with you. When you find her you will need a doctor".

Jason went to his tent and Marie to hers. She didn't know what to think of Jason. That he would risk his life for her was remarkable. His poor little limp body just being beaten senselessly and still not giving up.

Jason laid in his cot thinking about the day's events and to think he wanted to pay fifty thousand dollars not be here. He wasn't going to leave, and he thought he just might stay and help rebuild this country. He felt purpose. This was the first time in his life he had to fight for something and it felt good. It felt right. Jason left his tent and went knocking on Marie's door. Marie opened the door it was Jason. He looked terrible; there was a hematoma over his left eye, the size of a golf ball. He would have a scar on his forehead for the rest of his life, on his face shone the innocence of a boy who once thought he was a man.

"I want to help Marie, I know you don't really know me; all you know is the jerk. I want a chance to make a difference I have money lots of it. I can help".

"I understand Jason and I think you will, but now you need to rest. Get some sleep".

Did you take some pain meds or any anti-inflammatory?"

"I did, I did" replied Jason.

"Ok Jason we will talk about it tomorrow, please get some rest". He smiled and slowly walked away. Marie looked at him walking away.

The next morning, the local Police arrived and took a report. They would try and find the sister. But they said chances are very unlikely that they would find her. The Police said there were many stories like this and so few of them, Marie understood. She was not concerned about the police finding the girl as she knew the chances of them completing such a task was slim to none. The Police were outmanned and outgunned by the thugs on the streets. The US marines would have to go with her and they promised late the next evening they would.

Dr. Dupre was apologetic and concerned. He did not like being vulnerable to armed thugs. He ran a clinic not a boot camp. He was also very uncomfortable that Marie was in the possession of weapons on the compound without his knowledge. Yes they served a valuable purpose yesterday but the mere facts there were weapons on the premises made him very uncomfortable.

As they sat around the next morning Dr. Dupre brought up his concerns. He was also very concerned that Jason had been hurt and wanted him to possibly go volunteer at a safer location or return to the United States.

Marie explained the guns were not hers. They in fact belonged to her father. They were in her personal possessions because they were recovered from the house by Tonton. All his items and that of her mom's were securely locked away in a small combination safe in her trailer. The only reason she retrieved them was because of the gravity of the situation and the fact someone could have easily been killed.

Jason told Dr. Dupre that he wasn't going anywhere. He also chimed in he was glad Marie had the gun. They were all lucky she did as the other child could have been easily carried away. They all could have been shot and killed and the clinic looted. Dr. Dupre was silent, he knew they were right. He conceded and asked that they have an alarm system implemented should something like that ever occur again. They all agreed.

When Tonton came back and heard what had happened he was very angry, angry that no one had called him he told Marie. She should have called him right away. But Marie was glad she didn't. Tonton was not a very good person to talk when angry. She had seen the repercussions of his actions many times. He usually left many of the walking wounded when he was in conflict and no doubt if he was there it would have been very ugly.

Tonton went up to Jason "so I heard you were a hero my boy and your face sure tells a story, wanna hear a joke?"

"A real joke?" asked Jason "or another poke fun at me thingy that you do".

"No boy a real joke I'm telling you" said Tonton. "Once there was a church that had a bell that no one could ring. One day, a boy came and asked the priest if he could try. So the boy went up into the tower and ran straight faced-first into the bell. boom next thing you know the bell rigging all through Port au Prince. Hell! even I heard the bell. The Priest was so shocked he gave the boy a job right away. "Every Sunday my son you are responsible for rigging the bell and getting everyone to church." But one Sunday, he ran straight toward the bell with his face, missed and fell off the tower and died. The priest was devastated "Congregation," the priest asked before the next Sunday mass. "Did anybody know this boy's name? Because I didn't know him, but his face sure rings a bell. Well my boy, that's what I thought when I saw you. Can't remember your name but by looking at your face it sure rings a bell of someone you used to look like".

"Tonton that's just mean" said Marie.

But Jason was laughing "its ok" he told Marie "I'll get him back one day and they all started laughing."

It was late evening when the marines showed up for Marie. She asked the little girl who had been attacked to come with them. Jason was dressed to go with them but Dr. Dupre advised him against it. But Jason did not agree and when the marines said he couldn't ride with them, Tonton showed up and Jason went in his truck with his friends. Marie called Jason out the truck. Marie told Tonton it was a bad idea for Jason to go look for the girl as he is not from Haiti and if something happened to him there would lots of explaining to do. Jason became very upset.

"I wish everyone including you Dr. Dupre would stop speaking like I'm not standing right here, like I'm some five year old that needs protection. So what I got my butt kicked last night. I don't want to go on this trip for revenge. I know I can't fight those guys I'm a realist, I'm a Doctor. I'm going because when you find her and I know you will, she is going to need medical attention right away. If any of you get hurt I'll be there as much as you want to protect me. I want to protect you".

175

The idea of taking the Tap tap bus was scratched. Tonton and Jason got into the Marines jeep. As the jeep drove through the streets the mayhem was abundantly clear. There were even rotten corpses at the side of the road.

"Stop" said Marie the jeep stopped and she went over to an old man picking up cans and putting it into a bag on his bicycle. The old man hugged and kissed Marie then pointed to a south westerly direction. The little girl said the area looked familiar and she thought that is where they took her sister.

Marie jumping back into jeep and they headed in the direction the old man had pointed. He said most of the thieves and thugs were staying there. He told Marie he thought the escaped convicts had occupied the old school building, north of where they were and they have been taking young women of the streets and holding them there. The marines told Marie and Jason when we get there they wanted them to stay in the jeep and out of sight. Tonton was with them as he spoke creole and knew the area. Jason and Marie both nodded simultaneously. They drove around for about an hour before finding the old school and when they did find it what a surprise.

It was set up like a small village made up of tents. There were thousands of people some on the streets, some in tents. Fifty percent of the items looted probably were stored right in this one area. There were flat screen TV's still in boxes outside of tents, bicycles, stereos, refrigerators and there was one way in and one way out.

"I think we should return another time" said the marines. "This has the making of bad things."

"We at least have to give it one try" said Marie.

"Ok!" said one of the marines. "I have an idea" He pulled out the megaphone and started driving up making announcements in English and having Tonton do the same in Creole.

"We are not here to arrest anyone; we are just here to find a missing child".

"Nou pa isit la yo arete nenpòt moun nou yo se jis isit la jwenn yon timoun ki disparèt" said Tonton.

They kept repeating it over and over as they slowly drove up the street. Soon a small mob gathered behind the jeep as they continued to get closer to the school. After which they could go no further, there were tires blocking the street. One of the convicts who were occupying the school came out and on the rooftop they could see at least twenty men. They didn't know if they were armed or not.

The convict shouted "why are you here? Leave this place. We have nothing for you".

Then he turned to the mob and said "they come here to kill us. They want us dead…Death to the Americans". They started throwing bottles and cans and rocks at the jeep.

"Bad idea" said the marines we should have never drove in.

He looked at the other marine and replied "I'm not dying in here today; if I have to I'm plowing right through."

Marie grabbed the bull horn and jumped out the in the street. As she jumped out, a rock was thrown and hit her in the head causing blood to squirt from her forehead. Jason attempted to jump out the truck and Tonton grabbed him.

"They will kill you, and you will make it worse for her. If anyone can she can do this".

Blood was dripping down on her white shirt. She took a small piece of cloth gauze from her pocket and held it to her head.

"What is wrong with you?" she shouted in creole into the megaphone. "I am Haitian; I am your daughter like the girls trapped in that building. Does making me bleed make you a proud Haitian? Does the sight of my blood bring you joy? How many of our people have died in the past few days and how many more will die in the coming days? Take my life if you must because those children being raped and held as prisoners in that building will surely die".

"Our Haitian faith comes from God. We are one people united against overwhelming odds. You did not choose to be Haitian we are born Haitian. We do not choose our faith we are born with it, we do not choose to kill our children they are meant to live"…There was a hushed silence from the mob. You could hear a pin drop as she walked closer to them; she wanted them to see who she was, so they could see the blood gushing from her head. "These men are criminals, escaped convicts from Port au Prince who were jailed, who kill and rape our children and yet you stone me, the hands that would save them. Then you are not Haitian because Haitians do not kill babies. These are the men you should be stoning" she said, pointing at the school. The cloth she was holding to her head became heavy, her hands were tired and her lips were dry.

She then felt hands embracing her, they were holding her up and the voice said to the crowd "shame on you, shame on you. Do you know who this is? Yes you do! When she was born you partied in the streets. This is Marie DuPont Duvalier, daughter of Jean Pierre Duvalier". And then the old man started calling names and pointing people out in the crowd.

"Philippe when your mother died didn't Jean Pierre come to the funeral and bury her free of charge? Moel when your son got yellow fever didn't Jean Pierre took care of him and gave you money?" Then someone in the crowd turned to the gates of the school and shouted "Give Marie the children, Give Marie the Children, Give Marie the Children" the mob became incredibly angry and turned their rage on the convicts. They were throwing rocks and firebombs at the school, and they broke down the barrier. The old man helped Marie back to the jeep and the road was cleared. "Let's go!" said the marines "get her in".

Jason was attending to Marie. He stitched her up and gave her Gatorade.

"No!" said Marie "if you want, go without me but I'm not leaving without the children".

Tonton was on his phone, giving directions to his friends.

"I will bring the children" said the old man. He followed the mob who had already broken into the old school, they were beating the convicts and raining blows on them.

They came back with 15 young girls, age ranging from 12-17. "Are you here to help us?" asked one of the girls. "Yes! Yes!" replied Marie with tears pouring down her cheeks. Jason was checking the girls and helping them. Then Tonton's bus showed up, his friends were all armed with guns and machetes. He went in and took out his gun and hung it on his shoulder. He turned to Marie and replied "next time we do it Tonton's way". His friends moved all the rifles in the back to the front to make room for the girls. When everyone was safely inside the vehicles they drove away. Marie was tired, Jason held her in his arms but this time she didn't say let her go. She was a Duvalier, wow even he knew who the Duvalier's were in Haiti.

# CHAPTER 6

Marie's father Jean Pierre was an illegitimate son, but his mother brought him up the right way. His father, Papa Doc Duvalier, was born in Port-au-Prince, the son of Duval Duvalier, a justice of the peace, and to Ulyssia Abraham, a baker. Jean Pierre's father was raised by his aunt. He completed a degree in medicine from the University of Haiti in 1934 and served as a staff physician at several local hospitals. He went on to spend a year at the University of Michigan, studying public health. In 1943, he became active in a United States-sponsored campaign to control the spread of contagious tropical diseases, helping the poor to fight typhus, yaws, malaria and other tropical diseases that ravaged Haiti for years. And that was how he affectionately became known as "Papa Doc", a moniker that he used throughout his life.

Lucky enough to be schooled and literate in a country where few were educated, his father witnessed the political turmoil of Haiti. His father lived through the occupation of Haiti by the United States which began in 1915, followed by its incessant violent repressions of political dissent, which left a powerful impression on him. The one thing that bothered him the most was the lack of political power of the poor black majority and their resentment against the *gens de couleur*. Papa Doc Duvalier became actively involved in the négritude movement of Haitian author Dr. Jean Price-Mars. He began to practice the worship of Voodoo, the religion of his mother. He then co-founded the journal Les Griots. In 1939, Duvalier married Simone Ovide, with whom he had four children: Marie Denise, Nicole, Simone and Jean-Claude. He had 3 girls, and fearing he might never have a son Jean Pierre was born outside his marriage. After the birth of Jean-Perre, his wife became pregnant with Jean-Claude.

In 1946 Papa Doc aligned himself with President Dumarsais Estimé and was appointed Director General of the National Public Health Service. In 1949, Duvalier served as Minister of both Health and Labor, but when General Paul Magloire ousted President Estimé in a coup d'état, Duvalier left the government and was forced into hiding when President Magloire resigned and left Haiti to be ruled by a succession of provisional governments.

Papa Doc came out from hiding on 22 September 1957 and declared his candidacy for the President of Haiti. The elections pitted Louis Déjoie, a mulatto land-owner and industrialist from the north of Haiti against Duvalier, who was backed by the military. The *gens de couleur* did not want Papa Doc in power as they thought he was a dangerous tyrant and a Houngan. Papa Doc Duvalier campaigned as a populist, using a noiriste strategy of challenging the mulatto elite and appealing to the Afro-Haitian majority. He described his opponent as part of the ruling mulatto class that was making life difficult for the country's rural black majority and still practicing racism.

After being sworn in on 22nd October, President Papa Doc Duvalier exiled most of the major supporters of Déjoie and had a new constitution adopted in 1957. Jean Pierre as a child found his life had changed drastically in1957, as a child he lived alone with his mother. She lived with his grandparents and they lived a life of farmers. They were not poor, but struggled for necessary cash flow. Then one day all that stopped. His grandparents wanted to stay on the farm. Jean Pierre and his aunts all moved into a big house in Port au Prince. His mother no longer worked long hours and his uncle and aunts started working in the shipping business. His school changed, he had new friends and new toys. As he got older, his mother and his uncles all treated him with respect. He heard whispers, but never directly to him. One day, one of the children in his school asked if it was true, his father was the President. He laughed and told her no his father was dead.

President Duvalier promoted and patronized members of the black majority in the civil service and the army. Haiti became a semi Socialist State. Then as his power grew in mid-1958, the army, which had supported Duvalier earlier, tried to oust him in another coup, but his supporters failed. Those were the times when Jean Pierre knew he was different. Whenever there was trouble in the country a police vehicle would be stationed outside his mother's house. Outside his school outside his soccer matches. In response, Papa Doc replaced the chief-of-staff with a more reliable officer. He then proceeded to create his own power base within the army by turning the army's Presidential Guard into an elite corps, aimed at maintaining his power. After this, Duvalier dismissed the entire general staff and replaced it with officers who owed their positions and were loyal to him.

Then Papa Doc heard a rumor, three exiled Haitians and five Americans had landed armed to the teeth. The five American freebooters and three exiled Haitian army officers sailed from the Florida Keys in the good ship Mollie. They had been paid by Duvalier's Presidential opponent whom he had placed in exile. Their plan was to rally political dissidents to their side and take over Haiti. They came ashore at Deluge and seized a jeep which took them 45 miles into Port-au-Prince. Then around midnight, the eight men stalked into the downtown Dessalines Barracks shot an officer and captured 50 nonplused soldiers.

The Haitian rebels phoned around town to old army friends and even to the guard of President Francois Duvalier in the palace from across the street urging them to rise up. The rebels got no response. Duvalier called out loyal troops and armed civilians and then sent his forces in an overwhelming counterattack at the Dessalines Barracks. In the bloody fire-fight, all eight of the rebels were killed and Duvalier used this coup attempt as a lesson to all would-be attackers. The revolutionary meddling of five Americans -- led by Arthur Payne, a former deputy sheriff in Miami -- worsened the already touchy Haiti U.S. relations. The day before the abortive coup, a Haitian minister told newsmen in New York that U.S. Ambassador Gerald

Drew should be recalled because "he is going too far in our internal affairs". The State Department angrily denied that charge but then it turned around and apologized for the U.S. plotters. Duvalier accepted the apology grudgingly.

President Duvalier had lived in the United States, he knew their might and he knew their power. Unlike his predecessors, he covertly involved the United States in all his foreign affairs decisions. In 1959, Duvalier created a rural militia, the Milice Volontaires de la Sécurité Nationale (MVSN, English: National Security Volunteer Militia) which was locally known as the "Tonton Macoute" a Creole term for the bogeyman. This was created to extend and bolster support for the regime in the countryside. The Macoute, which by 1961 had twice the numbers of the regular army, never developed into a real military force, but still was more than a mere secret police. The Tonton Macoute's name was taken from the Italian Facist paramilitary organization (The Blackshirts).

During the time Papa Doc had spent in hiding, he learned about Benito Amilcare Andrea Mussolini and his fascist followers. How he consolidated power through a series of laws which transformed the nation into a one-party dictatorship. Within five years Benito had established a dictatorial authority by both legal and extraordinary means, aspiring to create a totalitarian state. He created squads called the Squadre d'Azione ("Black Shirts Action Squad") which were organized to destroy opposing political and economic organizations.

By the end of 1920, the Blackshirts were attacking and destroying organizations, not only of the opposition, but also of communists, republicans, Catholics, trade unionists and those in cooperatives. Hundreds of people were killed as the Fascist squads expanded in numbers into power. Benito then officially transformed the Blackshirts into a national militia, the Voluntary Fascist Militia for National Security. The black shirt was worn not only by these military Fascists, but also by other Fascists and their sympathizers, especially on patriotic occasions.

Papa Doc Duvalier then formed the *Tonton Macoute he made them wear blue shirts and straw hats.* He gave them the name because he knew what their jobs were and what he would have to do to stay in power. So they were the mythological *Tonton Macoute* (Uncle Gunnysack). The Bogeyman who kidnaps and punishes unruly children by snaring them in a Gunnysack (*macoute*) and carrying them off to be consumed at breakfast. Papa Doc authorized the Tonton Macoutes to commit systematic violence and murders in the name of the Republic Of Haiti. They were responsible for over 60,000 murders and rapes.

Duvalier employed the Tonton Macoute in a reign of terror against any opponents, including those who proposed progressive social systems. Those who spoke out against Duvalier would disappear at night, or were sometimes attacked in broad daylight. Tontons Macoutes often stoned and burnt people alive and many times the corpses were put on display, or often found hung on trees for everyone to see. Family members who tried to remove the bodies for proper burial often disappeared themselves, never to be seen again. They were believed to have been abducted and killed by the MVSN, who were also called the "Tontons Macoutes". Anyone who challenged the MVSN risked assassination.

It was during this time Jean Pierre met Tonton. He was older than Jean Pierre, about 18-19 yrs older and his job was to make sure nothing happened to Jean Pierre or his mother and to report anything suspicions back to Luckner Cambronne, the head of the Tonton Macoute.

Jean Pierre was beaten up one day by a bully at his school. When he returned home, he saw his mother and Tonton sitting inside the house. He also saw the kid who had beaten him up with his parents, surrounded by men in straw hats, blue shirts and sunglasses. The entire family was crying, the boy's father, and his mother all started to fall at his feet and begged him for forgiveness.

Jean Pierre was confused as to what had happened. Suddenly a van came for the family and they started to whimper. His mother turned to him and said

"please Jean Pierre tell them no".

Jean Pierre then turned to the men who were taking them away and said

"no bring them back" and just like that, in an instant, the family was brought back and the boy from his school hugged him. Tonton who was with his mom smiled, they were happy. He didn't understand why, how, what he did, but making his mother happy was all that mattered. She was everything to him.

Luckner Cambronne nicknamed the "Vampire of the Caribbean" was the right hand of Papa Doc Duvalier. His job was also to make sure Jean Pierre and his mother never wanted anything and was always safe. Luckner was the worst of his kind, profiteering by extortion, carried out by his henchmen and by supplying corpses and blood to Universities and hospitals in the United States. Luckner made sure some of the most important members of the Tonton Macoute were voodoo Mambos and Houngans and this religious affiliation gave the Macoutes a sense of unearthly authority in the eyes of the public.

The Tonton Macoutes wore straw hats, blue denim shirts and dark glasses, and were armed with machetes and guns. Both their allusions to the supernatural and their physical presentations were a tool to instill fear. Their unrestrained state terrorism was accompanied by corruption, extortion and personal aggrandizement among their leadership. The victims of Tonton Macoutes could range from a woman in the poorest of neighborhoods who had previously supported an opposing politician to a businessman who refused to "donate" money for public works (which were the source of profit for corrupt officials and even Papa Doc himself).

In the name of nationalism, Duvalier expelled almost all of Haiti's foreign-born bishops, an act that earned him excommunication from the Catholic Church. Then through very generous donations he managed to persuade the Holy See to allow him one-time permission to nominate the Catholic hierarchy for Haiti. This action solidified the change to the status-quo: no longer was Haiti under the grip of the minority rich mulattoes, protected by the military and supported by the church.

On May 23ʳᵈ a plot to kill President Duvalier took effect. The nurse in charge of his insulin shots was accompanied by a young doctor who quickly quadrupled his regular insulin shot. Its peak effect was to take effect within 2-4 hours under regular conditions, but when Papa Doc went into cardiac arrest his people knew something was wrong. He was supposedly in a coma for 9 hours, but he was not seen for two days. While recovering power was left in the hands of Clément Barbot, leader of the Tonton Macoutes. Upon his return, Duvalier accused Barbot of trying to supplant him as president and had him imprisoned. The President suspected someone had made an attempt on his life and secretly thought it was Barbot. Tonton was the only person allowed with him during this time and most people including those who attempted to kill him were amazed he lived. A few years later Barbot was released and began plotting to remove Duvalier from office by kidnapping his children.

Jean Pierre was scared, he was not allowed to go to school and his mother took him back to his grandparents' house to hide as men in blue shirts and straw hats stood guard outside their house. The plot failed and Duvalier subsequently ordered a massive search for Barbot and his fellow conspirators. During the search Duvalier was told that Barbot who was also a Houngan had transformed himself into a black dog. Duvalier ordered that all black dogs in Haiti be put to death. Barbot was later captured and shot by the Tonton Macoutes. Papa Doc then order the head of the other conspirator, packed in ice and brought to him.

After the insurrection, he hastily called a national election although his term was to expire in 1963 and the constitution prohibited re-election. The election was still conducted and the official tally showed 1,320,748 voted, which was the total amount of registered voters in Haiti at the time. All 1,320,748 voted for Papa Duvalier, with none opposed. Upon hearing the results, Duvalier proclaimed he was shocked:

"I accept the people's will. As a revolutionary, I have no right to disregard the will of the people. So from today onward I herby institute a constitutional referendum to ensure the will of the people is followed and I herby make myself "President for Life".

The new constitution granted Duvalier—or "Le Souverain," as he was called—absolute powers as well as the right to name his successor.

By this time Jean Pierre knew who he was, he chose rather than to be called by his full name Jean Pierre Duvalier, to be called Jean Pierre. Jean Pierre hated his father's family. His father was a murderer and a thief and the more he found about him the more he despised him. Jean Pierre went to College in the Dominican Republic. When President John F. Kennedy was assassinated on November 1963, Jean Pierre was in college and wrote a paper on violence having no place in Politics. He volunteered with the United Nations and promised himself to bring reform to Haiti and undo his father's atrocities.

He first saw Josephine in the Santo Domingo. He was captivated by her beauty. She was at a party and when he tried to talk to her she walked away. He kept trying until she said yes. He kept his family history from her until a very heated discussion ensued about her mother and the President of Haiti who was attempting to exploit tensions between the United States and Cuba. Papa Doc was emphasizing his anti-Communist credentials and Haiti's strategic location as a means of winning U.S. support:

"Communism has established centers of infection... No area in the world is as vital to American security as the Caribbean... We need a massive injection of money to reset the country on its feet, and this injection can come only from our great, capable friend and neighbor the United States."

Josephine wanted the US to give his father support against communism and he wanted his father to receive no help.

Josephine was astonished and upset he hadn't told her before, and now she was already in love with him. They kept the secret from her mother and got married in the Dominican Republic. Jean Pierre promised her he would undo the horror done by his father and he worked tirelessly with the United Nations. His father's relationship with the neighboring Dominican Republic was always tense. Papa Doc continued to re-emphasize the differences between the two countries. Jean Pierre continued working with the United Nations to bring democratic reform. In April 1963, relations were brought to the edge of war by the political enmity between Duvalier and the Dominican president Juan Bosch.

Bosch, a left-leaning democrat, had provided asylum to Jean Pierre and his entire family and support to Haitian exiles plotting against the Duvalier regime. Duvalier ordered his presidential guard to occupy the Dominican Embassy in Pétionville. President Juan Bosch reacted with outrage, publicly threatening to invade Haiti, and ordered army units to the frontier. However, as Dominican military commanders expressed little support for an invasion of Haiti the idea was soon abandoned. When the CIA visited Isabel she said yes. Her daughter was married to Jean Pierre Duvalier a good and honest man and so was Jean Pierre mother's family.

Isabel saw this as a course to change the direction of Haiti. She was in Germany at the time, so she flew to the Dominican Republic where she met with Josephine and Jean Pierre. Isabel challenged Jean Pierre to lead by his actions and not just his words. The CIA wanted the 5 Principles signed by him before helping him achieve power in Haiti. The CIA had orchestrated the demise of his father and it wasn't if but when.

The outlines for the new Government under Jean Pierre were clear.

1.  To establish a fully functioning Haitian National Police, and to revitalize Haiti's system of Justice.

To recognize the link between peace and development and a sustained commitment to the international community. To assist and support economic, social and institutional development of Haiti and indispensable long-term peace and stability in the country.

2. Support of the Haitian people's quest for stability, national reconciliation, lasting democracy, constitutional order and economic prosperity.

3. Establish measures to account and control the contribution of international financial institutions, including the Inter-American Development Bank, and the importance of their continued involvement in the development of Haiti.

4. Recognizing that the people of Haiti bear the ultimate responsibility for national reconciliation and the maintenance of a secure and stable environment and reconstruction of their country.

5. Install a process where elections are fair and the democratic election of a new President in Haiti every four years occurs peacefully with the transfer of power from one democratically elected President to another.

Jean Pierre refused to sign the 5 Principles which infuriated Isabel. Josephine could not understand Jean Pierre's refusal to sign the 5 Principles as they were what he had fought for. On the eve of Isabel's departure Jean Pierre approached her. She was not speaking to him or her daughter, she wasn't speaking to her daughter for failure to convince her husband to accept the proposal and to Jean Pierre because as she told him he couldn't sign the 5 principles because he was no different from his father.

Jean Pierre and Josephine had lost their first child due to a miscarriage, and his main concern was the safety and comfort of his wife and his family, they were first Haiti was second. As he addressed his mother in-law, he reminded her of Haiti's turbulent nature, of the occupation of the American's and if he signed that document he was no different than his father or any of the previous dictators who ruled Haiti. He told her the people must choose their leader, just liked they took themselves out from the yoke of slavery, they will shed this burden called his father in due time. His signing of the 5 Principles is a violation of the very principles itself. Why even put articles 4-5 in the Articles of Principle ….

He asked Isabel

"how can I sign a document then engage in an act of conspiracy to overthrow the current government and put myself in power?"

He wanted no part of that. Isabel disagreed but she understood. She told him

"sometimes we have to choose the lesser of two evils in life".

When Isabel died Josephine and the family were devastated. Isabel had come to not only accept Jean Pierre's decision but to respect him.

As she lay dying she said to Josephine,

"You have done well my daughter, now your journey begins."

Jean Pierre and Josephine wanted to go home back to Haiti but a faction of the military was gearing up to overthrow Duvalier around the same time. They detonated bombs around the Presidential Palace and started riots. President Duvalier quickly had the rebellion put down and had nineteen Presidential Guard officers shot in Fort Dimanche. In his next public speech during which he read the "attendance sheet" with names of all 19 officers killed.

After each name he said "absent". After reading the whole list, Duvalier remarked,

"All were shot."

The time had come to remove Papa Doc Duvalier. The process would be easier this time around, since the last orchestrated attack. Papa Doc was now ailing from prostate cancer, heart trouble and his old nemesis diabetes. He had become more careful and more paranoid, but his paranoia had left many in his camp feeling they would be next and they were uneasy. The attack had to be natural, with no suspicion.

Luckner Cambronne would stop at nothing to create a situation for garnering fame and glory in capturing and torturing Papa Doc's killer so he could be seen as a hero. Luckner wanted control of Haiti taking control of the country under the false pretense of a State of Emergency whereby the Minister of Security would have Presidential powers. Would be Haiti's worst nightmare, worse than the nightmare they were now living.

Potassium Chloride was one of the drugs used in Papa Doc's many prescriptions. Klor-Con, Klor-Con 8, Klor-Con 10, and Klor-Con/25, among others all broke down into its individual components of potassium and chlorine. Both which are found in the human body and the presence of either or both would not raise any suspicion by an attending physician or the coroner who would be carrying out the autopsy. The compound broke down into both potassium and chlorine, in which the chlorine (Cl) binds with the human body's naturally occurring sodium (Na) to create NaCl -- sodium chloride -- common table salt.

Papa Doc would have a heart attack and there will be no known cause. The autopsy will show doctors a slightly elevated level of NaCl. The excess potassium in his body will cause tachycardia (an abnormally fast heart-rate), which will then lead to ventricular fibrillation.

It was April 18th 1971 he was overdosed just before he was about to go to sleep. When they realized he was dead several Haitian priests were brought in to bring him back to life. Tonton was nowhere to be found this time. Papa Doc had fallen out of favor with the gods. By April 22nd, four days later, the realization that he was not coming back set in. The world learnt Papa Doc Duvalier was dead.

Jean Pierre and Josephine had already made up their minds to move back to Haiti. They felt they had overstayed their welcome in the Dominican Republic and it was time to return home. Jean Pierre wanted to return to his mother's house, but Josephine said no. She reminded him that her grandfather Rene had a house and some propriety in Port au Prince. It was a modest home and would give them a brand new start far and away from past troubles.

On the same day of the announcement of his father's death in April 1971, Jean Pierre's 19yr old brother assumed the presidency of Haiti, Jean-Claude Duvalier. There was terrible infighting. Jean- Claude wanted his older sister Marie-Denise Duvalier to have power, but Luckner Cambronne was having none of that. He had a greater influence over Jean-Claude and could easily manipulate him he convinced them this was the last request of Papa Doc.

Jean-Claude agreed he would leave substantive and administrative matters in the hands of his mother, Simone Ovide Duvalier, and a committee led by Luckner Cambronne, his father's Interior Minister while he attend to ceremonial functions as the leader of Haiti.

Jean-Claude was invested with near-absolute power by the constitution. He took some steps to reform the regime by releasing some political prisoners and easing press censorship. However, there were no substantive changes to the regime's basic character. Opposition was not tolerated, and the legislature remained a rubber stamp. The money to Jean-Claude and the regime continued to flow uninterrupted, the money came from the Régie du Tabac (Tobacco Administration). They used this "non-fiscal account", established decades earlier, as a tobacco monopoly. It was later expanded to include the proceeds from other government enterprises and used it as a slush fund with no balance sheets.

Jean Pierre was back in Haiti, helping set up the network for the United Nations for projects like clean water, power, livestock and grain. He wanted no part of politics, his life was social work and attending to the needs of farmers. Things in Haiti were getting better, and the Nixon administration restored the US aid program for Haiti after Papa Doc's death.

A few years later his brother Jean Claude decided to marry his high school crush Michèle Bennett. Josephine and Michèle were best of friends; both their parents belonged to *gens de couleur*. Michèle and Josephine were both born at the same hospital and their parents had the same doctors. Michèle's dad Ernest Bennett was a Haitian businessman, and descendant of Henri Christophe who was once the President and self proclaimed King of Haiti. But like the DuPont's they too owned thousands of acres of land and were well known in the circle of the gens de couleur.

Michelle's uncle was Haiti's Roman Catholic Archbishop Monsignor François-Wolff Ligondé. During the time Josephine was in Germany with her mother, Michèle moved to New York. Michèle went on to work as a secretary at a slipper company in the garment district in New York City. She first married Alix Pasquet, the son of Captain Alix Pasquet, a well-known mulatto officer and Tuskegee Airman who in 1958 led a coup attempt against François Duvalier. With Pasquet she had two children, Alix Jr. and Sacha. After her 1978 divorce from Pasquet she had a career in public relations for Habitation LeClerc, an upscale hotel in Port-au-Prince and whilst in Haiti she rekindled her friendship with Josephine. They both knew Jean Claude from school and called him "rolly polly" because of his chubby cheeks. When Michelle found out Josephine was married to Jean Pierre's brother she laughed. Jean Pierre did not dislike his brother; they knew each other and were cordial.

One day, at a United Nations breakfast meeting, at the hotel, Josephine introduced Jean Claude to Michèle. Their romance blossomed; Jean Claude was smitten and proposed to Michèle. Their wedding was Haiti's social event of the decade. It cost an unprecedented US$3 million and was received enthusiastically by the majority of Haitians. The wedding began with a 101-gun salute and the exploding of $100,000 worth of fireworks which greeted Haiti's President for

Life Jean-Claude ("Baby Doc") Duvalier and his new bride Michèle Bennett. The couple emerged under crossed sabers from the freshly refurbished cathedral of Port-au-Prince to which Michelle's uncle Archbishop Monsignor François-Wolff Ligondé presided over the ceremonies, it was Haiti's most lavish social event in two decades. Michelle promised the nation things would change "We'll make lots of children and live happily ever after." She said.

Papier-mâché roses decked the dusty streets of the capital. Free bouillon and champagne, soup and rum were distributed to all who lined the streets.

Michelle at first endeared herself to the population by distributing clothes and food to the needy as well as opening several medical clinics and schools for the poor. Michèle and Jean-Claude toured Haiti, turning up unannounced at meetings, marketplaces, and other gathering places, which garnered "approving glances and words most everywhere".

On a visit to Haiti, Mother Teresa remarked that she had "never seen the poor people being so familiar with their head of state as they were with the Duvaliers.

As time passed Michelle had her first child for Jean Claude little Francois Nicolas and Josephine and Jean Pierre finally had their first child Marie. There were celebrations for the two births Francois Nicolas Duvalier and Marie DuPont Duvalier.

The marriage represented a symbolic alliance with the *gens de couleur* the very families Jean-Claude's father had opposed. This resulted in her husband's mother, Simone Duvalier (who opposed the match), being sidelined politically, which in turn created new factional alliances within the ruling group since the Duvalierist Old Guard opined that the new First Lady's power appeared to exceed her husband's. While Jean-Claude often dozed through Cabinet meetings, his wife, frustrated at his political ineptitude, reprimanded the ministers.

But Jean-Claude miscalculated the ramifications of his May 27, 1980 wedding to Michèle Bennett. Although Jean-Claude was light-skinned, his father's legacy of support for the black middle class and antipathy toward the lighter-skinned elite had enhanced the appeal of Duvalierism among the black majority of the population. With this marriage to Michelle, Jean-Claude appeared to be abandoning the informal bond that his father had labored to establish with black Haitians.

The extravagance of the couple's wedding, which cost an estimated US$3 million, further alienated the population. Discontent among the business community and elite intensified in response to increased corruption among the Duvaliers and the Bennetts, as well as the repulsive nature of the Bennetts' dealings, which included selling Haitian cadavers to foreign medical schools and trafficking in narcotics. Increased political repression added to the volatility of the situation. The marriage also estranged the old-line Duvalierists in the government from the younger technocrats whom Jean-Claude had appointed, Jean-Marie Chanoine, Frantz Merceron, Frantz-Robert Monde, and Theo Achille all friends of Josephine and Michele.

Jean-Claude's mother, Simone Ovide Duvalier, was expelled from Haiti, at the request of Michèle. Josephine and Jean Pierre watched the change in their friends their social engagements became less frequent.

Josephine was more concerned about Marie and putting her in the right environment. Whilst Michelle was concern about Givenchy, emeralds, Boucheron and the luxury store Hermes.

Then came the outbreak of African swine fever virus on the island, the United Nations advised Jean Pierre they would have to totally eradicate all of Haiti's pig population. The Program for the Eradication of Porcine Swine Fever and for the Development of Pig Raising (PEPPADEP) caused widespread hardship among the peasant population, who bred pigs as their main source of income. Widespread discontent began in March 1983, when Pope John Paul II visited Haiti. The pontiff declared that "Something must change here."

Pope John went on to call for a more equitable distribution of income, a more egalitarian social structure, more concern among the elite for the well-being of the masses, and increased popular participation in public life.

This started a revolt in the provinces, Jean-Claude responded with a 10 percent cut in staple food prices, the closing of independent radio stations, a cabinet reshuffle, and a crackdown by police and army units, but these moves failed to dampen the momentum of the popular uprising against the dynastic dictatorship. Jean-Claude's wife and advisers, intent on maintaining their grip on power, urged him to put down the rebellion and remain in office. In January 1986, the Reagan administration began to pressure Jean-Claude to renounce his rule and leave Haiti.

Josephine and Jean Pierre knew Jean Claude and Michele's downfall was near; they had completely stopped associating with them. Jean Claude and Michele no longer cared for the people of Haiti.

As Marie lay in his arms, Jason listened to Tonton telling the story to the marines. Marie was the queen of Haiti he told them. Jason felt privileged in his hands he held the most beautiful woman in the world. And she was way above his pay grade, now it all made sense.

# CHAPTER 7

They got back to camp exhausted, emotionally and physically. Marie was doing a little better, she was happy to have gotten the girls out. She had a slight headache but all in all she was much better. Dr Dupre took charge of the girls they brought back, whilst they went back to their tents to recoup. Later on that evening, they came back out for dinner. As they quietly ate that night, looking up at the sky into the starry night Jason said

"When I was a young boy I wanted to be a Pilot, to fly the skies and see the world from up above"

"And why didn't you?" asked Marie.

"Because I lived my life for my parents and realized their goals not mine. "And you, Marie why did you become a nurse?"

"It was either a nurse or school teacher, I chose to be a nurse. My father showed me the most direct way to make impact in someone's life is to do something you like and make a difference whilst doing it".

"How come you are not married or don't have any kids?" asked Jason.

"I just haven't found the right person and I won't sacrifice my values. And I say that because I know how Americans think, every Haitian girl needs a green card or to be saved. I'm not one of them. I don't need to be saved, and the last thing I want is a green card".

"I know Marie, trust me I know, I have no doubt that is the least of your interest."

"Now Jacqueline here" well..

"Please!" said Jacqueline "my father is Puerto Rican I had my American Passport the day I was born". They all started laughing.

"How is your head?" asked Dr. Dupre interrupting the laughter.

"Its fine!" said Marie "it was a small gash".

"Well you need to stop getting banged up, I do have work for you to do" said Dr. Dupre.

"I'm sure you do" said Marie.

"No! Seriously I do. Things were pretty bad around here today. I got in more suspected cases of Cholera; I isolated them from the others".

The next morning Dr. Dupre woke them up.

"I think we have 10 more cases of Cholera. We are going to have to do something. I need to talk to the Health Minister or someone in the health ministry".

"I can help in locating the source. You need to go get some rest and lie down a little Marie" said Jason.

"Thank you Jason but I'm fine. You should be the one getting some rest."

"What you don't like me now? I have this beautiful black eye" said Jason with a big silly grin on his face.

"I never liked you" said Marie "and now with the black eye ewewwwwww".

Jason laughed at Marie.

"Marie I have an idea, get me a stool sample please"

"What do you have planned Jason?"

"I'm going to try and do a rapid test to identify the cholerae."

"How is the test done Jason?"

"This is sort of rapid test depends on the ability of the vibrios to multiply in a specially designed medium in the presence of other intestinal bacteria and to agglutinate against specific antisera directly. The culture medium consisted of 2 parts: agar and broth. The thing is Aseptic condition is not required. If I add about 0.5 ml amount of a diluted stool suspension to an equal volume of molten agar in a freeze drying glass ampules and left to set, the ampule will incubate. Now all I have to do is wait until a slight turbidity of bacterial growth is visible which will take about 24 hours and then boom like magic we will know."

"You know Jason; you just sounded like Dr. House. Right now, how about we freshen up and eat something and let Dr. Dupre know our plans."

Jacqueline called out to Marie and Dr. Dupre.

When they went over to see her on the ground in the medical supply tent were four open boxes, 2 packed with dry ice and Omaha Steaks. The other box contained 12 bottles of Pinot Noir and the last one was packed with frozen chicken breast.

"Oh my! Please call the delivery officer of medical supplies at the airport" said Marie

"I did" said Jacqueline,

"the delivery officer confirmed they were delivered in error."

"He said you are right ma'am, they were delivered in error and they do belong to someone else. The problem is these items were ordered prior to the Earthquake and the shipment was delayed.

The business that these boxes were to be delivered to is no longer standing and the owner is nowhere to be found. So the Marine officers who were assigned to you yesterday said if anyone deserved this precious cargo your camp did. "

"Oh well in that case did you say Thank you" replied Dr. Dupre.

Laughter broke out.

"Isn't this camp on the grounds of the Ministry of sports?" asked Marie

"It is, and the building that was destroyed was the sports administration building" replied Dr. Dupre.

"Well I guess it's yours now" said Jason "consider it a gift from the US Marines."

"This is so wrong" said Marie.

"Why?" asked Jason "what makes this wrong, actually this is so right."

"You are impossible Jason, do you know that?" "Yup something like that" he said looking at Marie smiling.

"We have work to do people, stop milling around thinking of red wine and steaks" said Dr. Dupre.

"Jason you seem to have an expansive knowledge in infectious diseases can you share with the rest of us what you know about Cholera and what we should be looking for?"

"Of course Dr. Dupre' replied Jason but Marie has a informational meeting set up for this evening with everyone before dinner can we do it then?"

'Absolutely "thanks Marie" said Dr. Dupre "as usual you are ahead of the game."

Jacqueline had driven down to the Ministry of Health and was meeting with the Chief Surgeon of Hospitals for Haiti.

"We think there is definitely an outbreak of Cholera at our camp, in addition, today at our camp, a band of escaped prisoners from the jail attacked the camp and raped and beat a little girl. We need some sort of protection at the camp."

"I understand Jacqueline" said the minister, "there are similar stories throughout Port au Prince and things are very chaotic. I will have a talk with our Security Minister to see if we have the man power to spare someone at your camp. It may not be for 24 hours but definitely at night. Just a few hours ago Prime Minister Bellerive and I discussed this situation; many people are in grave danger. Therefore we are working with the United Nations. Our police and remaining security forces will work together with them. I will make it a priority that you have some sort of security at the camp. How is the young American Doctor working out for Dr. Dupre? Your camp is fortunate to have two Doctors. Many camps have only one and many others are spread out in the countryside."

"We are indeed grateful" said Jacqueline "and Dr. Dupre and the American are doing a fine job together. They are putting together a program as we speak to deal with the cholera outbreak".

"Ok Jacqueline…please keep us updated".

When Jacqueline got back Marie called the camp workers and volunteers.

"I have spoken to Dr. Bramer or Jason as he likes to be called. This evening he wants to give us a quick lesson or shall I say preventative education on Cholera. Now I don't want anyone to panic, we are not certain this is Cholera and the last time we had Cholera here on the Island was over 100yrs ago. So Jason the ball is in your court."

"Ok so this is a bit long, but you know as you say here in Haiti "Pa pèdi founo pou yon grenn pen". (Don't lose the oven for bread.)

"Jason please just give us the info and stop with Haitians sayings already, you are spending way too much time with Tonton."

"You're right Marie" Jason chuckled "as a matter of fact why don't you help me with this. I'll do the first part and you can do the second part".

"No Jason you just get going because we're hungry."

"Ok here is what we are looking for."

"Ok we will be setting up isolation tents. This is what we are looking for when they come in. Their symptoms will begin with the sudden onset of painless watery diarrhea that may quickly become voluminous and may be followed by vomiting. Some may experience accompanying abdominal cramps, probably from distention in their small bowels as a result of the large volume of intestinal secretions.

If there's no fever don't bother checking temps. However, most Vibrio cholerae infections are asymptomatic; here is where our problem is. This cholera infection may not be clinically distinguishable from other causes of gastroenteritis. So it's important we are able to distinguish between the two".

Diarrhea. Profuse watery diarrhea is a hallmark of cholera. Cholera should be suspected when a patient older than 5 years develops severe dehydration or if the kid looks weak (usually without vomiting) or in any patient older than 2 years who has acute watery diarrhea and there is nothing else wrong with them.

Vomiting. Vomiting which is a symptom of Cholera may not always be present. Early in the course of the disease, vomiting is caused by decreased gastric and intestinal motility; later in the course of the disease they may start throwing up.

Dehydration, If we don't detect these cases early they are going to die. Die and die fast. This is what we call isotonic dehydration.

What can we do? ... Water! Water! Water! I'm not sure, but Jacqueline you have yon sèl boutèy dlo (tons of bottled water) Did I say that right?"

"No you did not" said Jacqueline; "you just told everyone you have one bottle of water coming".

"I'm going to strangle Tonton. He has been teaching me Creole and I think he has been misleading me. Before we went to the meeting I was standing outside the tent, he came by and asked me how I was doing. I said fine then 3 aid workers were walking by, he grabbed my arm and told me say:

"Mwen se yon doktè moun sòt ak mwatye nan yon nan sèvo", which means hi how are you have a wonderful day. But then they looked at me really weird and then started laughing. And he said to me it was the way I said it with my American accent."

"Listen here Jason, as of today, no more hanging out with Tonton and anything he tells you please come and ask us before you repeat it."

"OMG!" exclaimed Jason Marie please tell me what I said".

You told those ladies "Hi I am an idiot doctor with half a brain"

"Arhhhhhh!!!" exclaimed Jason "this guy has issues."

"Jason why would you listen to Tonton of all people? Please just stick to English, stay on track and finish the presentation please we are hungry."

Jacqueline and Marie were both laughing, tears filled their eyes.

"Ok, ok" replied Jason "ok well education and environmental control is critical for the prevention of cholera. The source of cholerae in nature is human excrement and the most common vehicle of infection is water. Environmental control must focus on keeping these elements apart. What I'm going to do in the next few days is trace this and find the source then we can stop it. Key public health planning, clean water conservation and usage and proper sewage disposal, Jacqueline that's up your alley with the Government. Marie you and I can track, trace and resolve this. Dr. Dupre and the rest of the team will heal and take preventive measures.

What Marie and I must do is find that source to stop the cycle of infection, excretion, and re-infection. We are gonna have to share some kind of pamphlet about the sterilization of water and hand-washing. Contamination via food like water used to wash foods. Water contamination occurs via sewage or soil that is used to fertilize crops. So Jacqueline once these results come back and I'm like 90% certain on everything we have seen that we have a Cholera problem. In this situation, training food handlers is necessary.

"Ok I'm done. It's dinner time Ms. Marie."

"Thanks Doctor Bramer for allowing us to eat."

"Marie, rumor has it you prepared the steaks" said Jacqueline.

"Well Jacqueline, let that remain a rumor because I'm not cooking around here", as laughter broke out. "Yes and we should give thanks and enjoy because tomorrow I am donating all the chicken to the camp in Jacmel."

"And here I am thinking I was in charge of this camp" said Dr. Dupre

"Sometimes you are" said Marie for - Medical purposes.

(All breaking out in laughter)

They went to bed that night hoping they didn't have a Cholera outbreak but knowing in their hearts they did. When Marie went to wake Jason he was already up in his makeshift lab with Dr. Dupre. He turned to Marie "see how the agglutination appears as a suspension of fine particles, its cholera".

"Dr. Dupre is there a phone I can use to call the United States?" asked Jason.

"Yes use mine" replied Dr. Dupre.

Jason called his buddy David in infectious diseases.

"David, its Jason I need a huge favor. I'm sending you a sample. I need infectious disease to run a trace through the CDC as soon as possible. We have a Cholera outbreak here in Haiti and we need to find its source".

"Ok Jason no problem, how about you are, you ok, is everything fine?" "Everything is great David just trying to get a handle on this Cholera issue. I'll have the sample out on the first plane then we will touch base".

# CHAPTER 8

Jason and Marie left early that morning. Their goal was to track the area where most of the sick people who were coming to their camp came from. Tonton was their driver. Before Marie could get a word in, Tonton said to Marie "you spending a lot of time with that boy". "That boy risked his life not once, but twice, not just for me, but for some unknown children. Tonton he may not be the sharpest knife in the draw as far as common sense is concerned, but as far as being a doctor and having a heart, that more than makes up for it".

"Ok, Ok Ms. Marie" he said smiling as Jason got into the bus.

"Tonton we need your help" said Jason "all the sick people we have received have come from the communes of Grande Saline, St-Marc, Desdune, Petite-Rivière-de-l'Artibonite, Dessaline, and Verrettes. In the last 3 days the rise has been continuous."

"I have someone who has asked to meet you" said Tonton. "It's a mother and her child she knows two children who recently died and lived in the Bocozel commune of St-Marc, they all had diarrhea for days before their death".

"Where was this?" asked Marie

"In Bocozel" replied Toton.

"We have to go there now. Marie please call Jacqueline, if what Tonton is saying is true we may have an epidemic on our hands."

When they arrived at Bocozel they were told there were many sick people, most were being sent to a hospital in Dessalines and there were many deaths caused by severe diarrhea. Jacqueline met them in Dessalines and the news was the same in many places diarrhea, vomiting and death. Jacqueline also told him some faxes had come in from the USA for him. The one connection to all the people who were sick was the Artibonite River, from which most of the sick people had been drinking water.

Tonton got a small boat for them to ride up the river, as they got close to one of tributaries they saw a UN military base at the mouth of the tributary. It was the home to peacekeepers from Nepal. Marie asked Tonton to take them closer to the base. When they arrived, they were greeted by the head of the Nepalese command who asked to see their credentials.

Jacqueline showed him her credentials and told him they were trying to find the source of some contamination in the water. He was very accommodating and told her since they opened their camp he has seen many Haitians using the river by the thousands and it was possible they may have unknowingly put some contaminant in the water.

Jason thanked him and asked if it was ok if they stayed on the banks around the camp and looked around, he agreed. As they scoured the banks, Marie noticed two six inch pipes that drained into the river close to some dwellings. Marie went to talk to the neighbors whilst Jacqueline and Jason walked the banks of the river.

Marie came running down to them saying "it's the Nepalese base". Jason looked at her perplexed, and Jacqueline told her to be careful of making such a statement without proof. "Listen guys" said Marie "I spoke to the neighbors, they said since the camp came, the sickness came and there have been deaths about four to five of them having died from vomiting and diarrhea".

"Marie let's take samples from the pipe and around it, I'm going to talk to their medical staff. They won't lie, and it will put an end to all this speculation".

Jason went up to the camp and met the head of the Nepalese medical staff. She assured Jason they were not infecting the river with contaminants.

"It's not contaminants Dr. Ayusha, its Cholera" replied Jason. "These patients are dying from Cholera".

Dr. Ayusha was stunned. She confessed six members of the team who came were sick with gastro-like systems and were eventually sent back to Nepal. No one has been sick since, but for the last couple weeks a total of 15 members of the team were sick with diarrhea and vomiting.

"I believe you may have unknowingly brought Cholera to these people. I know as a physician you will help me do everything possible to resolve this situation. Do you know of any recent outbreaks of Cholera in Nepal?"

"Yes we do!" said Dr. Ayusha. "There was an outbreak in Nepalgunj, a city on the border with India earlier this year. It was detected early, at first it was endemic but within a couple weeks we were able to get it under control and now it's at controllable or normal routine levels.

In Nepal our biggest issue is the monsoon season, during which time diarrhea-related illnesses normally spike because of contaminated water sources, so we are always on the lookout. So it's fairly difficult to distinguish between the two, normal gastrointestinal – diarrhea and dysentery. "Ok here is our biggest problem" said Jason he was now joined by Marie and Jacueline, "we have to see how far this river runs and map the source of the contamination, then notify the Minster of Health. We have, well Marie has in her possession several samples. We have to find its DNA fingerprint to know what we are dealing with. Some of this has already been done; the results are awaiting us back at base camp."

"Well Doctor Bramer, what I can tell you about its fingerprint from what I know is that it's the Vibro cholerae serogroup O1, serotype Ogawa, a strain found in South Asia. So when the many different analyses of the strain are complete, it may be possible to identify the origin of the strain to see if they match".

"Ok!" said Marie "well it's getting late and we shouldn't be out on the river in the dark, and we have a long way to go and in addition to mapping the infected areas. Also, I have set up a meeting with the Health Ministry. Jason, they want to meet with you and find out what you know, because tomorrow they would like to issue warnings and education material."

That evening up and down the river they stopped at various locations to take samples. Dr. Ayusha had decided to accompany them. For the next four hours they spoke to over 300 people who use the river at different locations. Everyone downstream had the same symptoms vomiting, diarrhea and eventually death. They got back to camp and Jason went to prepare the report for the next day as Marie and Jacqueline broke the news to Dr. Dupre.

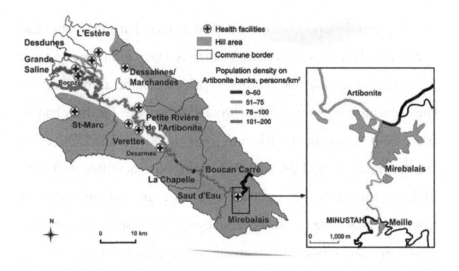

The next morning Jason stood in front of the Ministry of Health and delivered his report..

"A couple days ago I ran rapid test on a couple patients from our camp for Cholera because all the signs were symptomatic to Cholera. The test confirmed it was indeed Cholera. I then had the samples sent back to the US Centers for Disease Control and Prevention to indentify and confirm the strain".

"Dr. Dupre and Marie from our camp confirmed that you had not had Cholera in Haiti in over 100 years which is a very long time and that this outbreak represented the first significant outbreak of Cholera. The one common denominator with each patient was that they had all drank from the Artibonite River or lived close to it. The CDC DNA fingerprinting showed the samples I sent were identified as Vibrio cholerae serogroup O1; serotype Ogawa, a strain found in South Asia. This may have consequences beyond Haiti, since this strain is more hardy and virulent, with an increased resistance to antibiotics. I then went with members from our camp and combed the bank of the Artibonite River and found the Nepali peacekeeping base. The base is on the river and a few of their peace keeping forces were in fact sick and had been sent home, they never suspected Cholera and thought they had gotten ill from the conditions after the Earthquake".

"As a priority, right now, rehydration in the treatment of cholera. Rehydration is accomplished in 2 phases: rehydration and maintenance. This information must get out to the people as soon as possible. The goal of the rehydration phase is to restore normal hydration status, which should take no more than 4 hours. The goal of the maintenance phase is to maintain normal hydration status by replacing ongoing losses. The oral route is preferred and the use of oral rehydration solution (ORS) at a rate of 500-1000 mL/hr is recommended. The goal has to be saving lives, we found many people have died and though we have no specific information that Cholera attributed to these deaths it is suspected it did."

"The United Nations has the ability to bring in Antimicrobial therapy to treat this cholera. It's sort of an adjunct to fluid therapy and it is not an essential therapeutic component. But what I do know is that an effective antibiotic can reduce the volume of diarrhea in patients with severe cholera and shorten the period during which Vibrio cholerae O1 is excreted. In addition, it usually stops the diarrhea within 48 hours, thus shortening the period of hospitalization. The reality is there are no other drugs besides antibiotics which can be used in Cholera treatment".

"What is critical is to follow up on what I have just said. If we do decide to use antimicrobial therapy as a treatment, it should only be given when the patient is first seen and cholera is suspected. I mean at this point all we can do is wait for culture and susceptibility reports, capabilities which we currently don't have. We know Furazolidone has been the agent routinely used in the treatment of cholera in children;

however, resistance has been reported and ampicillin, erythromycin, and fluoroquinolones are potentially effective alternatives. I think Marie is taking over the other part of this presentation because it's going to deal with different areas, what we found and how we think things can precede, Marie".

"Thank you Dr. Bramer. During the last 24 hours, new alerts were registered from 10 health centers and hospitals located in each commune covering the lower course of the Artibonite River. From Desarmes to the seashore, several more cases up and down the river have been identified. I do believe some of the recent deaths could be attributed to this outbreak. No cholera cases had been reported in the Lower Artibonite area before the Nepalese Camp was set up."

"After the camp was set up, a couple cases were recorded in the communes of Saut d'Eau (no case), Boucan Carre (no case), and La Chapelle (2 cases). Only a few hamlets of these 3 communes located between Mirebalais and the Artibonite delta are crossed by the Artibonite River, so population density on its banks is pretty low. Similarly, only 1 case, imported from Lower Artibonite, was reported initially in Gonaïve".

"I'm not sure how many of you are aware of this, but my Uncle Tonton reminded me of this yesterday. Gonaïve is built in a floodplain, adjacent to the Artibonite delta, but watered by a different river running from the north. When we rode down the river, we found that a strong correlation was found between the epidemic curves of the communes of the delta but not with that of Mirebalais. The correlation was at a maximum between St-Marc and Grande Saline, the 2 seashore communes bordering the main branch of the Artibonite River".

"As for our camp, the first case was noticed seven days ago. Dr. Dupre noticing the pattern took the initiative and notified 14 additional communes, most of them in the mountainous regions bordering the Artibonite plain and in Port-au-Prince. We visited several of these communes (Gonaïve, Ennery, Plaisance, Saint-Michel-de-l'Attalaye, and Port-au-Prince) and investigated the circumstances of the onset of cholera outbreaks within the last two days. In each case, cholera started after the arrival of patients who fled from the ravaging epidemic in the Artibonite delta. Numerous persons from bordering communes who worked in the rice fields, salt marshes and road construction were being infected. Most of the people knew there was an epidemic, but had no idea what was making them sick. Most of these camps also saw the same pattern soon after the first case was identified, and then the outbreaks started."

"But with all that said, the southern half of Haiti remains relatively free of infections, which really means these are staggered clusters occurring North-West, Port-au-Prince, which are roughly equidistant from the Artibonite delta."

"I hope I'm not boring everyone with all this information, but it's really important in stopping this spread. It really is the difference between life and death for everyone who lives along the river. In North, the most suspected cases occurred in the main cities located in the floodplains, especially Cap Haitien and Gonaïve. But numerous cases have been recorded in the mountainous areas between Artibonite plain and northern coast".

"Thank you Dr. Bramer and thank you Marie. We appreciate everything you have done, we will take control from here and make the necessary arrangement for medication for the various camps and follow up with more testing. Soon we will have forthcoming elections. It is important to project a united front because we are not happy with this discovery. We will fix the problem quietly and efficiently and we give some sort of compensation whichever way we can, then give help to the families affected by this. We have been doing our own investigations, but I agree wholeheartedly, we have found the source we will provide the necessary support. But we must move forward diplomatically. No good will come from pointing fingers and making accusations. Haiti needs all the help it can get right now isolation is not an option".

Jason, Jacqueline and Marie left the meeting feeling they had done all they could. Back at the camp Dr. Dupre was awaiting their arrival. He had been overwhelmed; they were now up to 100 cases of suspected cases of Cholera.

# CHAPTER 9

Jason remembered a story a friend of his told him some years ago, she said

"I remember, 17 years ago, walking into my backyard and picking a lime from our tree. I asked the tree for it first, which my grandfather always said we must do before picking anything, as all trees were alive. And as I wiggled in, to get a beautiful lime, I got stuck probably 3-4 times by the thorns and same as I came back out with it. But it was one of those moments, I felt the sting, but the strangest thing happened. For some reason, it dawned on me, how many people in their whole lives would never have the joy, and well, pain in my case, of actually picking a fruit in their backyard. And it was this appreciation of what I had on my hands, that made all the things I never had growing up seem non-existent. And to this day, I still start by appreciating the small things, and thanking God, not only for them, but that I can realize that they are important".

So Haiti was his lime tree, it could be painful at times but it had life, and there was purpose in this life. A few days had passed; the Ministry had released the information to the citizens of Haiti. The nation was coping as best as they could, but the backlash was fierce, the people were fed-up to compound the Earthquake, now Cholera, they were tired.

The mobs continued elections were close and the politics became part of the process. And as if to complicate matters further, musician Wyclef Jean, who left Haiti for the United States at the age of 9, said he was qualified to run for President and was in Haiti to initiate the legal process with lawyers and have his fingerprints taken by the judicial police to run for president. Rumors started, Wyclef's popularity with the youth of Haiti could help him easily win the presidential election if his candidacy were approved.

Marie was disgusted she called it the circus and would vent daily to Jason. Here they were dealing with death and destruction, healing people and the Politicians were playing games. Marie was tired she was ready to leave Haiti.

"Europe" she told Jason as they sat drinking a glass of wine.

"Yes you should" said Jason "but you won't. You love your people and you love this Island. Now if it was me yeah I'd be gone in sixty seconds."

"Jason Bramer you need a wife and some children and to settle down."

"I agree Marie but I'm holding out for you"

"You are a busy man Jason you're waiting on me Jacqueline, Ayusha and who else?"

"Is there anything that you don't see Marie? And Jacqueline no, I was giving her some assistance with some real-estate issues she had with her dad, Ayusha I'm working on."

"Good night Dr. Bramer" and Marie retired for the night.

Over the forthcoming days the Health Ministry tried to offer alternative explanations, but it seemed only good enough yesterday. Crowds in Hinche began to assault Nepalese troops with bottles and rocks, wounding six. In Cap-Haitien, the country's second city, a police sub-station was torched, roads were blocked and shots were fired at the UN.

They were targeting and fighting with Minustah and so Tonton told Marie to warn everyone in the camp. If they see white people, they can rush to judge and target them too because they were part of the plot to kill the Haitian people. Crazy rumors started to spread. The UN was shooting back at Haitians, at least two were dead, there were no confirmations, but everyone knew someone who knew someone who had seen them shooting Haitians. The Haitians needed to fire their guns too. The UN dispatched Spanish soldiers to Cap-Haitien and blocked it off, no one was allowed to enter or leave. The residents of the City had blocked the entrance with burning barricades across roads and metal barriers welded to the bridge leading to the airport.

Dr. Dupre had become very frustrated with the current events. The UN had sent an assigned team to guard the camp. They were swamped with seriously ill patients who were dying and the Politicians were trying to score points and capitalize on it.

Tonton had volunteered to pick up badly needed supplies from the ministry. When he got back everyone was awaiting his arrival. They unpacked the saline and badly needed fluids for the patients. After they were finished unpacking Tonton told one of his jokes.

"This one is about these Politicians" he said.

"Little Jacques wanted $50 really bad so he prayed and prayed but nothing happened. Then he decided to write God a letter requesting the $50. When they received the letter at the Port au Prince post office they didn't know what to do with it. The letter was addressed to God of Haiti, they decided to send it to President of Haiti. The President was so impressed, touched, and amused that he instructed his secretary to send Jacques $5.00 bill. The President of Haiti thought this would appear to be a lot of money to a little boy. Well Jacques was happy with the $5.00 and sat down to write a thank you note to God, which read:

Dear God,

Thank you very much for sending the money, however, I noticed that for some reason you had to send it through The Capital Port au Prince and, as usual, what do you know those thieves took $45 of the money you sent can you please send the rest directly to me.

Thanks, Jacques

They laughed and thanked Tonton he always found a way to put a smile on their faces.

The UN released a statement blaming the violence on Political agitators and those trying to gain political mileage during a time in the nation's crisis. They refuted any charge of troops firing on civilians. UN troops are only authorized to fire in self-defense. "Minustah urges the population to remain vigilant and not to allow themselves to be manipulated by the enemies of stability and democracy in the country. The controversy has shone a new light on what has been regarded internationally as a successful mission. Despite all the adversity, poverty and destruction Haiti remains relatively peaceful."

"The Haitian opposition maintained the cholera came from the Nepalese and that the UN will do its best to hide it because if it is confirmed to be from them this will be damaging for the UN and their peacekeeping all over the world. In comparison, US troops who briefly led relief efforts and many Haitains wanted them back.

The UN maintained their mission was to stop rampaging criminal gangs and chaos and implement stability and normalcy. But the protests in the streets continued. People were burning tires and now asking Minustah the local name given to the UN peace keepers to leave.

Jason had been leaving camp on evenings and spending time with Dr. Ayusha at the Nepalese camp, he assured everyone it was just research work. Marie warned him about going to the base as there had been clashes between rioters and troops which had left two dead, dozens injured foreigners in hiding and an awful question hanging in the tear-gassed air: did the UN mission, known as Minustah, bring cholera to Haiti?

The boys and men hurled rocks and bottles and fired shots at foreign soldiers in the northern towns of Cap-Haitien and Hinche. And had no doubt, nor did the residents of Port-au-Prince who greeted UN convoys with sullen stares and insults. "Minustah merde!" they shouted, as the UN trucks passed yelling at a passing pick-up with blue helmets. Jason assured Marie and Dr. Dupre he would be fine. He would be with Tonton. When Jason and Tonton arrived to pick up Dr. Ayusha there was utter chaos. Barbed wire protected the entrance and people were protesting outside the base.

After a lengthy discussion he and Ayusha decided it was best they not venture out that evening. As he was leaving her camp, Jason asked her for a 10 ml test tube. He wanted a sample of the water as he had been tracking the levels of bacteria in the water. As he walked down to the bank and scooped the water into the test tube, he didn't realize he was being followed. He turned around long enough to see the long shaft of a steel shank. It was an ice pick used in Haiti to chip large chunks of ice. The first stab pierced his lung, he gasped for air, the second stab pierced the soft tissue in his shoulder, touching the cartilage, and the third stab pierced the rhomboid major causing him anguish and discomfort. He felt the sole of someone's feet kicking him in the back as he slipped into the water, he felt no pain. The stabs were numerous; they had stabbed him 15 times. As he laid face first in the water, something funny came to mind. Irony he thought here he was dying slowly, drowning not from the water in the Artibonite River. His autopsy would read: drowning, but few would know it was from the blood in his lungs and secondly shanked in the streets, who gets shanked in the streets? This might be a first. Usually a person who is shanked is in jail and then his eyes closed and he sunk to the bottom of the river.

Tonton had watched Jason go down to the river to fill up his tube. It was a routine since he had started dating the Nepalese girl. Tonton was glad it was the Napalese girl and not Marie. The first night he took them to KoKoYe Restaurant Grill and bar and he told Jason to try the local rum Barbancourt. He had to lift Jason into the back of his bus and take him back to camp. His Napalese girlfriend was just as bad. They were both so drunk they tried to go skinny dipping in the river. It was like babysitting children, but Tonton loved it. He remembered as a youth this was how Haiti was. Tourist abound, it was beautiful and safe.

Five minutes had gone by "Jason should have been on his way back to the truck by now" . He ran down to the bank of the river and did not see him, as he got closer he saw a shadow sunken in the water. Tonton jumped in and pulled Jason's body out the water. He pulled him onto the bank and tried to compress the water out of his lungs but blood kept coming out his mouth. There was no water in his lungs just blood.

Tonton knew what he had to do. He ran up the embankment and called out to Ayusha. She came back with several of the peace keepers. Tears welled in her eyes as they continued CPR but Ayusha pronounced him dead. Tonton asked for one of the UN ambulances to take Jason's body back to his camp. The news reached Marie around midnight; she was in disbelief, tears poured down her cheeks. She ran over to Jacqueline's tent but she already knew, everyone was up in the camp. Everyone was crying. It was probably the worst news Marie had received other than her mother's death. She had grown fond of Jason. She actually felt a little jealousy when he decided to go out with Ayusha. But she was happy because he was happy, and he was finally having a good time a reprieve from the chaos which had become their daily lives.

Jacqueline asked Dr. Dupre if he had a contact for his next of kin. Dr. Dupre told her no but he would be in contact with his hospital once the body arrived. The UN ambulance arrived with the body of Dr. Jason Bramer. Ayusha came with them, she was visibly upset. Marie did not want to see his body, neither did Jacqueline. Marie knew Jason did not deserve to die this way but Haiti was unforgiving at times and this one of these moments where it was.

# CHAPTER 10

As soon as the ambulance pulled into the camp Tonton jumped out and ran up to Dr. Dupre, they walked away in hushed tones. Tonton was a Bòkônon, he was also known as "Ifa" or sometimes as "Obò" or "Juju". Tonton's job was to bring peace and happiness to people. Tonton was a young boy, nineteen years old when Marie's father was a little boy. Marie was now twenty four, her father died at sixty. Which would make Toton somewhere close to eighty years old. Tonton looked no older than forty. It is said that Tonton was not born, but made in the back yard of a Mambo who was at war with the Orisha. It was a time of war and hardship for the slaves in Haiti so they formed a truce.

Through Syncretism the two religions' would combine for the peace of the people, any seemingly contradictory beliefs would be handled by the Bòkônon or Ifa. (Tonton) while melding practices of various schools of thought. This Syncretism involved the merger and analogizing of several original discrete traditions, especially in theology and mythology, but it allowed for peace of the slaves and an underlying unity allowing for an inclusive approach to their faiths.

When Tonton pulled Jason out of the water he knew it was a matter of seconds, he pulled the asoke cloth from around his waist. Wrapped in the clothe was a vial with a chemical mixture containing tetrodotoxin (pufferfish venom) bufotoxin (toad venom) Datura stramonium

(Sedative from a plant)and one more ingredient which is only known to the Ifa that makes the body cold as ice. Jason was not dead; he was induced into a coma and became what is known in Haiti as a zombie (A medicinal practice that dates back to the 12th century) the urban phase of Ife before the rise of Oyo, known as the "golden age" of Ife.

In 2002, the process was introduced in western medicine as induced coma, used to stabilize patients with traumatic injury. The treatment is called therapeutic hypothermia and at its core is the simplest of technologies: Killing the patient before he dies. Once a patient's heartbeat is restored, emergency-room doctors, cardiologists and rescue squads a quickly apply ice and other coolants to moderately lower a patient's body temperature by several degrees. Then the patient is put in a drug-induced coma in intensive care for 24 hours before gradually being warmed back up to normal temperature.

Icing the body slows metabolism and protects the brain from damage. When the body is slowly brought to normal temperatures, the restoration of blood flow triggers a cascade of responses over the following minutes and hours, which can induce cell rejuvenation and bring injured tissues back to life giving the patient a chance to heal.

Dr. Dupre came back and asked Marie to scrub up; he asked Dr. Ayusha if she would be willing to help.

"I'm sorry Dr. Dupre" she said "I don't do autopsies and with Jason I don't think I will be able to help. I'm not emotionally stable enough to handle this situation right now".

Marie was absolutely confused and so was Jacqueline. Marie, Dr. Dupre and Ellen went into the surgical tent. To most westerners there is considerable confusion between what is known as Voodoo and Bò.

Bò is an occult science whose priest is called Bòkônon or Bòkôtônon in opposition to Voodunsim. Effusion and Diffusion are the two ways that gases mix with other gases. In Diffusion, two gases combine to form a uniform mixture. In Effusion, one gas passes from one medium to another remaining the same gas.

Anyone can become a Mambo (voodoo female priestess) or a Houngans (voodoo male priest) but not everyone or anyone can become a Bòkônon or Ifa. Tonton was a Bòkônon.

Their camp was not a surgical camp. Most of the surgeries were sent to hospitals in different areas, but Dr. Dupre was going to intubate Jason and perform a bedside Thoracentesis (Thoracentesis is a procedure to remove fluid from the space between the lungs and the chest wall). He told Marie if Jason was going to live this was the only way he would make it. Marie was confused because Ayusha confirmed to her twice he was dead, no heart beat no pulse, nothing. Now Dr. Dupre was talking about him being alive.

Dr. Dupre turned Jason on his side and with their help he pulled what appeared to be 20cc's of blood with a long syringe from the pleural cavity where the blood had built up in his lungs. They bandaged up the rest of his wounds and laid him in a semi-elevated position. Then they intubated him and put him on the respirator machine. The machine showed Jason's heart was beating at 30 bpm, which was impossible, the normal heart beats at 60–100 bpm.

First it was impossible for the body to sustain such a slow heart rhythm without completely falling into Congestive Cardiac failure (CCF). There was no math to this. When the heart is unable to provide sufficient pump action to maintain blood flow to meet the needs of the body, you suffer a heart attack and die. But Jason was alive or barely and had now been this way for over two hours.

He will stay this way for 24 hours. "Tomorrow we will attempt to revive him Marie. You should pray for him tonight". Marie did not respond to Dr. Dupre, the confusion, the chaos. She needed answers and she knew where to get them.

Dr. Ayusha and Jacqueline were waiting outside. She asked what was the cause of death.

"Jason is not dead" Marie told them. "He is in an induced coma and healing as per Dr. Dupre. He will try awakening him tomorrow around the same time".

Dr, Ayusha was stunned and turned as white as a ghost, she lost her footing, and she fell. Marie rushed over and held her. She was placed in a chair to sit. Tonton rushed over with a cup of water and Marie gave him the death stare. She was not talking to him.

Jacqueline was speechless… "I thought all these procedures were to speed up the process to send his body back to America and notify his relatives" said Jacqueline.

"Apparently not!" replied Marie "we now have to wait on Dr. Dupre and pray and hope for the best, but he has a heartbeat and he is indeed alive".

"Tonton I'm not talking to you, but I want a shot of that Barbancourt you keep under your seat please". Dr. Dupre had sat down with the group.

"Make that two" said Dr. Dupre.

"Just bring the bottle" said Jacqueline.

When Tonton came back Marie confronted him.

"Ms. Marie this is not the time or place, soon you and I will talk".

"It is the right time and place" said Marie.

"Everyone here can get in trouble or go to jail if Jason dies. We need the truth not just for ourselves but we owe to Jason and his family if he dies."

Tonton turned to Dr. Dupre who looked at Tonton and nodded his head.

"Drink plenty rum" he told Marie "because after tonight your lives will not be the same. Some people call me Tonton some people call me Ifa. I cannot remember my mother and father or what part of Haiti I was born. I remember your father Marie and his father and so the same for Dr. Dupre. You don't see me all the time because usually I'm in different parts of Haiti and the Dominican Republic".

"I am what you may call a faith healer; many jokes are made about me because I'm short black and ugly and resemble Bo in my religion. Even if the origin of humanity and the world are explained to you tonight, here it will not be a centered question of the faith. Because we – I believe that the answer to such question is beyond human reach or comprehension. I was nineteen when I met your father Marie, he was a boy. He died at age of sixty; I was there for his death. I don't know how, but I was called back to this place to be here for his death, to bury his body in your garden".

"So many years have passed, but I was asked to return for the earthquake. Somehow I knew you would be here and I would have to take your mother from under the rubble. This is my job, the task I have been assigned in my life. I was there for the death of Papa Doc Duvalier, the first time and the second time. The first time he was poisoned it took 24 hours to heal and cure him and to put him back in power. The second time, I did not go because he had fallen out of favor with the gods. Papa Doc was chosen to rule Haiti by the Orisha's. He was brutal yes and he killed many Haitians but less than the Americans, less than the French, less than the British and less than the Spaniards".

"In my religion, remember priority is given to the ancestors. With them interceding on behalf of their families and descendant towards the Almighty.

When the Almighty creator is recognized or spoken to in the Voodoo pantheon, the worshipers cannot address themselves to that particular deity. So it is my job to protect these people. The French boiled our people in molasses and rolled them down barrels with spikes and threw them into the Arbonite River with sacks over their heads and hands tied behind their backs. And when they rebelled the Haitians were made to Pay 150,000,000 Million gold gourds. It was your great great Grandfather who interceded on behalf of Haiti and lowered the price to 90,000,000 which impoverished us for over a Century".

"When we finally regained our wealth, the United States on the verge of a depression invaded us and reintroduced slavery which they called forced labor under the Gendarmerie. They took our cotton, coffee, cocoa and sugar cane and said of the 500,000,000 dollars in the National Bank De Republique they could only find 500,000 but were going to keep the said 500,000 in NY for safe keeping. No gold bullions were ever found. Seventeen years later after the Great Depression the Haitian people got their bank back and the Treasury was empty. I am Ifa the spirit of our people.

And so my friends, our people again called to the Loas, the messengers, for help. But in order to communicate and pray, every clan or family must have their own God, sometimes called Assanyì or what you call ancestors. It's like praying to your grandmother or grandfather and asking for help. You wouldn't want to ask Jason's grandparents for help now would you? You must ask your own family to help you the spirit of those who have passed before us."

"So Marie, there is no black science or magic contrary to popular beliefs, there are no spells to cast upon anyone. I am Bòkônon, Ifa, Houngan, Mambo, Uncle Tonton or Eshu, a messenger who relays messages between the human world and the world of the Orisha's. This is why they make fun of me. Because I look like the depiction in the books of an old dark, short man with a large staff and a pipe. Known as the mediator between the gods and the living, I maintain balance, order, peace and communication bringing laughter and joy to the soul.

My religion, our religion, Haiti's religion is only a spiritual cult in which an important part is devoted to the cult of our ancestors. Based on spirituality, often associated with a known higher spirit, but is distinctive to each family. There are also different elements to this spirituality, the elements of divine essence that governs the Earth. In Trinidad it's known as Shango, Puerto Rico, Cuba and Venezuela, Ṣàngó, Xangô or Changó. It is a hierarchy that ranges in power, from major deities governing the forces of nature and human society to the spirits of individual streams, trees and rocks, as well as dozens of ethnic defenders of a certain family's clan, tribe, or nation."

"I am here to protect you Marie and anyone who surrounds you, the same goes for Dr. Dupre and countless families on this side of the Island and the other. Do you think you were brought to this camp by accident Marie or when you worked at the Hospital with Dr. Dupre it was coincidental? My daughter you are sadly mistaken. I am at the center of all things Orisha, the centre of your spiritual life. Similarly in many ways, to your doctrines, such as the intercession of saints and angels all this is being said so you can understand nothing bad is happening to Jason because you are young, your minds are young, and your faith is young. If you cannot see it then you don't believe it. So we emphasize ancestor worship and hold that the spirits of the dead live side by side with the world of the living. Jason is neither dead nor alive; he is side by side with the dead and the living."

"So there is a pattern of worship like Christians do to Mary and Jesus, and King David and Moses and you sing and say Psalms and read the bible. Our Patterns of worship follows the same various dialects, practices, songs and rituals recognizing one God with many helpers called Orisha's. A single divine creator called various names, but representing the same Mawu or Nana. In some sects it is Buluku who bore seven children and gave each rule over a realm of nature - animals, earth, and sea - these children are inter-ethnic and related to natural phenomena or to historical or mythical individuals. Like the Christian God who took six days to create the Earth but rested on the seventh day. The creator embodies a dual cosmogonic principle of which Mawu, the moon, and Lisa, the sun, are respectively the female and male aspects, often portrayed as the twin children of our Creator".

"So tonight you pray to god and your saints for Jason, but I will pray to Mawu's youngest child, Legba, who acts as a go-between with her other children: in some places he is young and virile whilst here in Haiti he is known to take the form an old man. Then there is Mami Wata, goddesses of the waters, Gu, ruling iron and smithcraft, Sakpata, who rules diseases and many others. All creation is considered divine and therefore contains the power of the divine".

"This is how our medicines and herbal remedies came into being and is understood, and explains the ubiquitous use of mundane objects in our religious ritual. Things such as talismans, or objects such as statues or dried animal parts, powders and potions that are sold for their healing and spiritually rejuvenating properties. So Jason was given the white potion of the dead tonight so he can heal, tomorrow he will be given the black potion of the living so he can live".

When Tonton finished with his story everyone was asleep except for Dr. Dupre. Toton had slipped the potion from the root of the moab (family to valerian root) into the bottle. This was known to contribute to a restful night and blank memories the next day.

The trio slept well into the morning. When Marie awoke she went to inquire about Jason. Dr. Dupre said he was doing much better and they would be able to see him in a few hours.

It was 4: pm when they entered the surgical tent. Jason's eyes were open and he was smiling. He motioned he could not talk because his throat hurt. Dr. Dupre explained to the group it would take a couple hours before his throat would be completely healed, they hugged him.

Marie kissed him and Tonton stood smiling telling Jason when he was better he had a joke for him. Dr. Dupre told the group when Jason was strong enough the marines would be taking him back to the US. Arrangements had been made to fly him to LA to his parents' house to recoup.

Later that evening they returned Jason was up and talking slowly and with a slightly raspy voice. Dr. Ayusha had stopped by earlier to say goodbye because of the ongoing violence the Nepalese peacekeepers were being evacuated.

Later that evening when they returned Jason turned to Marie and said, "so this is what has to happen for me to get a kiss from you mmmmm?"

Marie's cheeks became flushed with embarrassment.

"Maybe"

Jacqueline laughed at them both and said "Jason tell us what happened?"

Jason told them he went down to collect samples like he and Marie had been doing when he was attacked. He felt the piercing of his flesh and a boot kicking him in the back then he fell into the water and blacked out.

"And where was Tonton?" asked Marie.

Jason smile "telling jokes, no but seriously Tonton saved my life and I don't know how because medically I should be dead. I am humbled and grateful Tonton, I owe you a debt that can never be repaid."

Tonton took his hand "you were destined to come here and find the cause of death to our people. I knew you were here before you came and my job was to protect you, there are no coincidences in life. I am happy to be of service to you and Marie. And the man who stabbed you has been found and will never commit this type of harm to another so says the gods of the Orisha"

Jason Looked at Tonton Perplexed and then blurted out "do you feel ok Tonton you didn't poke fun at me, that scares me is there something I should know, like did you put laxatives in my food or something, you passing up on an opportunity to make fun of me naaaaahh"

Tonton smiled "well I did save one joke for you."

Marie chimed in "Tonton Tonton NO!"

"It's ok Marie" said Jason I need a laugh.

Tonton started "It was Friday, and four nuns went to the priest at the local Catholic church to ask for the weekend off. They argued back and forth for a few minutes. Finally the priest agreed to let them leave the convent for the weekend.

"However", he said, "as soon as you get back Monday morning I want you to confess to me what you did over the weekend." The four nuns agree, and run off. Monday comes, and the four nuns return. The first nun goes to the priest and says, "Forgive me, Father, for I have sinned." The priest asks, "What did you do, Sister?"

She replies, "I watched an R-rated movie." The priest looks up at heaven for a few seconds, then replies, "You are forgiven. Go and drink the holy water." The first nun leaves, and the fourth nun begins to chuckle quietly under her breath. The second nun then goes up to the priest and says, "Forgive me, Father, for I have sinned." The priest replies, "OK, what happened?" She says, "I was driving my brother's car down the street in front of his house, and I hit a neighbors dog and killed it." The priest looks up to heaven for half a minute, then says, "You are forgiven. Go and drink the holy water."

The second nun goes out. By this time, the fourth nun is laughing quite audibly.

Then the third nun walks to the priest and says, "Forgive me, Father, for I have sinned." The priest asks, "Out with it. What did you do?" She says, "Last night, I ran naked up and down Main Street." The priest looks up at heaven for a full five minutes before responding, "God forgives you. Go and drink the holy water." She leaves. The fourth nun falls on the floor, laughing so hard tears run down her cheeks. The priest asks her, "OK. What did you do that was so bloody funny?"

The fourth nun replies, "I peed in the holy water..."

"That was good one Tonton" said Marie.

"I agree" said Jason "but so you guys know I'm going to miss you all an I promise to come back. When I'm all healed up." A tear rolled down his cheek.

"I have learned so much in these past few months, lessons for a lifetime."

And then he looked at Marie and said.

"I have to return there is something I want from Haiti, but it is something I have to earn, because it is something I am willing to cherish for a lifetime. I have always gotten everything easy in life, but this requires work, dedication, patience and love, so I will be back."

The silence in the room was deafening. Then Marie said.

"Well Dr. Jason Bramer hurry up and get better, time is of the essence. The good things in life never really cost a lot, it just requires honesty, hard work and commitment."

"You two sound like a romance novel said Jacqueline, please everyone knows you like Marie Jason and Marie you are too stubborn to give him the time of day. Hope this shows you both life is short and precious. Marie you should have been Puerto Rican by now he would have gotten some Bodequa love and all that Ayusha nonsense, him going all the way over there to get stabbed smh"

Marie looked at Jacqueline and laughed she was so crazy and that's why she had grown to love her. No messing around it is what it is with Jacqueline. And with that said Jacqueline herded everyone out the tent. 'You to Tonton" she said.

Then on que everyone left the tent except Marie. She held Jason's hand and they spoke for the first time. The following week the Marines took Jason back to the US. The months flew by they worked harder than ever at the camp and then they received the report from the United Nations on the Cholera outbreak. Marie was leaving the camp for a 3 week vacation she was taking Jacqueline with her six months had gone by. Jason frequently called the camp to check on them, sending packages and gifts ever so often. He couldn't fly until his lungs were completely healed. Jacqueline and Marie were not going to Europe on vacation they were on their way to Orlando.

"Tell my friend I said hi said Tonton, "after dropping Marie and Jacqueline off at the airport.

"Tonton who told you I'm going to see Jason, Jacqueline and I are going shopping in Orlando" said Marie.

"The twinkling in your eyes and the beating of your heart" said Tonton as he smiled and drove away. Back at the Camp Dr. Dupre read the final report on the outbreak of the Cholera from the independent commission.

The 12 January 2010 earthquake was the latest and most devastating of many major sudden-impact natural disasters affecting Haiti in the last 10 years. It was also one of a series of sudden emergencies that mobilized the international community on a global scale.

The response to Haiti, especially in the health sector, has been generous, even overwhelming. This internal and external response met considerable challenges and problems, some of its own making. As was the case in the response to the Indian Ocean tsunami and the Pakistan earthquake, not all those challenges were met effectively.

The objective of this Report is to draw the lessons to be learned for improving the health response in future sudden-onset disasters. We know that massive earthquakes will occur again and some will devastate metropolitan areas or even the capital city, as was the case in Haiti. Haiti is the subject of this study, hopefully not the object, as Haiti has had her share of catastrophes.

The scope of the book is limited to the health response, health being defined in its broad sense, not merely medical care or disease control. The review is confined to the immediate and early response in the first three months, the period during which most of the international assistance was mobilized and influences, for better or worse, rehabilitation and reconstruction.

269

Love & Cholera focuses specially but not exclusively on those lessons that are of general interest, i.e., not specific to the special case of Haiti. The international community has much to learn from the response in Haiti where it has shown an ability to repeat its errors and shortcomings from past disasters.

The poorest country in the Western Hemisphere, Haiti has been affected by political violence for most of its recent history. Poverty, corruption, lack of export industries, a large deficit and severe environmental deterioration and deforestation, are among Haiti's most serious disadvantages.

Haiti prior to the earthquake

This initial report summarizes the situation in Haiti prior to the earthquake. Whenever possible, it offers a comparison with Haiti's neighbor, the Dominican Republic (to place the country in a regional context), and with three countries affected in the last decade by large, sudden-onset natural disasters and recipients of massive international assistance: Indonesia and Sri Lanka (Indian Ocean tsunami in 2004) and Pakistan (earthquake in Kashmir in 2005).

Haiti, a French- and Creole-speaking country located in the middle of the Caribbean basin, has a population estimated at 10 million inhabitants. It takes up one-third of the island of Hispaniola, the rest being occupied by the Dominican Republic, which has a comparable population.

Half of the population lives in urban areas, the largest being the capital metropolitan area (Port-au-Prince "agglomeration"), with a population estimated at 2.3 million.

Sources for this report: Institut Haitien de Statistique et Informatique (IHSI 2010); World Bank, Haiti at a glance (2006);

The absence of such basic information as agreed upon census data in Haiti illustrates the lack of reliable or accurate data on many aspects of the country's public life. For this reason, figures are rounded in this publication.

Social, political, and economic determinants.

Characteristics of Haiti affecting disaster response

Disadvantages for response:

- A small country, among the poorest of the world, and therefore with limited response capacity;
- Weak institutions with little control over thousands of donor-supported NGOs;
- Lack of governance and a high level of corruption;
- The absence of armed forces.

Advantages for response:

- Easy access by land and water;
- Presence of peacekeeping forces, UN agencies, and a large number of humanitarian NGOs.

In 1991, a military coup paralyzed the development of the country, leading in 1993 to an OAS/UN embargo. One of the first decisions of the newly elected, democratic Government in 1994, was to dismantle the army—the cause of so many military coups in Haiti—leaving the police force as the only national institution in charge of security.

Following a long series of political upheavals, the United Nations Stabilization Mission in Haiti (MINUSTAH) was set up in 2004.3 While the Haitian National Police was progressively emerging as a law enforcement body, foreign military forces under MINUSTAH ensured basic security both for the population, which was increasingly ambivalent to this presence, and for an increasingly large UN humanitarian and development community. MINUSTAH was the only entity with significant assets and discipline for logistic support to the humanitarian community in case of sudden-onset disasters. However, this function was not included in its mandate. It should be noted that the presence of a peacekeeping force in absence of civil war or conflict subjected the UN actors to particularly constraining security rules.

Haiti's socio-economic situation at the time of the earthquake can be described in a nutshell:

- One of poorest and smallest countries in the world and the least developed in the American region;
- A high level of corruption, inequity, and inequality;
- Severe environmental deterioration and deforestation;
- Lack of export industries and a large deficit;
- An ongoing brain drain, primarily to the United States, Canada, and France;

MINUSTAH was originally established through the UN Security Council Resolution 1542 of 30 April 2004, to "support the Transitional Government in ensuring a secure and stable environment; to assist in monitoring, restructuring and reforming the Haitian National Police; to help with comprehensive and sustainable Disarmament, Demobilization and Reintegration (DDR) programmes; to assist with the restoration and maintenance of the rule of law, public safety and public order in Haiti; to protect United Nations personnel, facilities, installations and equipment and to protect civilians under imminent threat of physical violence; to support the constitutional and political processes; to assist in organizing, monitoring, and carrying out free and fair municipal, parliamentary and presidential elections; to support the Transitional Government as well as Haitian human rights institutions and groups in their efforts to promote and protect human rights; and to monitor and report on the human rights situation in the country. ... In extending the mission's mandate for another year on 13 October 2009, the Security Council, by its resolution 1892, further tasked MINUSTAH with providing logistical and security assistance for elections anticipated for 2010" (UN 2011).

Most services delivered by NGOs with token supervision and consultation from the Government. Haiti has been called a "Republic of NGOs".

Haiti stands in stark contrast to its neighbor, the Dominican Republic, and to other developing countries recently affected by sudden-onset disasters that triggered massive foreign assistance. While Haiti can be compared to Sri Lanka in terms of size, its level of development is far lower. Haiti's development level is comparable to that of Pakistan but the size of the latter country and extent of its resources are very dissimilar.

Gross national income (GNI) per capita (formerly GNP per capita) is the gross national income, converted to U.S. dollars, divided by the midyear population. It comprises the value of all products and services generated within a country in one year (i.e., its gross domestic product), together with its net income received from other countries (notably interest and dividends). Figures are from World Bank Databank (2010).

The Multidimensional Poverty Index (Alkire and Santos 2010) uses 10 indicators to measure critical dimensions of poverty at the household level. The MPI value summarizes information on multiple deprivations into a single number.

The Corruption Index ranks countries on a scale from 10 (highly clean) to 0 (highly corrupt); ranking in world is in parentheses (Transparency International 2011).

Haiti

Note: The Rule of Law Index is one of six indicators used to assess the quality of governance in countries. These indicators aggregate the views on the quality of governance provided by a large number of enterprise, citizen and expert survey respondents in industrialized and developing countries. Figure compiled from the World Bank Worldwide Governance Indicators website:

Health status

Health characteristics of Haiti

Negative aspects:

- Lack of reliable baseline health statistics;
- High level of most communicable diseases;

- Only half of the population has access to poor quality health services, water, or sanitation;
- 75% of health services are delivered by NGOs and faith groups, most of which are unwilling to follow Ministry of Health norms and guidelines.

Positive aspects:

- A strong pharmaceutical and supply system which is internationally administered;
- On-site presence of external medical organizations (NGOs or bilateral).

Health situation in the Americas, basic indicators 2009; Haiti, PDNA (analytical matrix) (2010).

A governance review of the health sector carried out by the Ministry of Health in 2007 shows that leadership and regulatory functions in Haiti were "weak or very weak" at the central, departmental, and periphery levels (MSPP 2007). At the crosssectoral level, donors must share in responsibility for a situation that enables NGOs to decline to comply with norms and standards or tentative attempts of coordination from the Ministry of Health.

On the information management side, there is a lack of adequate information to support analysis and decision making at strategic and operational levels. The absence of acceptable baseline data complicates any monitoring effort of the response. Health indicators, when available in Haiti, show a picture of excessive morbidity/ mortality with poor preventive and curative services.

For all indicators, Haiti demonstrates greater vulnerability or weakness than her neighbors. Life expectancy is over 10 years less in Haiti than in the region; mortality in children under 5 years old is twice the regional average and three times that of the Dominican Republic.

Communicable diseases include, among others, acute diarrheal disease,5 the highest incidence of tuberculosis in the Americas, a generalized HIV epidemic, and dengue (presence of serotypes in 85% of Port-au-Prince population). Tropical diseases such as leprosy, lymphatic filariasis, and anthrax remain prevalent.

Vaccine-preventable diseases remain all too frequent due to the very low coverage that has been achieved.

Delivery of health services

The existing health system is mostly private, with a very small public sector. Health institutions linked to faith-based groups and NGOs provide most of the health care, complemented by the Cuban Medical Brigades, which supply an average of 400 doctors in rural areas.

Together, these organizations provide an estimated 75% of the care. In the capital and major cities, private, for-profit health clinics and pharmacies offer health services for those who can pay. The elite often seek treatment in the United States or other foreign countries.

In real terms, 47% of the Haitian population lacks access to basic health care. This figure rises to over 50% for women. Accessibility is low due to financial barriers; when accessible, services are of poor quality.

Specialized services such as rehabilitation, mental health, and blood banks are far below the level of neighboring countries. Mental health services in Haiti have been centered on two understaffed and under-equipped psychiatric hospitals, a situation that is far from the community-based approach recommended by WHO.

In addition to a striving private pharmaceutical industry, PROMESS (Programme de Médicaments Essentiels), managed by the Pan American Health Organization, serves as the national pharmacy, offering essential supplies and drugs at or below cost.

Water and sanitation

Only 58% of the population has some access to improved drinking-water sources (Schuftan, Hoogendoorn, Capdegelle 2007). The access is notoriously better in urban settings (70%). Access to improved sanitation and disposal of excreta is extremely poor (total 19%, urban 29%, rural 12%). In brief, 8 million of the country's population of 10 million lacks access to water and/or sanitation.

Nutrition

The levels of global acute malnutrition as well as those of stunting (chronic malnutrition) are high but markedly under those considered a humanitarian emergency. The focus of ongoing projects has not been sufficiently aligned with Haiti's priority nutrition security problems or with international best practices. Above all, malnutrition in Haiti is the end result of extreme poverty associated with low education level. It is primarily an economic and equity issue rather than a health one.

Violence and criminality

The rate of violence is very high in Haiti. Reliable figures are unavailable or at best spotty. Gender-based violence is endemic and underreported. There is little follow-up, be it from law enforcement or the health services, on reported cases of gender-based violence.

Dominican Republic at a glance.

The health status of Haiti prior to the earthquake is particularly bleak when compared to its neighbor or other countries affected by sudden-onset catastrophes.

The services remain very poor despite considerable investment by NGOs and the higher density of medical doctors and hospitals beds in the country compared, for instance, to Indonesia.

Finally, the "singularity or exceptionality" of Haiti in the Region of the Americas should be noted. It is the only independent, French/Creole-speaking country in the Caribbean or Latin America. Haiti has a social, economic, and political culture comparable to no other. Although it is making a consistent effort to join regional institutions, few if any other members share the same challenges or background, or even understand its culture. Haiti is not fully integrated as an equal member in the Caribbean or Latin America. It is an orphan without siblings, but with many foster parents.

Disaster vulnerability, risk reduction including preparedness.

Vulnerability

Haiti is particularly vulnerable to disasters. The main factors causing this vulnerability are social and economic.

The focus of preparedness in Haiti was overwhelmingly on seasonal climatic events. Rare, but catastrophic events were not contemplated.

The poorest countries are the least able and willing to invest in risk reduction, including in preparedness. Considering the urgency of every day needs faced by these countries, the onus for risk reduction and disaster preparedness should be more on the international community.

International agencies and donors should increase their efforts to focus the attention of health authorities on credible scenarios of major sudden-onset disasters.

Among the many factors affecting Haiti's vulnerability to disasters are the concentration of population (39%) and resources (66% of GDP) in and around the capital (West Department), deforestation, the presence of communities living on plains which are prone to flooding, high urban population density, and a proliferation of seismically unsafe buildings and infrastructure constructed on unstable soils.

Environmental vulnerability and social factors like poverty, political instability, rapid urbanization, and the fragile nature of the Haitian State exacerbate the damaging effects of natural events.

These observations have been confirmed by the alarming trend in successive disasters: 56 internationally recognized disasters, including 20 major disasters in the 20th century and 3 catastrophic hurricane seasons in just the last decade

| GDP | | Affected | Deaths |
|---|---|---|---|
| 2004: Hurricane Jeanne | 7% | 300,000 | 5,000 |
| 2007: Hurricanes Dean and Noel | 2% | 194,000 | 330 |
| 2008: Tropical storms Fay and Gustav and Hurricane Ike | 15% | 1,000,000 | 800 |

Risk reduction

Although risk reduction includes preparedness, this aspect will be treated separately.

The risk of earthquake was not unknown by the health sector and was stressed in the Country's health profile.

"Haiti is . . . extremely vulnerable to earthquakes. The country has eight fault lines; two of the most important are located as follows: one in the far north and the other crossing east to west. Seismic activity in Haiti in 2003–2005 has revived the specter of a possible major earthquake (7–8 on the Richter scale), which experts have been forecasting for several years. The extremely high rate of urbanization that has left the metropolitan region of Port-au-Prince with slightly more than two million inhabitants (10,000–18,000 persons per km) will worsen the damage."

As noted by François Grünewald, the earthquake "has taken place in a context where the most frequent problems obscure the most serious problems. Though Haiti experienced earthquakes which destroyed

Cap Haïtien in 1840 and Port-au-Prince in 1700, these tragedies of the past only had a marginal influence on the national strategy for managing risks".

As often is the case, important issues (preparing for major but rare events) were overshadowed by more pressing immediate priorities (attending to daily and seasonal emergencies). Haiti's Directorate for Civil Protection (DPC) started to work on building standards for critical facilities before the earthquake and on a disaster risk reduction strategy. They were planning to initiate a building code project in January 2010. Reduction of seismic risk through adoption and enforcement of construction norms and standards had never been enacted before.

The easiest and least expensive way to protect health (and other) facilities from seismic risk is by including strict norms in new construction. However, few if any new health facilities had been built in Haiti in recent years. The retrofitting of existing facilities is a technically more complicated and more expensive approach and was never seriously considered as a feasible and cost-effective measure by the Ministry of Health or donor community.

No serious attention was given by the health sector to the possible scenario of a severe earthquake. The modest efforts focused on seasonal hurricanes. Admittedly, Haiti has the highest index of vulnerability to cyclones of all the developing small island states. An estimated 96% of the population of Haiti lives in constant danger of two or more risks. Furthermore, being part of an island in the middle of the Caribbean indeed increases the risks linked to rising sea level and those related to the possible impacts of changing patterns in the El Niño/La Niña phenomena (DARA 2010).

The seismic recurrence interval was estimated at about 150 years.

At the multi-sectoral level, major donors (World Bank and European donors) provided significant support at the end of the last decade to strengthen the national Directorate for Civil Protection. The focus was initially at the national level and shifted later toward decentralization and strengthening of the department level.

Cyclones are known as hurricanes in the Caribbean or typhoons in the Pacific Ocean.

Based on the estimated number of people killed per year (per million exposed) (World Bank 2005).

Health sector preparedness

In the health sector, training and other technical cooperation was regularly provided to the Haitian Ministry of Health within the limits of the modest funding allocated by donors to disaster preparedness. Principles of mass casualty management in the aftermath of earthquakes were periodically promoted in Haiti and other countries in the Caribbean.

The outcomes and impact of regional preparedness efforts in Haiti remained limited. The disaster preparedness program in the health sector never received the priority, authority, or resources required for the task. No effective planning and preparedness measures took place in Haiti on health facilities. Then again, investing for mass casualties may seem somewhat unrealistic when daily emergencies cannot be attended properly.

On 12 January 2010, a 7.0 earthquake on the Modified Mercalli Scale shook Haiti. It was the most powerful earthquake to hit the country in 200 years.

The impact was unprecedented; more so if we take into account that it affected the most densely populated area of the country and also its economic and administrative center, hindering an already meager response capacity.

The earthquake:12 January 2010

The impact of the Haiti earthquake was truly unprecedented among recent natural disasters:

- The magnitude of damage and losses in absolute terms, but above all compared to the size and poverty of the country precluding any backup capacity;

- The destruction of the capital and its effect on the government apparatus;
- The leadership losses incurred by the UN peacekeeping forces, UN agencies, and other potential actors;
- The impact on logistics of severe damage to both the major airport and seaport.

On 12 January 2010, shortly before 5 PM, an earthquake with a magnitude of 7.0 on the MMS scale shook Haiti for 35 seconds.11 It was the most powerful earthquake to hit the country in 200 years. The earthquake's hypocenter was close to the Earth's surface (13 km below) and its epicenter was approximately 25 km southwest of Port-au-Prince, the capital, in the West Department. Although the South-East and Nippes Departments were also affected, only a limited, albeit densely populated, area (45 km radius) was hit by the earthquake.

11 Initial estimates indicated a magnitude of 7.3 on the Richter scale. U.S. Geological Survey and other sources suggest a magnitude of 7.0. Part of the reason for the discrepancy is the increasing use of the Moment Magnitude Scale (MMS) which differs slightly from the Richter scale. As with the Richter scale, an increase of one step on this logarithmic scale corresponds to a $101.5 \approx 32$ times increase in the amount of energy released, and an increase of two steps corresponds to a 103 (i.e., 1,000 times) increase in energy. It should be noted that the Richter scale is notoriously less accurate in measuring severe earthquakes.

According to a study by the U.S. Geological Survey, the fault initially thought to have triggered this devastating earthquake is likely still under considerable strain and continues to pose a significant seismic hazard. This puts to rest the common misconception that an area affected by a major seismic event is vulnerable to milder aftershocks but protected from more severe earthquakes.

The Port-au-Prince metropolitan area suffered enormous damage. Eighty percent of the town of Léogâne (17 km southwest of Port-au-Prince) was destroyed.

The earthquake created an unprecedented situation, amplified by the fact that it affected the most densely populated area of the country and also its economic and administrative center. It also severely affected the international organizations in Haiti (including MINUSTAH, UN agencies, and NGOs).

Rural areas in the West and South-East Departments, including the mountainous areas were also badly affected. Thousands of rural houses in remote, hard-to-reach areas were destroyed and earthquake-triggered landslides were frequent.

The extent of damage and losses reflect the particularly high vulnerability of Haiti. While the U.S. Geological Survey recorded 22 magnitude-7.0 or larger earthquakes in 2010, almost all the fatalities were produced by the 12 January earthquake in Haiti. In 2010, about

227,000 people were killed due to earthquakes, with over 98% from the Haiti event.

This large, shallow earthquake produced violent shaking that can cause damage even to well-built buildings anywhere in the world. In Haiti, this high-intensity shaking together with buildings vulnerable to earthquakes and high population exposure resulted in catastrophe.

The Post-Disaster Needs Assessment (PDNA)

As is systematically done after such an event, the Haitian Government and the international community launched a Post-Disaster Needs Assessment (PDNA) involving UNDP, the World Bank, the European Commission, and other donors.

"The objectives for the PDNA, a cross-sectoral exercise to provide a financial estimate of the damage and needs, were multifold, each actor stressing a particular one:

- "A tool for decision making and priority setting by donors and agencies due to meet at the Donor Conference in New York (31 March 2010);
- "A new vision for in-depth reform, making use of the window for opportunities opened briefly following major disasters; however, some questioned whether an incremental approach

to 'build back better' was not more realistic than a costly new vision;

- "A step toward developing an action plan and strategy for the sectors; this is a result that was achieved in the health sector, although not fully implemented;
- "A necessary statistical record for global comparison and documentation for the significant investment in the reconstruction process" (Griekspoor 2010).

U.S. Geological Survey geologist Carol Prentice led a team of scientists to Haiti immediately after the earthquake to search for traces of ground rupture. The researchers sought evidence of deformation from the 2010 quake and determined that the main strand of the Enriquillo-Plantain Garden (EPG) Fault did not rupture in the January quake, as was initially thought. They also documented evidence of geologically young ground ruptures on the EPG Fault, which they believe may have formed during earthquakes that struck Haiti in 1751 and 1770. Because the EPG Fault did not rupture the surface, little, if any, accumulated strain on that fault was released during the quake and the hazard remains high ((Koontz 2010).

Including the communes of Port-au-Prince, Carrefour, Pétionville, Delmas, Tabarre, Cité Soleil, and Kenscoff.

A magnitude-8.8 offshore earthquake that hit Chile on 27 February was the largest recorded in the world in 2010. An estimated 577 died;

about half of those deaths resulted from an earthquake-generated tsunami. The energy released by the Chilean earthquake was more than 500 times greater than the one that hit Haiti. However, fatalities were far lower in Chile due to that country's strict building codes and lower maximum shaking intensities (USGS 2011).

Overall impact on infrastructure. The earthquake caused massive infrastructure destruction. According to the survey carried out by the Post-Disaster Needs Assessment (PDNA), some 105,000 homes were completely destroyed and more than 208,000 damaged. Over 1,300 educational establishments and over 50 hospitals and health centers collapsed or were left unusable. Part of the country's main port was not operational. Damage to the airport guidance system limited the early arrival of essential response, leading the Government of Haiti to delegate authority over its airspace and airport to the U.S. military.

The President's Palace, Parliament, the Law Courts, many other landmarks of the Haitian nation, and most of the ministry and public administration buildings, including the Ministry of Health, were destroyed. This damage further crippled the limited capacity of the government to lead a forceful response.

The only natural disaster that came close to this level of devastating governance capacity and administrative structures was the Managua earthquake (Nicaragua, 23 December

The primary source for this section is: Haiti earthquake PDNA: assessment of damages, losses, sectoral and general needs, published by the Haitian Government, March 2010.

(1972). Two-thirds of the capital's population was displaced. However, there were significant differences from the Haiti earthquake:

- Managua had a population of 325,000 compared to the 2.5 million in Port-au-Prince;
- Fatalities were relatively few (3,000 to 7,000) compared to over 200,000 deaths in Haiti;
- There was a strong dictatorial government in Nicaragua compared to a fragile but democratic government in Haiti.

Economic impact

- The earthquake set back the economic development of Haiti by 10 years;
- The economic valuation process of damage and losses does not reflect the magnitude of human losses and suffering;
- When translated into monetary value, the social losses represent only a relatively modest economic cost.

The health sector does not operate in a vacuum. It is entirely dependent on the economic health of the country and its population.

An impact of the earthquake on economic well-being is an impact on public health.

The disaster impact on economic performance, employment, and poverty can be assessed from two measures:

1. The damage: that is, the replacement value of physical assets wholly or partially destroyed;
2. The losses: the economic flows resulting from the temporary absence of damaged assets.

According to the PDNA, the total value of damage and losses caused by the earthquake on 12 January 2010 is estimated at US$ 7.804 billion, surpassing the country's GDP in 2009. This is the first time in 35 years of applying the assessment methodology developed by the UN Economic Commission for Latin America and the Caribbean16 for estimating damage and losses that the cost of a disaster is so high in economic terms in relation to a country's GDP.

The private sector (including not-for-profit) sustained most of the damage and losses (US$ 5.722 billion, 73% of the total), whereas the public sector's share totaled US$ 2.081 billion, or 27%. There are two exceptions: the health sector, where only 40% of the health damage/losses were borne by the private sector. The Damage and Loss Assessment (DaLA) methodology was initially developed by the UN Economic Commission for Latin America and the Caribbean

(UN-ECLAC) in 1972. It has since been improved through close cooperation of the World Bank, Inter-American Development Bank, UNESCO, and ILO to capture the closest approximation of damage and losses due to disaster events. It is a flexible tool that can be adapted to specific disaster types and government ownership requirements. The DaLA methodology bases its assessments on the overall economy of the affected country.

Including for-profit and not-for-profit) and the environment sector (primarily for waste and debris disposal) where the losses are borne almost entirely by the public sector.

The value of material assets destroyed, including housing, schools, hospitals, roads and bridges, ports, and airports, has been estimated at US$ 4.302 billion (55% of the total losses due to the disaster). The variation in economic flows (lost production, fall in turnover, job and salary losses, increased production costs, etc.) has reached US$ 3.561 billion (equivalent to 45% of the total).

Housing is the sector that has been most affected by the earthquake (damage is US$ 2.3 billion). Comparatively, the economic impact (damage and losses) in the social sector is modest in monetary terms. Health and education sectors represent only 6% each of the economic impact.

Damage and losses from the 2010 Haiti earthquake (rounded to millions of US dollars)

| Sectors | Public | Private | Total |
|---|---|---|---|
| Social | 352 (23.2%) | 1,161 (76.8%) | 1,513 (19.4%) |
| Water and sanitation | 29 (12.3%) | 206 (87.7%) | 235 (3%) |
| Health | 282 (60%) | 188 (40%) | 470 (6%) |
| Education | 40 (8.4%) | 437 (91.6%) | 477 (6.1%) |
| Food safety and nutrition | 0 | 330 (100%) | 330 (4.2%) |
| Infrastructure, including housing | 1,402 (31.4%) | 3,059 (68.6%) | 4,461 (57.2%) |
| Production sectors | 3 | 1,327 (100%) | 1,330 (17%) |
| Environmenta | 324 (64.3%) | 175 (35.7%) | 499 (6.4%) |
| TOTAL | 2,081 (26.7%) | 5,722 (73.3%) | 7,803 (100%) |

Source: Adapted from figures presented in Table 2 of the PDNA (Haiti 2010, 7).

a Damage and losses to the environment sector mostly include solid waste removal (debris, hospital waste, hazardous substances, etc.).

The PDNA estimated that:

- The central government's overall deficit would likely rise from 4.4% of GDP for the 2008/09 financial year17 to 7.1% of GDP during the financial year 2009/10, despite a marked increase in overall income over the years preceding the impact date.
- The earthquake will entail a loss of 8.5% of existing jobs in the immediate future.
- Poverty indices have returned to 2001 levels (71% in moderate poverty and 50% in extreme poverty), canceling all modest progress made in the last decade.18

All these factors bear a direct short- and long-term impact on public health.

The fiscal or financial year in Haiti runs from 1 October to 30 September.

This projection does not take into account the promising prospects of the reconstruction activities.

UN Headquarters

Photo: UN, Logan Abassl

Impact on international and bilateral organizations

- The UN and peacekeeping forces lost their leaders and headquarters.
- Many international agencies were directly impacted by the earthquake and unable to respond as promptly as expected.

The offices of most international or bilateral agencies present in Haiti were located in Port-au-Prince. Many of them suffered infrastructure and staff losses.

The UN mission (MINUSTAH) loss was considerable: 102 international UN employees lost their lives, among whom were the Special Representative and the Head of Mission, 7 other top civilian staff, 36 military staff, and 7 UN police officers.

Although the loss represents less than 1% of the entire UN staff in Haiti, the command structure of MINUSTAH and operating capacity of some UN agencies were temporarily affected. The destruction of the Hotel Christopher which housed the MINUSTAH Headquarters, resulted in the loss of most commanding officers and left the operations in chaos. UN Mission search and rescue efforts focused primarily on its own leaders and staff. Their transportation assets, for the most part, remained unaffected by the earthquake.

The offices of many of the UN agencies were either damaged or deemed unsecure, while part of their staff lost their accommodations.

Several bilateral cooperation agencies as well as international NGOs suffered material as well as human losses. The building of the Delegation of the European Commission, for instance, became unsuitable and the staff was evacuated to Santo Domingo.

Losses, material and human, of such a magnitude that affected external agencies contributed to making the rapid organization of an emergency response all the more precarious and more dependent on headquarters outside of Haiti.

As noted in the PDNA, by striking at the very heart of the Haitian economy and administration, the earthquake had an acute effect on the human and institutional response capacity both of the public and the private sectors, of international technical and financial partners, and certain NGOs.

In the affected area, 30 out of 49 hospitals were damaged or destroyed. Haiti's University and Educational Hospital (HUEH), the country's largest hospital, suffered serious physical as well as functional losses. The hospital lost several staff during the earthquake.

The health impact

Most of the health losses were the result of an extreme vulnerability to disasters, the deterioration of the medical care system, and dysfunctional public health programs.

According to the Post-Disaster Needs Assessment (PDNA) carried out jointly by the Haitian Government and international partners in February–March 2010:19

- Some 1.5 million people, representing 15% of the nation's population, were directly affected.
- More than 220,000 lost their lives and more than 300,000 were injured.
- Some 1.3 million lived in temporary shelters in the Port-au-Prince metropolitan area in the months following the impact.
- Over 600,000 left the disaster zone to seek refuge elsewhere in the country.

Problems that already existed in terms of access to health care, food, and basic services were thereby exacerbated nationwide.

The health impact in Haiti was of a much higher order of magnitude than in the tsunami-affected countries or in Pakistan.

It should be noted that all of these statistics have been intensely questioned and remain a matter of debate. The tsunami in 2004 claimed over 228,000 lives in 14 countries (Telford, Cosgrave, Houghton 2006).

Mortality

- The international community attaches far too much importance to the mortality figure.
- Donations should not be linked to the number of fatalities but rather to the number of survivors and the extent of their needs.
- Techniques and methods are available to estimate objectively the number of persons killed. They must be used when a complete census is not possible.
- The endorsement of exaggerated official statistics by the humanitarian community is counterproductive and damaging.

If development (health or others) statistics are lacking or unreliable in normal times, data following massive disasters are notoriously inaccurate. Initial estimates of number of deaths or injuries rarely result from individual body counts, detailed listings from facilities or humanitarian organizations, or censuses or surveys conducted at a later stage.

In the aftermath of most disasters, the number of deaths is a much-sought statistic by the mass media and the public. It is the most powerful figure to elicit emotions and generosity. The usefulness of mortality statistics to gauge the magnitude of the needs (of survivors) is overstated.

After earthquakes, an initial rough estimate is usually announced in the first few days. Then, reported numbers rapidly increase day after day, occasionally suddenly soaring to accommodate higher and conflicting estimates advanced by humanitarian organizations (for example, the Red Cross societies) or a public statement from higher authorities.

In Haiti, the reporting of estimated numbers of deaths by the Directorate for Civil Protection (and endorsed, de facto, by the UN Office for the Co-ordination of Humanitarian Affairs [OCHA] and the international community) followed the same pattern. An initial rough estimate of 75,000 killed was provided after one week, progressively increasing to 112,392 on Day 13. No further official revisions were offered for another 10 days. On 4 February, Day 24 of the disaster, the Prime Minister made a public statement that "the number of killed could be as high as 200,000 and that of injured above 300,000." The tally was increased to 212,000 and the counter started rising again to reach 222,570 deaths. Reported deaths by days since earthquake impact

Fatalities reported 250,000.

The Prime Minister made a statement increasing the death toll to over 200,000 on 4 February 2010 (Day 24).

Do estimated mortality figures reflect reality?

Scientists routinely question the accuracy of estimates of deaths following major disasters. Divergence in opinion is usually on a reasonable order and does not question the credibility of the whole process.

In the Indian Ocean tsunami, initial estimates in Indonesia and Sri Lanka calculated bodies recovered and missing persons separately. The latter figure was exceptionally high due to the number washed away by the waves or buried under tons of mud and debris. As bodies were recovered days and weeks later, the first number (dead bodies) increased rapidly while the number of missing remained unchanged, because no identification was attempted in either country. Mass media and agencies rapidly combined both figures into one. The final statistics clearly included significant double counting.

In the case of the Pakistan earthquake in 2005, the remoteness of most affected areas resulted in a very approximate figure probably reflecting the death toll within reasonable margins. There was limited opportunity for surveys or controversy.

The Bam earthquake in Islamic Republic of Iran in 2003, which was a shallow, localized earthquake of manageable size, offers us an illustration of a correct approach. As usual, initial estimates overstated the number of casualties: For months the official mortality figure was above 41,000 killed. Following a special census, the authorities formally corrected the earlier estimate down to 26,271 out of a total of 142,376 people in the affected areas. No other example of correction is reported.

In Haiti, it is accepted that the number of deaths (and missing) caused by the earthquake was extraordinarily high. How high remains an issue.

It was not until the publication of several studies carried out months after the impact that the official process of reporting mortality figures was thrown into controversy, questioning its integrity and credibility. A survey by the University of Michigan and later a study commissioned by USAID/Haiti suggested lower but statistically more credible estimates of the number killed: It is unclear whether and when the relief authorities were informed of the results of this survey published only nine months after the impact. The Government of Haiti unexpectedly raised further the official figure to over 300,000 when commemorating the first anniversary of the earthquake, almost five times the lowest scientific estimate. Despite the methodological differences of the two studies, they offer significantly lower figures than those officially issued by national authorities.

Haitian fatalities: two surveys dispute official tolls USAID study

The death toll was determined based on two sources of information: The color-coded building assessment carried out by Haiti's Ministry of Public Works, Transport, Communication (MTPTC) through an international entity22 and the Building Assessments and Rubble Removal (BARR) survey in which people were asked how many of the residents in each of the houses assessed died, among other questions. The group calculated the deaths per residence by using average occupancy per house (5.2) and average death rate by yellow, green, and red houses. The study concludes that the number of people killed in the earthquake was 65,575 (the range of the estimate at p < .01 is 46,190 to 84,961 dead) (Schwartz, Pierre, Calpas 2011).

University of Michigan study

The mortality rate is established comparing two surveys: 1) a 2009 survey (pre-earthquake) carried out by the University of Michigan, sampling 1,800 households in the Port-au-Prince area; and 2) a post-earthquake survey conducted in 2010, in which 1,732 (93.1%) of the 2009 sampled household members were located. Using population estimates for the greater area of Port-AuPrince of 2,713,599 and an average of 5.7 persons per household, they calculated 158,679 deaths: 111,794 died during or immediately after the earthquake, 37,301 died as result of the injuries, and 9,583 died of an illness in a period of six weeks following the impact (Kolbe et al. 2010).

*Jeff Benjamin*

| Source | Number killed |
| --- | --- |
| Government (2010) | 222,570 |
| Government (Jan 2011) | 300,000 |
| Univ. of Michigan study | 149,095 |
| USAID study | 65,575 |

It is important to note that the absence of data disaggregated by age and gender in official statistics had some impact on both the understanding of the quake and its effects, as well as on programming the relief efforts in Haiti.

This figure does not include the estimated number of deaths from illness unrelated to the earthquake.

Miyamota International trained 270 Haitian engineers in building assessment techniques, using a color-coded system: Green = safe; Yellow = inhabit after repairs; and Red = unsafe for occupancy. From February 2010 to January 2011 the team evaluated 382,256 Port-au-Prince buildings with the following results: 205,539 green (54%), 99,043 yellow (26%), and 77,674 red (20%). This initiative was endorsed by the Ministry of Public Works, Transport, and Communication, UN Office for Project Services (UNOPS) and the Pan American Development Foundation (PADF).

Very partial data in Indonesia suggest that mortality among women resulting from the tsunami was significantly higher in some fishing villages.

The main lesson for future disasters is not what the best estimate in Haiti was, it is the need for a transparent methodology to produce the official statistics. The credibility of the international humanitarian community is also at stake: Although many international staff privately questioned the credibility of the figures, all agencies and the mass media welcomed the highest figures possible for their own purposes (for fund raising, readership, or other motives).

In many catastrophes, the management of death figures, a difficult technical task under any circumstances, is handled politically. What is new in the case of Haiti is the significant and rising discrepancy between the official figures and the scientific estimates. This has led, more than a year after the event, to a public controversy, since the amount of funding that a disaster deserves is closely linked in the public's eyes to the number of persons killed.24 It is indeed the recognition of this linkage which incites governments and agencies to opt for the highest figures possible.

This perception needs to be changed: the main criteria for assistance should be the number of people in need (the dead are not in need of assistance) and the urgency and magnitude of their need.

Regardless of the controversy, the mortality rate was very high (almost 10% of the population in the metropolitan capital area if the official figure of 220,000 is accepted). The question is: why?

The Richter scale reading alone of an earthquake is a poor predictor of the expected morbidity/mortality. Everything is a matter of geological context (type of soil, epicenter, and hypocenter) and physical and socio-economic vulnerability. The triggering event is natural, the disaster itself is not natural.

All estimates are fairly illustrative of the gravity of the tragedy, as well as suitable for purposes of public information and fund raising. Whether fewer than 100,000 casualties or surpassing 300,000, the impact is an immense tragedy for a poor country the size of Haiti (6.5 to 30 deaths per 1,000 inhabitants according to the figure selected). Comparatively, the mortality of the Indian Ocean tsunami was 1.8/1,000 in Sri Lanka and 0.7/1,000 in Indonesia. Few families or institutions in Port-au-Prince were spared fatalities.

First, such a high mortality rate is not uncommon for a shallow earthquake directly under a densely populated area. In the Bam, Iran, earthquake in 2003, 18% of the population was killed.

Other factors affecting vulnerability are mentioned in a study by Mompelat (2010):

- Extreme vulnerability of constructions;
- High occupation density of dwellings;
- Highly instable soil (slopes);

24 See, for example, the article "U.S. Reduces Estimates of Homeless in Haiti Quake", New York Times, 31 May 2011.

- Severe damage to facilities with high occupancy (schools, universities, administration);
- Mortality in the narrow streets;
- Lack of access to medical care.

Most of those factors could have been minimized by the adoption of a risk-reduction approach including land use management and construction norms.

On the positive side, the timing (4:53 PM) contributed to minimize the impact. Many adults and children were in the streets. One hour earlier, public offices and schools would have been occupied; a few hours later, most Haitians would have been at home.

Immediate morbidity

- The number of injuries by type and gravity is a critical statistic lacking in most disasters.
- A very simple list detailing the type of injuries to be reported in the aftermath of disasters needs to be developed urgently at the global level.

This section reviews the immediate impact on health, that is, primarily in terms of injuries and traumas. Delayed impact such as on disease transmission, mental health, violence, and nutrition is later discussed.

Estimates of the number of persons injured are also notoriously inaccurate in most severe disasters in less developed countries. They offer at best a reasonable guess of the magnitude of the problem. In Haiti, offering a scientific estimate on the number of injuries was almost impossible. There was no registry of patients and no information system in most of the facilities. The situation can best be illustrated by the observation of a team arriving in Port-au-Prince 10 days after the earthquake with the mission to restore surgical services to the University Hospital (Peranteau et al. 2010):

"No patient identifiers were present and there were no physical reports accompanying patients to indicate their diagnoses, operations or care plan . . . At first we used scraps of papers or cardboard taped to the patient indicating name and injury . . . as paper became available, a single sheet became the makeshift chart taped to the edge of the stretcher."

If such a situation prevailed after two weeks in the country's largest hospital, it is not surprising that, with the exception of self-sustained military facilities, no compiled data were available for overall management or reporting.

Although the number of injured is a critical indicator of the need for assistance, the external pressure for updated figures was far less than for mortality data. Consequently, those statistics were less frequently released by Haiti's Directorate for Civil Protection. As was true for mortality, the morbidity figure evolved over time, starting with a rough estimate of more than 200,000 injured on Day 9 (20 January) to be readjusted down to 194,000 on Day 15, and increased to 196,501 the next day an estimate of "over 300,000 injured" was announced publicly by the Prime Minister and adopted officially by the Directorate for Civil Protection effective on 6 February (Day 26). These figures must be considered with caution and are only indicative of the magnitude of the impact.

The challenge of estimating the numbers and types of injuries remain:

- What defines an injured person, and the methodology used to calculate the figures are unknown.
- There was no systematic collection of data from the many medical teams attending to the injured.

Disaggregation by age, sex, or type of injuries was only available from some of the best-organized foreign medical teams or hospitals. Their patients represent a very small and biased sample. Often, these data were analyzed retrospectively after the intervention and the findings could be shared only after being published in peer-reviewed journals.

Table 3.3 shows the distribution of patients by type of injury for the patients admitted to the University of Miami Global Institute/ Project Medishare field hospital in Port-au-Prince over a three-month period (CDC 2011b, 1675). This field hospital also served as a referral treatment center and the data presented may not be fully representative of the overall pathology. In particular, the most severe diagnosis groups (head/spine, crush syndrome) are probably over-represented among the patients. The rate of 5.6% crush syndrome cannot be generalized to the entire injured population although there is evidence that the incidence of crush syndrome can reach 2% to 5% overall among disaster victims (Sheng 1987).

Distribution of patients by type of injury admitted to a field hospital, 21 January–28 May 2010.

| Injury diagnosis groups | Number admitted | % |
| --- | --- | --- |
| Head/Spine | 142 | 16.6 |
| Fracture: Extremity | 188 | 21.9 |
| Burn | 40 | 4.7 |
| Penetrating injury | 27 | 3.1 |
| Fracture: Non-extremity | 43 | 5.0 |
| Crush/Compartment syndrome | 48 | 5.6 |
| Sprain/Strain/Contusion | 18 | 2.1 |
| Wound infection/Abscess | 158 | 18.4 |
| Abrasion/Laceration/Cut | 133 | 15.5 |
| Traumatic avulsion/Amputation | 22 | 2.6 |

| Other | 38 | 4.4 |
| Total | 857 | 100 |

Source: CDC 2011b, 1675.

The health authorities established a National Sentinel Surveillance Site (NSSS) system to complement the routine sentinel surveillance system (COSE) to address specific post-earthquake conditions. The NSSS was set up with support from PAHO/WHO and CDC. From 25 January (almost two weeks after impact) 51 surveillance sites within and outside the affected area reported new admissions segregated by main cause, diseases as well as injuries. Both NSSS and COSE continue to function.

25 January –24 April 2010

| Type of injury | Age group (years) | | | Total |
|---|---|---|---|---|
| | < 5 years | > 5 years | Unknown | |
| Trauma | 141 | 947 | 60 | 1,148 (22.7%) |
| Fracture | 61 | 321 | 85 | 467 (9.2%) |
| Head injury | 2 | 23 | 2 | 27 (0.5%) |
| Weapon or dagger injury | 4 | 96 | 11 | 111 (2.2%) |
| Burns | 37 | 99 | 13 | 149 (2.9%) |
| Infected wounds | 195 | 2,691 | 175 | 3,061 (60.4%) |
| Crush syndrome | 5 | 78 | 5 | 88 (1.7%) |
| Amputations | 3 | 11 | 0 | 14 (0.2%) |
| Total | 448 | 4,266 | 351 | 5,065 |

Source: Adapted from Magloire et al. 2010.

As reported by Magloire et al. (2010) the surveillance system could not describe the immediate trauma effects of the earthquake as many victims died or were treated before the reporting mechanism was established. It is important to note that the 51 reporting sites were selected from among existing facilities associated with the U.S. President's Emergency Plan for AIDS Relief (PEPFAR). They offered general care for a fee but were not equipped for emergency trauma care. Specialized field hospitals and teams were not included among reporting sites. Finally, the data include all injuries whether or not related to the earthquake. It should be noted that traffic accidents and violence are major sources of daily injuries in Haiti.

First, the 5,065 cases of trauma reported represented only 12% of the total of new patients with reportable conditions (16 additional infectious and non-infectious conditions were included).

As noted by Magloire et al., in the two departments near the epicenter, injuries accounted for 9.2%, while in the eight departments further from the epicenter, they accounted for 15.2%. The migration of the population, the competing presence of trauma teams and hospitals in the affected departments, and the generally poor public attendance at the reporting sites may explain this surprising result.

Nevertheless, the data are valuable for guidance of foreign teams arriving two weeks or more after an earthquake:

- Infected wounds are the main condition past the immediate emergency;
- Fractures remain a serious burden even two weeks after the impact;
- Demand for routine normal pathology rapidly exceeds that for treatment of earthquake-related trauma.

Another source of data is the consolidated survey by Handicap International (Calvot and Shivji, forthcoming). It provides the best picture of the situation based on visits to 17 hospitals with interviews and review of almost 2,600 patients. As with any other partial data, they are not fully representative. Among their observations (Table 3.5) is the relatively higher incidence of injuries among the working age group (18–59 years old). In this group, women were particularly vulnerable (57% women versus 43% men).

The same study describes the distribution by type of injury. As shown in Table 3.6, approximately half were fractures and 16% were amputations.

Table 3.6 Type of injury in persons visited in hospitals in Haiti,

January 2010

| Type of injury | Number | Percentage |
|---|---|---|
| Fractures | 1,233 | 48% |

| | | |
|---|---|---|
| Amputations | 407 | 16% |
| Spinal cord and traumatic brain injuries | 41 | 2% |
| Burns | 27 | 1% |
| Eye injuries | 20 | 1% |
| Other, unspecified | 866 | 33% |
| Total | 2,594 | 100% |

Note: See note for Table 3.5; reproduced with permission of the authors (Calvot and Shivji, forthcoming).

Compiling the statistics from medical teams, if and when available, is further complicated by the absence of standard nomenclature and definitions of type of injuries.

Crush syndrome

Crush syndrome continues to be underreported in most disasters worldwide.

Crush syndrome is a condition caused by prolonged compression of skeletal muscles leading to renal failure. There is no consolidated single source on the incidence of this condition after the earthquake in Haiti. In addition to the 48 cases referred to the Miami University field hospital and the 88 reported by the surveillance system,[25] the Renal Disaster Relief Task Force of the International Society of Nephrology working through Médecins Sans Frontières (MSF) tallied 51 cases of acute kidney injury (AKI) (Vanholder et al. 2010).

Whether those cases are distinct from those reported elsewhere is unknown.

When comparing the 51 acute kidney injury patients with crush injuries in the Haiti event with injury in other disasters, the specialized Renal Task Force found that prevalence of AKI was low in Haiti. In assessing these results, the Task Force (Vanholder et al. 2011) observed:

". . . several factors may have influenced this, such as: the fact that it occurred during the day, when people are up and about, favoring head and chest trauma and decreasing the compression trauma to muscles; the presence of many buildings which were not sturdy enough to cause severe muscle trauma; difficulties encountered with early rescue; the extrication of most victims by neighbors or family members resulting in a selection of less heavily wounded people, and a lack of immediate medical help for the occasional severely affected victim."

Another plausible explanation may be high mortality associated with severe underreporting due to the absence of centralized data collection in the first two weeks.

Spinal cord injuries

There is scarce information on the number of spinal cord injury (SCI) patients who survived the first days after the earthquake. A survey by Handicap International (Calvot and Shavji, forthcoming) estimated the number to be above 100, later revised closer to 150. Information in the Haiti SCI database26 in mid-2011 indicates over 200 beneficiaries, of which 135 sustained a SCI directly as a result of the earthquake; the majority of patients presented complete paraplegia. Statistics continue to be collected and this number will increase. The death toll amongst this group remains unknown.

Most of the severe cases (cervical lesions or multi-trauma) probably did not survive the rough handling by bystanders and the initial lack of medical care (Burns et al. 2010).

It is important to recall the fact that many injured were not sent to health facilities in time because of the difficulties of moving in the destroyed city during the first night (electricity was cut in most areas). Many may have died in the street despite the fact that neighbors and relatives removed them from the rubble. The very low level of "first aid" culture increased the on-site mortality as most simple, life-saving acts were by and large unknown.

Impact on health services

Impact on health infrastructure

- The immediate impact on the capacity of the health services has been dramatic, both in terms of infrastructure and health workers.

- The capacity of the public and private sector to offer immediate medical assistance was considerably reduced at a time when it was most needed.

Within the affected departments, 30 out of 49 hospitals were damaged or destroyed. The ability of the health care system to respond has been permanently affected by the destruction, and delivery of service is disorganized. The Ministry of Health was unable to fulfill its leadership role, primarily because its main building was completely destroyed.

The damage predominantly affected the secondary and tertiary facilities, while 90% of primary health care centers in the affected departments remained intact or suffered only light damage 26 The confidential Haiti SCI Database was created in March 2010 and continues to be administered by Healing Hands for Haiti/Haiti Hospital Appeal.

Specialized facilities were also affected:

- Before the earthquake, there were at least four hemodialysis units across Haiti, treating approximately 100 chronic patients. One unit was lost during the earthquake.
- The earthquake destroyed the buildings housing the National Center for Transfusions and the National Blood Safety

Program. For the first eight days after the earthquake, no Haitian blood was available for transfusion.

• The sole hospital for chronic mental disease was seriously damaged in the earthquake. Most of the 76 patients slept on the hospital grounds with no protection for a sustained period of time.

In several facilities, personnel refused to re-enter premises they deemed unsafe in spite of structurally minor or cosmetic damages and reassurance from engineers. This is not uncommon. The same reluctance to reoccupy facilities that were emptied too hastily was observed after the earthquakes in Mexico City (1985) and El Salvador (2001). It is far easier to take the decision to evacuate a hospital than to reoccupy it. The long-term solution is to carry out risk reduction prior to an earthquake through a careful structural and nonstructural assessment of critical facilities to determine which are at risk and may need evacuation. Those considered resilient to earthquakes should not be evacuated at the first sign of seismic activity. Few facilities in Port-au-Prince would fit in this category.

NGOs are major stakeholders in the provision of medical care in Haiti. They have not been spared by the impact. All MSF structures (except one emergency facility) were severely damaged, some with patients and staff members trapped inside.

Haiti's University and Educational Hospital (HUEH—also known as General Hospital), the country's largest, suffered serious physical as well as functional losses

Haiti's University and Educational Hospital

Haiti University Hospital (HUEH)

Buildings entirely unsafe    Buildings safe and usable

Department of Surgery Outpatient consultation Pediatric department    Administration

Most of internal medicine

Most of emergency services

Maternity

New facilities (urology and dermatology) Radiology

The HUEH engineers ordered immediate evacuation of all premises in case of aftershock. This recommendation was reportedly confirmed later by separate assessments by USAID, U.S. Army Corps of Engineers and Spain's Fire Brigade experts. After the second aftershock, the use of emergency services was reduced. After the third aftershock, the patients refused to re-enter the buildings and the medical personnel expressed fear about working in the oldest buildings. Consequently, the decision was made to place all patients and most of the operating rooms under tents.

This reaction was not limited to public facilities run by the Ministry of Health. Most MSF hospitals were damaged and unusable, and where still intact, patients and staff were too frightened to enter, so all MSF services and hospitals were placed in tents.

Abstracted and translated from a report from the HUEH director to the Minister of Health.

PROMESS, the central pharmaceutical warehouse, remained mostly intact. Fortunately, its stock had been replenished at the end of 2009.

Impact on health personnel

The earthquake did not spare Ministry of Health personnel. Very high but unconfirmed estimates of losses were circulated and occasionally published. These figures were shown to be inaccurate by a retrospective survey on the impact of the earthquake on the health staff carried out two months after the impact by the Human Services Directorate of the Ministry of Health (MSPP 2010a).

In this survey, a census was conducted in the three affected departments. Of 6,812 employees, 5,879 health workers (86%) were identified based on questionnaires sent to all Ministry of Health institutions. Of the 5,879, 61 were reported killed; 59 of these were in West Department, where the capital is located. These figures include Ministry employees only. They do not cover students (medical or nursing), whose mortality was presumably higher due to the collapse of the nursing school, among other causes.28 The reasons for the relatively low mortality figure are simple: as mentioned earlier, at the time of the earthquake, office workers had mainly left their workplaces and were on their way home.

Most practicing doctors divide their working time between official duties in a public facility and private practice. This is a life necessity given the meager and irregular 28 The nursing school at Lumière University—one of three official nursing schools in the country—was reduced to rubble, killing an estimated 150 students (UNFPA 2010).

Salaries paid by the Government. Relatively few physicians were present in the health facilities at the time of the impact. For instance, in the main tertiary level facility, the University Hospital, only the night shift was present.

In addition, the Ministry of Health survey found that 245 (2.2%) of Ministry staff lost a member of their immediate family (spouse or children) and 3,955 (67%) were technically homeless (30% of their houses were destroyed and 37% were damaged and potentially unsecure). The fact that many Ministry staff were reported absent for some time is largely attributed to the fact that they had to find relatives and organize for their survival before reporting to their duty stations.

It was estimated that 50% of the health workers were living under tents for a sustained period of time.

Impact on population displacement

- Reasonable estimates on size and place of displacements are essential for planning the delivery of health, water, and sanitation services.
- Statistics on displacement tend to be on the high side initially and are contested later.
- The health effects of displacement are not limited to areas physically affected by the earthquake.

The level of destruction and loss of employment and homes led many people to seek shelter in temporary settlements. The concentration of displaced families in thousands of small camps and settlements presented a health risk in itself and a challenge for the provision of health services because it caused a massive redistribution of catchment areas. The situation was quite distinct from that observed in other countries where space allowed for organized, medium-scale settlements (10,000 persons or more). There was no vacant land in Port-au-Prince itself and all small public spaces were overcrowded, initially leaving only 2 or 3 square meters per person. Common facilities (water, electricity, waste disposal) were non-existent and would compete for space.

Monitoring the constant flux of displaced households under the conditions in Haiti was particularly prone to inaccuracy. The number of camps was close to 1,200, some housing only a few hundred persons. Families (or some of their members) shifted from place to place according to the benefits (aid) to be expected. A detailed description of the registration strategy used by the Camp Coordination and Camp Management "Cluster" was circulated by the International Organization for Migration (IOM) in April 2010.

An official number of internally displaced after the earthquake (1.5 million in temporary camps) was released by IOM and accepted initially by all partners, only to be questioned one year later by scientists (and mass media). Discrepancies between sources as well as internal inconsistencies are illustrated.

Numbers of persons living in temporary shelters in Haiti after earthquake, by source

Source Data

PDNA (March 2010)    1.5 M persons directly affected

Around 1.3 M living in temporary shelters in the metropolitan Port-au-Prince area; 500,000 moved into the rest of the country

IOM Registration Strategy (April 2010)    450,000 households living in sheltersa (i.e., at least 2 M persons)

IOM Press Briefing Note (Dec 2010)    Peak figure in the camps was 1.5 M

USAID survey (Schwartz et al. 2011)    Estimated number of people who went to camps in January is 866,412 to 894,588 (p < .01)

By April 2010, approximately half of those who had gone to camps or the countryside had returned home according to the IOM, household size is estimated between 5.2 and 5.7 persons.

The lesson is that any statistic, not only mortality data, can only be a rough estimate likely to be subject to questioning. The key again is to resist the temptation to err systematically to the higher side and to share the methodology adopted as was done in this case. There is no real benefit for the affected population to adopt the higher end of all measurements. A middle road approach will more likely make divergence between experts a matter of scientific debate rather than a public crisis affecting the credibility of an agency.

Faced with the situation in Port-au-Prince, the Government encouraged migration to non-affected departments, and buses were rapidly made ready to transport people. Since roads in the affected area were impassable, buses were located at the periphery. Movements of people away from the capital started spontaneously, during the night of 12 January; the first arrivals of the injured were reported in the early morning of 13 January at Saint Mars and Gonaïves hospitals. The flow of "evacuated injured people" continued for a few days, rapidly overstretching the response capacities of these facilities. Health services in the receiving areas, which were already insufficient to meet the most basic needs of the local population, had to attend to a flux of reportedly between 500,000 and 600,000 disaster-affected individuals, many with injuries and emergency treatment needs. These health facilities normally charged for services, habitually saw only a few patients daily, and had no stocks of supplies to serve the increase in patients. How long the extra medical burden on non-affected departments lasted is unclear.

If efforts were made by the Government to encourage and monitor the initial movement out of Port-au-Prince, few data were sought by or provided to the humanitarian community on the return of those displaced.

The Rapid Initial Needs Assessment for Haiti (RINAH) is one of the few studies that explored this issue in some depth.29 Another survey commissioned by UNFPA confirms that more than a quarter of the population of the metropolitan area left after the January earthquake (Haiti Data Services 2010). Half migrated into urban areas unaffected. However, the study went further and enquired on the duration of this displacement: "The data show that those who left after 12 January have returned soon after. Around one out of three (27.7%) have been away less than one month and 55% between one and three months. In conclusion, less than 20% stayed more than three months outside the metropolitan area.

The massive international distribution of goods and services in the metropolitan area influenced or determined this reflux. Material assistance indeed became much more accessible in Port-au-Prince, inciting the return of displaced populations. As distributions were organized in temporary settlements, some of the beneficiaries were not those affected by the earthquake but actually the economically vulnerable seeking better opportunities (shelter, food, water, health, and education opportunities). What is not known is the importance of this factor.

It is rather enlightening to note another finding of the UNFPA survey: The municipality of Cité Soleil, the poorest area of the city but one of the less affected by the impact, received the smallest proportion of displaced from other municipalities (2.9%) but has the highest rate of displacement. More than 20% of the residents migrated into other (more affected) municipalities.

Figure 3.3 Internal migration following the Haiti earthquake.

Haitians living abroad (the 'diaspora') and neighboring countries played a significant role in the response. Humanitarian actors already working in Haiti, as well as foreign medical teams, also became a valuable asset during mus aut untem et eaque retibea prae Git etthe relief operation.

Who provided assistance?

- While the impact of the earthquake in Haiti was unprecedented, the short-term response had all the strengths and weaknesses noted in evaluations of earlier disasters.
- Lessons from the past have not been learned.

The logistical challenges faced by the responders were overwhelming:

- International access: The airport facility, briefly closed, was reopened thanks to U.S. military intervention. However, its use was initially reserved for U.S. military troop movement and selected bilateral relief assistance or evacuations. The harbor was severely damaged.

- Land transportation: The lack of vehicles, especially considering the unavailability of the MINUSTAH fleet for 7 days,31 was compounded by chaotic traffic conditions. It often took several hours to move from one meeting place to the next within Port-au-Prince.

- Power: Modern relief is dependent on a reliable source of electricity, a condition rarely met even months after the impact in Haiti.

As noted in Chapter 1, the MINUSTAH mandate did not consider logistic support to the humanitarian agencies.

Communications: Fixed telephone lines, that were unreliable in normal times, were suspended; mobile phone lines were unavailable most of the time, satellite telephone circuits were overloaded, and internet access was limited.

- Language: The language barrier was a significant obstacle for some foreign teams that found themselves unable to communicate properly in French or Creole with their local partners and beneficiaries.

Administrative obstacles: A cumbersome process for both customs clearance in Haiti and approval of movement and arrangement for escort, when required by UN security rules, causing difficulties and delays.

Substantially increasing the number of personnel, to coordinate and manage the health sector response without increasing logistical support, would not have resulted in a more effective response.

The humanitarian actors

- If the impact of the earthquake was unprecedented, the response was not. It followed the trend observed in past disasters.
- National professionals and neighboring countries played a significant role. The foreign response was extremely generous.

The earliest and therefore most effective responders were those already in Haiti and especially in Port-au-Prince: relatives and neighbors, local health services, and the many humanitarian agencies already on site. How many lives, for instance, neighbors and relatives have saved will never be known. The local contribution was invaluable but overshadowed by international actors better skilled in public relations.

The Haitian actors. According to most accounts, the solidarity among the Haitians was massive, with people helping each other in the ruins, sharing the little they had, and trying to get as many people as they could out of the debris. Despite a few unruly incidents during supply distribution, which were overblown by the media, the many stories of solidarity confirm once more that rampant social disorder and violence after natural disasters is, indeed, just a myth.

Local health personnel

In all disasters, local health services play a key role, especially the first few days before assistance can arrive. Haiti was no exception.

A much debated issue is the conflict in roles for health workers between caring for their own families and their professional obligations. How did that play out in Haiti?

In Haiti, local health facilities and services were understaffed and some were even closed for several days. These isolated observations are overshadowed by the number of those who worked on the front lines, salvaging medicines and dressing supplies from damaged and destroyed private pharmacies or health facilities.

The early situation at the University Hospital has been well documented: "On the morning of Day 2, key staff reported to HUEH and following public announcements on the radio, nursing and support personnel progressively and partially returned."[32]

Reasons for medical staff not reporting in the first days were many:

- Some had suffered severe personal losses (family and housing) and could not contribute;
- Others were providing emergency care in their own neighborhoods;

- Transport within the city was nearly impossible (loss of vehicles, no public transport, and roads often blocked by rubble).

Those nationals who reported to work operated in extremely difficult professional and personal conditions which did not compare with those of the better equipped and self-sustained foreign teams progressively entering the area. Among the priority needs expressed by HUEH in the first days were funds for the staff ("for transport and feeding their families") as well as for tents for their accommodation.

There are no quantified data on the Haitian personnel on duty during this initial period. Two months after the event, a survey carried out by the Ministry of Health offered the first statistics on the availability of human resources (MSPP 2010a). This survey shows that 79% of the Ministry's personnel were reporting to duty seven weeks after the impact. However, in the most affected department (West), only 48% of the medical doctors were present.33 Most of the missing medical personnel were from the three main hospitals or maternity hospital; 190 medical doctors did not report to duty at the University Hospital (HUEH). Special mention is therefore due to the nursing staff whose continuous presence was so critical.

Factors that help to explain the low number of medical doctors reporting in government facilities two months after the impact are:

- A number may have accompanied the 600,000 people who moved to the non-affected departments or migrated abroad.
- More significantly, a large number were recruited by humanitarian agencies at salaries several times above their pre-disaster incomes. This practice of international "poaching" is very common in humanitarian response. Although these health workers opted to work where they could get necessary equipment, supplies, and

Dr. Alex Larsen (HUEH), (nd), Rapport au Ministre de la Sante publique et de la Population. [Translated from the French.]

There are no data on the "normal" absenteeism rate, which should also be relatively high.

Remuneration by international NGOs is four or five times higher than the salary paid by the Ministry.

In the post-earthquake period, MSF had 372 international and 2,960 national staff. Should a large number of those local health employees be released, one can question the ability of the Ministry of Health to absorb them.

Support to serve the population for a given period of time, the practice does weaken national institutions and may hamper recovery.

The key point is that reduced staffing in public facilities does not necessarily mean that the missing doctors and health workers were not helping their population.

In the private, non-profit sector (NGO and faith-based organizations), absenteeism was not an issue as illustrated by one agency comment: "Despite the tremendous personal losses sustained by many national staff members, and despite the chaos that followed the earthquake, the majority of MSF's surviving Haitian staff immediately set to work helping their countrymen and continued to do so throughout this difficult period" (MSF 2011, 7).

More surprisingly in the harsh economic context of Haiti, the for-profit sector did not lag far behind in generosity. Private, for-profit hospitals and clinics opened their doors, offered their services, and shared their supplies from the time of the impact. The staff of several clinics immediately provided care at no cost and acted as field hospitals.

Haitians from abroad

Associations of expatriated health personnel can play a major role. However, they should plan ahead and take the lead in coordinating and facilitating the efforts of their members.

The importance of the presence of Haitian expatriates (the so-called "diaspora") during the post-disaster period has been well documented. Their knowledge of Haitian culture, language, and customs, coupled with their wide range of technical and professional skills, gave them a unique advantage over other groups during the health response.

Though the international teams deployed to Haiti made numerous references to the work of national and expatriate Haitians, it is rare to find numbers or precise descriptions of their contribution. For example, the University of Miami Global Institute/Project Medishare (UMGI/PM), which has a 15-year relationship with Haitian physicians, observed that one of the key characteristics of this operation was the participation of Haitian professionals and technicians both living in Haiti and abroad. However, there are no specific figures regarding this phenomenon.

This summarizes the few data available to the authors on the participation of national staff and expatriate Haitians with selected groups involved in the post-disaster health operation. The Ministry of Health developed guidelines for the payment of Haitian public staff by international actors. Agencies found it difficult to change their salary scales, creating discrepancies within their local staff (based on whether the date of a contract was before or after the guidelines were issued) and were reluctant to further complicate their competitive search for scarce local skills. For the most part the guidelines were ignored.

The Alliance for International Medical Action (ALIMA), an international NGO arriving a few days after the disaster, had pre-earthquake contact with the private Clinique Lambert and decided to support it. The international staff involved in this operation was impressed by the sense of dedication of the clinic's Haitian staff, who worked 24 hours/day, 7days/week in very difficult conditions.

Although the expertise and contribution of expatriate Haitians were appreciated by the employing agencies, competing local interests (family, social, or political) did occasionally complicate their integration in the team.

Participation of local and expatriate Haitians in health response following the earthquake

Organization    Local Haitians    Expatriate

The American Red Cross recruited, trained, and equipped 70 Creole-speaking volunteers from across the United States who supported medical staff as translators aboard the USNS Comfort, a U.S. Navy hospital ship.

"Nurses from the Haitian American Nursing Association (HANA) participating in the Medishare initiative."

Humanitarian actors already in Haiti

The presence in Port-au-Prince of a strong national Red Cross Society, specialized medical NGOs, a large number of Cuban doctors, and many others became a specific asset in Haiti.

Haiti is the country with one of the highest densities per capita of local or international NGOs, UN agencies, and bilateral projects. Figures of between 9,000 and 10,000 NGOs are cited. The number of local NGOs and faith-based institutions with activities in the health sector prior to the impact is also high but figures are difficult to find.

As indicated earlier, an estimated 75% of the health services prior to impact were delivered by the private non-profit sector, 5% by the for-profit sector, and the rest by the Government. In other countries affected by disasters (Indonesia, Sri Lanka, and Pakistan), the balance is reversed, with the public health sector providing most of the services and the NGOs filling some of the gaps.

Some of those actors were affected by the earthquake but most could mobilize rapidly to meet the most immediate and pressing needs. A few hours after the quake, all sections of MSF present in the country organized their first reconnaissance mission in the city (even though it was already night time) and started to operate on the injured. The International Committee of the Red Cross (ICRC) in-country medical supplies.

That were stockpiled for urban tensions and hurricane response, were immediately mobilized and put into use the following morning.

Others more directly and severely affected such as the UN Mission, some UN agencies, and others needed time to address the critical needs of their own staff and to restore their capacity (materially and psychologically). They its office and many of the staff lost their homes. Without clinical responsibilities, skills, or equipment, the first night was spent accounting for the safety and welfare of its entire staff (national or expatriate), reestablishing contact with the health authorities, and finding facilities where it could resume operations. Not much productive work could be done overnight by technical or coordinating agencies that were deprived of offices and communication.

The direct impact on agencies that normally lead the international response was specific to the Haitian disaster. In other countries affected by sudden disasters, the UN capacity to assist, respond, and coordinate was not affected. However, planning for future scenarios of urban disaster should include this aspect.

Bilateral agencies confronted the same challenges. They faced an additional and competing priority from their obligation to care for their nationals (resident or visitors) who were missing or injured. This legitimate concern influenced greatly the priorities of their strategic and operational involvement (transport, air traffic control, search and rescue, medical care, etc.). Many dispatched SAR and medical teams, funded other actors, and provided supplies.

External actors

The Tsunami Evaluation Coalition (TEC) assessment of the international response (Telford, Cosgrave, Houghton 2006, 55) remains valid for Haiti:

"The number of international agencies involved in the response grew unabated. Well-resourced agencies and very small ones, competent and incompetent, well-prepared and unprepared, secular and faith-based, reputable and disreputable, household names and unknown, ambitious and humble, opportunistic and committed, governmental and nongovernmental, national and international, bilateral and multilateral, well-established and just-formed—they all turned up."

Foreign teams arriving in the country to provide health assistance in the aftermath of the earthquake belonged to one of the following groups:

- Medical components of urban search and rescue (USAR) teams. More than 30 countries sent USAR teams, many of them with some health equipment (from very basic stabilization boxes to full-fledged emergency field hospitals). This represented the first response of many bilateral government agencies (the traditional humanitarian donors but also Caribbean and Latin American countries and many others from around the world).

- Bilateral government medical teams. These arrived from many countries, including from the Caribbean. Often more than one institution from a country was present. For example, United States assistance included the Office for Foreign Disaster Assistance (State Department), the military (Department of Defense), and teams from the U.S. Health and Human Services Department, to name only a few;

As mentioned earlier, land-line telephone service was suspended, mobile systems were mostly unavailable, satellite phones were rapidly overloaded ("no circuit"). Only hand-held radios provided some support in most locations. Internet and Skype services were intermittently available.

By 19 February, an estimated 27,199 American citizens had returned to the U.S., most with the logistical assistance of the U.S. Government.

- UN or UN related agencies, UNICEF, UN Population Fund (UNFPA), World Food Programme (WFP), and the International Organization for Migration (IOM);
- Red Cross system (IFRC, ICRC and many participating national societies). The Red Cross system mobilized its six health Emergency Response Units (ERU) which consist of

"health services in a box" to be dispatched in less than 24 hours with specialized and support (logistics) staff;

- International NGOs (from the most established and experienced to the small or less known);
- Bilateral, non-State institutions (hospitals or universities, for example), many with ongoing activities and established Haitian counterparts;
- Teams from social or religious associations. This category included many small actors but with the advantage of having existing, one-to-one relationships at the local level;
- Ad hoc initiatives by individuals or groups set up only for the event (the "mushroom" NGOs that pop up overnight after each major crisis).

Over the last decade, the number of those actors has grown rapidly and without a strategy or master plan, leading the World Disaster Report of the IFRC (2004) to call the humanitarian community the "largest unregulated industry." Mass media play an important role in this wild expansion. If the far-reaching mass media contribute to generating global generosity and compassion on behalf of the affected population, they also represent an almost irresistible incentive for politicization of the process or its exploitation for the sake of publicity (or even proselytism by some faith groups, as occurred in Haiti).

Effectiveness is a matter of context

The results of the proliferation of health responders were atypical in Haiti compared to other past (and probably most future) disasters:

- In Haiti, the magnitude of the needs, the poor state of services prior to the impact, and the absence of national back-up capacity after the event resulted in many of those actors providing significant assistance to the population.
- In other disasters (Indian Ocean tsunami, earthquakes in Iran or Pakistan), most of those teams were more a burden than assistance.

This proliferation of international organizations is far from new (as already noted in the tsunami evaluation), suggesting that not much has been learned.

The number of small, short-duration medical missions in Haiti is unknown but likely to be high due to the visibility of the earthquake and proximity to North America. In an assessment of volunteerism in Haiti, Kathleen Jobe (2011) spelled out the conditions for those teams to be effective: "Short-term medical missions should be familiar with the broader public health messages that are determined by in-country public health officials and established in-country NGOs". In the same vein, C. Bajkiewicz (2009) observes:

"Volunteers are well served by evaluating not only the personal benefit they derive from participating in the mission, but also the overall impact of the mission on local health care and public health priorities."

## The close neighbors

The traditional bilateral humanitarian actors played a major role in the health response. Among them was the United States Department of Health and Human Services (HHS), an agency providing a large array of services, including the National Disaster Medical System (NDMS) and the Centers for Disease Control and Prevention (CDC), both of which were activated in Haiti. As noted in the box, the variety and extent of services was unusual compared to past disasters in the world.

Examples of support from the U.S. Department of Health and Human Services

Medical care: Deployed the medical assets of the NDMS, consisting of almost 1,000 health responders over the 42-day mission;

Evacuation: Assisted returning U.S. citizens and arranged for referral of injured Haitians to tertiary care institutions in the United States;

Disease surveillance: Provided assistance for epidemiological surveillance and laboratory support; Dead bodies: Storage, identification, and repatriation of bodies of U.S. citizens.

Many Latin American or Caribbean countries provided substantial assistance. Of the latter, two countries were particularly well placed to play an important health role during the first days: Cuba and the Dominican Republic, due to their medical presence or geographic proximity.

Cuba

Cuba has maintained a strong medical presence in Haiti since 1998. Over this period, more than 6,000 health personnel have served in the country, often in difficult rural environments. At the time of the impact, the Cuban Medical Brigades had more than 330 primary health care professionals in the country. Those experts provided an immediate source of medical personnel familiar with the conditions of the country. They reported seeing their first patients less than 90 minutes after the impact and completed 1,000 emergency consultations within the first 24 hours. At the end, more than 1,500 personnel contributed to the response. A summary of the reported activities in the first 10 days is presented in Table 4.2.

Table 4.2 Cuban medical assistance in Haiti, 12–22 January 2010

| Affected area | Number | | | | | | |
|---|---|---|---|---|---|---|---|
| | Surgery | | | Deaths | | | |
| | | Minor | Major | Total | Children | Adults | Total |
| Port-au-Prince | 11,354 | 113 | 622 | 735 | 19 | 49 | 68 |
| Suburban areas | 3,553 | 63 | 80 | 143 | 37 | 28 | 65 |
| Others | 5,188 | 896 | 180 | 1,076 | 1 | 14 | 15 |
| Total | 20,095 | 1,072 | 882 | 1,954 | 57 | 91 | 148 |

Dominican Republic

The Dominican Republic, a country with occasionally tense relations with its poorer neighbor, has played several roles:

- First, the Dominican Republic received tens of thousands of refugees, many seeking urgent surgical care. The country provided health assistance at all major border crossing points (especially Jimaní).
- It rapidly deployed a civil protection team to Port-au-Prince in order to provide assistance and expertise at the site of the disaster.
- For the first few weeks, the Dominican Republic was a vital lifeline for the relief operations in Haiti. Santo Domingo became a major hub for most of the foreign assistance as the access to Port-au-Prince airport was constrained by the deployment of the U.S. military, Civil Protection, and consular

operations (evacuations). There were few exceptions and those that were allowed to land in Port-au-Prince had to undergo a complex clearance process. In addition, the Port-au-Prince sea port remained inaccessible due to severe damage and after repairs were made it was congested. Landing in Santo Domingo and moving overland to Haiti border crossings became the normal procedure. The Dominican Republic facilitated or waived customs and immigration procedures at both the Santo Domingo airport and at the Jimaní border crossing.

The number of people seeking shelter and medical care in the Dominican Republic was overwhelming and required the support of the entire Dominican health system. It is a few hours' drive in normal circumstances from the Haitian capital (62 km) to Jimaní, a primary border town on the Dominican side (see map). For the Dominican Republic, it was not a minor, localized emergency but a major mass casualty event that exceeded its normal response capacity. It was a local disaster that took place in parallel to the larger one in Port-au-Prince. There could be no guidance or support from the authorities of the affected country. The Dominican Republic did handle it on its own.

As we will see, the disaster in Haiti followed a now well-known pattern of shifting priorities from life-saving trauma care to post-operative concerns and welfare. The response to the "border disaster" followed a similar pattern but was greatly accelerated. The timing was closer to that observed in other disasters when a whole country stands behind the assistance to a small part of its population. For instance, epidemiological surveillance and other communicable disease measures were already adopted at the Dominican Republic's central level on Day 3, an early warning system was activated on Day 4, and field visits of epidemiologists were made to temporary settlements on Day 5 (PAHO/WHO 2010b). In Haiti, two weeks passed before the first systems for surveillance and control of communicable disease could actually be set up.

Clearly, the scale of needs was far greater in Port-au-Prince than in Jimaní. Nevertheless, the magnitude of the task faced by the Dominican health services and Civil Defense cannot be underestimated. From 18 to 23 January, reports indicate a severe overload of the health services in all border provinces in the Dominican Republic. For 10 days, key staff remained on duty without relief and on Day 15, the hospitals in the border departments still had more Haitian patients than local ones.

The exodus of affected families and people toward the Dominican Republic slowed after 10 days, and the number of new patients started to decline. During January, the Dominican health services attended to 1,985 patients, performed a high number of amputations (212), immobilized 121 fractures, and registered 15 deaths in hospitals (PAHO/WHO 2010b).

The credit for the achievements in Jimaní should be shared with the countries and NGOs backing up the Dominican Republic with teams at the border. Little outside support was received from the donors.

Other countries from the region

- Many Latin American or Caribbean countries did not report their assistance to the OCHA Financial Tracking System. They lost an opportunity for a permanent record of the nature and value of their in-kind contributions.
- Some of the countries new to international medical relief would benefit from organizing their own "lessons learned" exercise and increasing their preparedness and training.

In addition to the special roles played by Cuba and the Dominican Republic, there was probably not one country in Latin America and the Caribbean that did not contribute in one way or another to saving lives and providing care to the affected population in Haiti. The contributions took diverse forms: from the deployment of search and rescue teams, the deployment of field or ship hospitals, the dispatch of medical teams, or the secondment of individual volunteers for the management of incoming supplies or experts to assist one of the humanitarian organizations. The response to the Haiti earthquake was global, but it was also truly regional.

Information on the regional medical response comes primarily from interviews and to a lesser extent from media reports. There is a serious lack of administrative information (reporting of in-kind donations to the UN/OCHA on-line financial tracking system, technical documentation, or scientific analysis) on these activities. Of the 280 peer-reviewed articles listed in Medline, none addressed lessons learned or activities of Latin American or Caribbean medical teams. This needs to be addressed both from an educational and public relations point of view.

Regional organizations

The supportive role at the operational level of the regional organizations to which Haiti belongs should be noted. Within 24 hours, the Caribbean Disaster Emergency Management Agency (CDEMA) supported the Government of Jamaica to mobilize its medical personnel. Jamaica became a staging area for further Caribbean assistance. As early as 14 January (Day 3), the Caribbean Community (CARICOM) identified the health sector as the agreed area of focus for the coordinated regional intervention. The modest Caribbean resources were complemented by Australia, which channeled AUS$ 1 million to CDEMA (i.e., 10% of the initial pledge from this country).

How much more effective would the response of the Dominican Republic and other Caribbean countries have been had other donors followed this example?

A literature review was conducted of articles in the U.S. National Library of Medicine's MEDLINE database on 7 August 2011.

An editorial on lessons learned in Haiti was published in the West Indian Medical Journal (Vaughan 2010).

Medical care at the Haiti/Dominican border

Photo:PAHOAVHOActorArlsaln

Institutional bilateral assistance

- Prior experience in the affected country or close partnership with an established, on-site NGO is essential.
- A significant commitment should be sustained both on the humanitarian but above all on the administrative, financial, and logistical sides.
- A mid-term view is critical. Improvised, overnight operations are not likely to be productive, regardless of the scientific credentials of the institution. Being a world-class academic or clinical center is not sufficient to become a major humanitarian actor.

The magnitude of the disaster and the proximity of Haiti to North America, among other factors, induced a very strong response by private (nongovernmental) health institutions, particularly from the

U.S. Some but not all of these institutions had ongoing health projects in the country. A similar response was not observed after the Indian Ocean tsunami or the Pakistan (Kashmir) earthquake.

Three of the largest and best documented responses from academic institutions in the United States were organized by medical centers in Chicago, hospitals affiliated with Harvard University, and the University of Miami Project Medishare (see box). These initiatives shared many features that were critical for their success:

- The participation of various global health initiatives or international emergency medicine programs at these institutions;
- Preexisting partnership with large NGOs through which the medical staff was deployed in Haiti (Chicago) or pre-existing standing projects in the country;
- A mid-term view (several months);
- Strong administrative, logistics, and communication support;43
- A systematic debriefing (lessons learned) process for all volunteers;
- The participation of a large number of Haitians (local or expatriate);
- Geographical proximity of Haiti (an important albeit not critical factor).

Examples of response from teaching institutions Chicago Medical Response

This initiative was formed by six academic medical centers from the city of Chicago. As of 1 April it had deployed 158 medical volunteers to work with established NGOs in Haiti. The minimum duration of deployment required was two weeks. The initiative supported the University Hospital (HUEH), staffed several mobile clinics, and collaborated with the post-operative station in Fond Parisien near the Dominican border.

Harvard Humanitarian Program

Partners in Health (PIH), a not-for-profit Harvard affiliate with an established presence in Haiti took the lead in university-related medical assistance. The group operated nine medical sites in Haiti. By 19 June, 50 medical and surgical personnel had been deployed in Haiti from Harvard-affiliated hospitals. Harvard teaching hospitals sent planeloads of medical supplies, including surgical and anesthesia equipment.

The University of Miami Global Institute/Project Medishare (UMGI/PM)

During the first nine days after the earthquake the Project Medishare hospital functioned inside the United Nations compound with 250 beds, 12 staff, and no critical-care units or organized operating rooms.

Sanitation and other working conditions in the first few days were dire. The hospital was later set up at the Port-au-Prince airport in a four-tent facility, with three fully organized operating rooms and 17 critical-care beds. It was staffed by 220 volunteers from the United States and Canada who served in 7-day rotations. There was strong administrative and logistics support in Haiti as well as in Miami. The group coordinated flights to transport medical staff, supplies, equipment, and victims between Haiti and the United States. This support included tele-medicine consultations and communications (see Ginzburg et al. 2010).

## A proliferation of international organizations

In Banda Aceh, Indonesia, approximately 180 agencies (representing all sectors) registered with the UN following the tsunami. In addition, the TEC estimated that "there may have been as many as 200 small international agencies that stayed only a few weeks" (Telford, Cosgrave, Houghton 2006,).

It is estimated that Chicago institutions dedicated 1500 hours of faculty and administrative time to their operations in Haiti.

## Missionaries of Charity

In Port-au-Prince, the proliferation of international organizations was far greater than in Banda Aceh. In the health sector alone,

390 agencies, mostly international, registered with the external coordinating mechanism (Health Cluster) . Many more health actors did not register.

Health Cluster following the Haiti earthquake, the response to the Haiti earthquake was not an anomaly, an "unprecedented" glitch in an otherwise rational response. It was, rather, a confirmation and acceleration of a global humanitarian trend observed in recent sudden-onset disasters (the earthquake in Pakistan and the Indian Ocean tsunami). In the last decade, the only countries spared this chaotic situation were those with sufficient resources to meet most urgent needs or those able to monitor and regulate the flow of outside assistance and ensure that it complemented local efforts.

The following chart differentiates these findings according to their specificity to Haiti.

Lessons new or specific to Haiti

- A demand for medical care far exceeding the offer in the first few weeks.
- Rapid response of medical international NGOs and other humanitarian actors present prior to impact.
- Rapid arrival due to proximity (18 hours instead of 3 days).
- Large medical diaspora abroad respond as individuals.

- Lack of national military assets but massive U.S. military and UN peacekeeping intervention or presence.
- Strong and sustained health initiatives from major U.S. university hospitals.

Lessons noted in past disasters

- Very generous response leading to exponential increase in the number of health "partners".
- Significant number of unqualified or unprepared actors.
- External coordination mechanisms (Clusters) do not reflect local mandate of line ministries.
- Failure to involve and strengthen local government for timely transfer of responsibilities/ authority.
- Too much emphasis on coordination (meetings) rather than on intelligence gathering and strategic guidance.
- Increasing priority on "build back better" (linkage between relief, rehabilitation, and development).

In the Buen Samaritano hospital on the Dominican Republic border, relief priorities shifted day by day, although the disproportion between needs and resources was not as extreme as in Port-au-Prince.

The life-saving response.

The response phases.

The traditional disaster management cycle, from preparedness to reconstruction, has become too simplistic to describe modern humanitarian response. The respective boundaries between relief, early recovery, and reconstruction are becoming increasingly blurred. The emergency relief phase tends to linger as long as humanitarian funding is available. This is especially true in situations like Haiti, where crises succeed each other (when not overlapping), and where long-term development seems so elusive.

Disaster relief changes considerably over time. Relief priorities shift day by day: from search and rescue and life-saving medical interventions to water, food, temporary shelters, resumption of routine programs, and meeting needs of specific groups. Priorities and their timing vary from event to event.

In smaller and less overwhelming disasters these changes are accelerated, as was seen in Jimaní, the border city in the Dominican Republic. The imbalance between needs and resources was not as extreme in Jimaní as in Port-au-Prince: more orderly planning was possible, changes could be anticipated, and a calendar was rapidly agreed upon among the main actors. In Haiti, the magnitude of the impact and of the needs ensured that, with few exceptions, saving lives, provision of food, water, and shelter, and other priorities overlapped and competed for time and attention for a much longer period than usual.

We can identify two periods in the relief phase after the earthquake:

- An "immediate" life-saving phase, which, in Haiti, lasted approximately two weeks (16 days). The crucial activities were search and rescue (10 days) and emergency trauma care. Other concerns, although present, were secondary.
- A second phase—of still undefined duration—began when the focus shifted predominantly to postoperative care, rehabilitation, primary health care for displaced populations, resumption of key programs, and the welfare priorities of food, water, and shelter (including camp management), among others. Cross-cutting priorities such as gender issues and protection of human rights were raised in the first days after the earthquake by the relevant agencies or NGOs and progressively received the attention they deserved.

The turning point between the two phases seems to be on 28 January (Day 17) when, according to the Haiti Health Cluster Bulletin:

- "Reports indicate almost all people with injuries have received medical attention; however, some still require surgical care.
- "The current priorities of the Ministry of Health include post-operative care and rehabilitation of disabled people, primary care at internally displaced persons sites, and provision of medical services outside of Port-au-Prince."

There was increasing overlap between activities and priorities. Most of the welfare needs listed under the second phase were urgent and required attention in the first few days after the event. Even in the immediate phase, all agencies carried out their activities (whether they were critical or even relevant at that time), competing for resources and facilities. The lack of a coordinating body that was able and empowered to set and enforce clear priorities allowed every actor to determine its own agenda.

The "immediate" life-saving response

As is always true, the first response in Haiti was from the local population and health workers (nationals or expatriate Haitians present in the country).

Several health priorities dominated this first phase: search and rescue, trauma care, and disposal of bodies. Many other concerns and activities were concomitant: water, food, and shelter. These issues shifted to the top of the priority list once the life-saving activities ended. All those priorities shared the same requirements (or constraints) such as availability of data from rapid assessment, efficient logistics, and supply management.

*Jeff Benjamin*

Urban Search and Rescue (USAR): its impact on health

- The impact of international USAR in terms of lives saved is relatively low compared to other measures. Strengthening local SAR capacity should be a priority for future disasters.
- There are, however, other compelling human and institutional benefits and objectives in providing this costly form of assistance.

Search and rescue activities are not part of the health sector responsibility. They are however a life-saving activity with medical components. In addition, at the international level this "sector" has been systematically organized and strengthened, which offers potential lessons for improving the management of the health response.

44 The pattern of shifting priorities (from trauma to communicable diseases and primary health care) is common to many earthquakes. However, the phases are typically much shorter. The sheer number of injured and the poor local capacity in Haiti extended the surgical phase to more than two weeks instead of a few days, as is customary.

A decrease in the number of urgent surgical interventions was already noted on Day 10 (Health Cluster Bulletin No. 3, 22 January).

SAR contributions to saving lives

International USAR started within 24 hours of impact and ended on 22 January, when the Government declared the search and rescue phase over. No live rescues had been reported in the preceding days. Calling off search and rescue activities is always a difficult political decision. Survivors are known to have been rescued weeks after the impact. The factors influencing the duration of survival are many, but the most critical during structural collapse is the "formation of a viable void space (i.e., a 'pocket' or 'survival space' so the survivor escapes fatal injury as the rubble settles). This void space is most likely to occur in concrete reinforced buildings and the least probable in adobe constructions" (Macintyre, Barbera, Petinaux 2011).

There were 132 live rescues reported by international USAR teams. This is the second highest number ever saved by international teams. This outcome was the result of the work of over 60 USAR teams from 30 nations responding with more than 1,800 rescuers (UN/OCHA 2010).

The logistics challenges were formidable and the economic cost very high. Cost-effectiveness may be a controversial issue in humanitarian response where "no cost should be spared to save one life." However, resources are limited and funds used for one relief activity may not be available for another. The expected outcome for the beneficiaries of each alternative intervention should play a greater role in deciding which type of assistance to provide.

One country, a very strong promoter of the International Search and Rescue Advisory Group (INSARAG), decided not to send its USAR team, which had been placed on standby at the departing airport. The main factor in this decision was that the expected delay in deployment was projected to be over 50 hours. The country chose instead to shift its resources to deploy a medical team specializing in pediatrics and obstetrics. This pragmatic decision is credited in having saved the lives of 150 to 200 patients, many more than could have been rescued by the USAR team.

Cost-effectiveness does matter in relief activities but there are many important and legitimate considerations other than the number of lives saved in deciding whether or not to send a USAR team (SDC 2011).

Search and rescue is a time-sensitive activity (Macintyre et al. 2011). Its effectiveness declines rapidly hours and days after the impact. This explains why the two local teams from the Haitian Directorate for Civil Protection saved persons in spite of their limited skills and lack of equipment. That statistic is not mentioned in reports on USAR performance in Haiti.

USAR performance indicators ("live rescue") provoke some questions:

- Most of the foreign USAR teams concentrated their efforts on institutional venues, hotel facilities, and residential buildings. Many of these structures were built with reinforced concrete, where there is a higher chance of survival for those trapped.

More persons were rescued alive in the Turkey earthquake in 1999.

The U.S. search and rescue teams saved 34 persons at a cost over US$ 40 million.

It should be noted that public opinion in this donor country was initially against the decision not to send USAR teams..

This figure was cited in a presentation by the Director of the Haitian Directorate for Civil Protection at the INSARAG 2010 Global Meeting, Kobe, Japan, 14–16 September 2010. In addition to those 78 persons, a larger number were rescued by relatives and neighbors, although the numbers and outcomes are unknown.

The USAR teams do have an obligation to search for their own countrymen, and the occupants of these buildings were largely foreigners. No compiled information was made available regarding the nationality of the people rescued, but many local interlocutors believed that they were predominantly foreigners.

- Extricating someone alive is no guarantee that he or she will survive. Indeed, the medical capacity of the SAR teams was limited to initial care and stabilization and medical teams were overwhelmed with caring for acute patients. A few teams tracked the outcome of those survivors days or weeks later. How many of the live rescues may have succumbed to their injuries shortly after rescue is not known, but it should be kept in mind that many of the rescued are believed to have been foreigners who were rapidly evacuated by air to sophisticated medical facilities.

The most important health lesson from the international USAR process is that there must be a sustained effort to improve quality and coordination. Mechanisms used by INSARAG to address coordination challenges are described below.

- INSARAG is a network of disaster-prone and disaster-responding countries and organizations dedicated to urban search and rescue (USAR) and operational field coordination. It works to develop and promote internationally accepted procedures and systems for sustained cooperation between national USAR teams operating on the international scene.

- A voluntary, independent peer-review process of international USAR teams (the INSARAG External Classification—IEC), is a feature that does not exist but is needed for foreign medical teams. IEC is seen as a capacity-building tool and a means of ensuring that international minimum standards are recognized by USAR teams. It is also a work in progress: of the 60 to 70 USAR international teams in Haiti, only 8 were IEC classified while 8 were in the IEC queue for classification (UN/OCHA 2010, 25).

- An On-Site Operations Coordination Center (OSOCC) based on a concept originally developed by UNDAC as part of the INSARAG methodology was activated in Haiti. Its objective is to assist affected countries to coordinate international search-and-rescue efforts following an earthquake.

- A "virtual" OSOCC, a component of the OSOCC, was also established by UNDAC and activated with the first alert in Haiti. It facilitated the registration of "who, what, and when" (i.e, who had what resources, who was ready to go, and when they reached the disaster site). The virtual OSOCC attempts to register all incoming USAR groups while the OSOCC itself is deployed with reception units at the entry points of the disaster-affected country (principally airports or sea ports).

- A systematic attempt to evaluate these mechanisms takes place at After-Action Reviews (AAR). Results and recommendations from the review feed into the INSARAG guidelines.

The review undertaken by UNDAC at the After-Action Review Meeting reached this encouraging conclusion: "The IEC-classified teams in Haiti demonstrated professionalism, followed the INSARAG Guidelines throughout their deployment and made a genuine difference during the response to the earthquake. The meeting suggested actions to be taken to ensure that priority was given to IEC classified teams by the affected countries during an earthquake response" . How effective these mechanisms were in filtering out sub-standard teams in the very difficult context of the first week in Haiti is, however, not documented.

The health sector would benefit from reviewing and, where appropriate, emulating this process of quality control.

Trauma care

In this section, several issues will be discussed: the role and contribution of foreign medical teams (FMT) and foreign field hospitals (FFH, land- or sea-based), the application of triage techniques, surgical challenges, post-operative treatment, patient referral, and evacuation issues.

Earthquakes are unique among other disasters in that they can produce an enormous number of injuries in the matter of a few seconds or minutes. In tsunamis, relatively few survivors require medical care: most in the path of the wave are killed. The challenge to the health system posed by an earthquake is significantly different from conflict situations where casualties are often announced or predictable and spread over days or weeks. In earthquakes, the emergency services are taken by surprise (what-ever their level of preparedness) and may suffer themselves from the impact.

Before the 2010 earthquake, emergency medical services in the non-profit system (State or NGOs) in Haiti were ill-equipped and understaffed to respond even to a small-scale event with mass casualties. In spite of training courses on mass casualty management and other international cooperation initiatives for preparedness, they were unprepared to face large emergencies. The private for-profit sector was nearly as poorly equipped to treat more than a few patients with severe conditions. The direct impact of the earthquake further reduced this capacity.

Emergency trauma care remained the priority for over two weeks in Haiti until all patients received medical care supplied first by local personnel, followed by assistance from an increasing number of external partners.

The discrepancy between the number of injured persons (estimated at 300,000) and the data on the number of people treated (up to 173,000 "consultations" in 24 hospitals over the first four months) (Winter 2011),51 suggests that during the first days many people may have died from the lack of immediate medical attention and later from secondary infections. The University of Michigan survey provides an order of magnitude for this delayed mortality: For an estimated 111,794 killed on impact, an additional 37,301 would not have survived their injuries in the next six weeks. That is 12% of the estimated number of injuries (over 300,000) and one of four of the deaths attributable to the earthquake (Kolbe et al. 2010).

This figure is approximate and only illustrative of the fact that many may not have received medical attention.

For the first 24 hours: Haiti was on its own. The immediate response, for which there are no quantified data, came from the nationals and other actors already present in Port-au-Prince. Those actors experienced the incredible stress of a major earthquake; some had personal losses.

Ambulances, barely available to the general population before the impact, were not an option. Families gathered their injured relatives and delivered them to the nearest health facility or its location if it was destroyed. Some opted to travel to the border with the Dominican

Republic where intact and better-equipped facilities could be expected.

The first report from the University Hospital is illustrative of the difficult conditions of work in the remaining facilities:

"At the time of the earthquake, there were nearly 600 patients in the hospital. Within 30 minutes of the impact, approximately 800 persons entered the premises; most were injured, and 95% were trauma cases. All patients were on the grounds of the hospital as instructions were given to immediately evacuate the buildings. Fifteen hundred patients initially required care. At 5 PM, only night duty staff was present.

"With the arrival of the Director General of the Ministry of Health it was possible for the medical staff to overcome their fear and reluctance and enter the buildings, where stocks of medicines and consumable supplies (alcohol, gauze, dressings, disinfectant, cotton, etc.) could be found. The entire stock was used during the night. The pharmaceutical stocks of the emergency services, surgery and internal medicine departments, as well as the warehouse of the central pharmacy were emptied".

This situation repeated itself in many public or NGO health facilities. With night falling, many of the most severely injured were waiting to be attended or died. Many of the Haitian doctors, who at the time of impact were at their private practice or at home, attended to their neighbors. As noted earlier, reporting to their hospitals was not feasible: roads were blocked, power was down, communications (including mobile phones) were unavailable, and the demand for their skills in their own neighborhoods was urgent and pressing.

Humanitarian organizations, after a rapid inventory of the health of their staff and the condition of their own facilities, were coping with rising numbers of casualties showing up at their doors.

Admittedly, Haiti was not prepared for any type of mass casualties. But no country or system could have had an orderly response to a disaster of this magnitude that affected the political, administrative, and economic center of the country.

After the initial 24 hours, external assistance started to arrive while a flow of patients and affected population was building up at the Dominican Republic border and in non-affected departments.

By the end of the first week, MSF estimated it had treated more than 3,000 wounded people in the Haitian capital and performed more than 400 surgeries. Ultimately, MSF was one of the major actors in emergency surgical care among the 30 foreign field hospitals deployed during this first three-month emergency phase. MSF surgeons performed 5,707 major surgical procedures, 150 of which involved amputations (MSF 2011).

The testimony of a Handicap International expert familiar with Haiti summarizes the situation in Port-au-Prince:

"We spent approximately two weeks in some 17 different hospitals, clinics, and field hospitals evaluating the numbers/types of catastrophic injuries, the acute needs (for personnel and equipment/supplies), and assisting in planning longer term rehabilitation and care needs.

"The capacity of each location serving trauma patients varied tremendously—some sites had multiple teams on the premises, other sites had one provider only. . . Most of the hospital structures in the greater Port-au-Prince area had a mixture of local staff (doctors, nurses), international aid organizations (for example: Red Cross, MSF, Merlin) and small, independent groups or individuals who arrived with or without invitation to assist (hospital groups, church-based, etc.).

"There was—by all appearances and experience—little coordination between any of the sites. . . More often than not, an individual hospital had little idea what other facilities in the Port-au-Prince area could offer in terms of surgical services, how they could find out that information, or how to transport a patient to another site. At each hospital where multiple organizations were 'on the ground,' there was at times little communication even between those groups.

"By the second week, many of the hospitals had established patient tracking systems; each patient remaining was in a data-base. However, it appeared that this was not coordinated nationally—each hospital did its own thing. Each organization seemed to have its own patient information form.

"One of the issues I could see was that many responders had never been to Haiti, had no local cell phone, had no way to communicate with local authorities, and did not appear to know 'who was in charge'."

Incoming foreign medical teams and hospitals

- The number of foreign medical teams or field hospitals is increasing in every disaster as is the diversity of their place of origin.
- In Haiti, they arrived much earlier than in Indonesia or in Pakistan. Their effectiveness was also higher considering the exceptional gap between the needs and local medical resources.
- Guidelines were not generally applied. A different approach toward quality control of these resources is required.

Personal communication with Dr. Colleen O'Connell, MD, PMR, 31 January 2011.

As is true for most of the response activities in the first few weeks, there are no official data or records on the number, timing, and role of the various foreign medical teams (FMT) or field hospitals (FFH) arriving in Haiti in the aftermath of the earthquake.55 The PAHO/WHO Guidelines for the use of foreign field hospitals in the aftermath of sudden-impact disasters (2003) defined a field hospital as "a mobile, self-contained, self-sufficient health care facility capable of rapid deployment and expansion or contraction to meet immediate emergency requirements for a specified period of time".

The distinction between fully equipped medical teams and small field hospitals has progressively been blurred. Many self-sustained foreign medical teams operating under tents would indeed meet this definition of FFH. In part, this may explain why medical "teams" eager to deploy in the rare sudden-onset catastrophes in the world have often ignored those guidelines that are too specific for field hospitals.

The time lag for arrival of foreign medical teams is an essential factor in their effectiveness in saving lives. In Haiti, they did arrive and were operational relatively early (1 to 2 days) due to the proximity of major providers. In other disasters reviewed in this publication their arrival was considerably later (3 to 5 days), which significantly reduced their impact.

The time of arrival or deployment is also a matter of controversy. Many teams provide only the earliest time of arrival at the point of entry in the country, suggesting that they were operational at that time. Statements such as "We were able to offer emergency medical relief, provide medical staff, and establish the first field hospital within 24 hours after the earthquake," occur frequently in the literature.

Interviews with national authorities and international experts suggest that concrete service (care) was actually provided much later. This more transparent and practical presentation of the facts was adopted by some of the responders: "The hospital started operating 89 hours after the earthquake" (Bar-On et al. 2011). As seen in past disasters, providers of medical teams are not always fully transparent in this regard.

Day 10    40 health facilities, including 8 FFH

Day 13    48 health facilities including 12 FFH and 2 hospital ships

Day 15    One military hospital departs; several others scheduling their departure

Day 21    2 hospital ships arrive

Day 24    91 hospitals (59 in Port-au-Prince, including 21 FFH)

A chronology was tentatively reconstructed by the Karolinska Insititute in Sweden (Gerdin and Von Schreeb 2011).

The same issue has been noted in the promotion of field hospital capacity, where the short time for deployment is from "alert," to "ready," to "board the flight" status, which is very different from the delay between request and actual provision of on-site medical care.

Following the Bam (Iran) earthquake, foreign teams and facilities started offering services more than three days after the impact. That is, 24 hours after almost all trauma cases had been air evacuated and distributed around the 13 provinces of the country. This fact did not stop some providers from publishing claims of having performed triage and stabilization of the victims.

Haiti may have seen the highest number of field hospitals (land-based or on ship) providing assistance. Unlike the situation in the aftermath of almost all other disasters where those external facilities were under-utilized, hospital ships were working at near full capacity in Haiti and providing a most valuable, albeit short-term, replacement for secondary and tertiary level facilities lost in the impact (or that were lacking prior to the disaster). Due to the collapse of the Haitian health infrastructure, the USNS Comfort became the main tertiary level facility.

Specifications for hospital ships for which data are available are:

Hospital ships serving in Haiti after the earthquake

Colombiaa    Franceb    Mexicoc    Spaind    U.S.A.e

Ship    Cartagena de

Indias    Sirico    Huasteco    Castilla    USNS Comfort

| Arrival date | 22 Jan (Day 10) | 24 Jan (Day 12) | 20 Jan (Day 8) | 4 Feb (Day 23) | 20 Jan (Day 8) |
|---|---|---|---|---|---|
| Departure date | 14 Feb | 6 Feb | n/a | 4 May | 10 March |
| Stay (no. of days) | 23 | 10 | n/a | 64 | 36 |

Capacity    Multipurpose    50 beds    Multipurpose /
25 beds    70 beds    50 trauma-beds; 400 intermediate-care beds, 500
minimal-care beds

| Operating rooms | 1 | 2 | 1 | 2 | 10-12 |
|---|---|---|---|---|---|
| ICU | No | No | n/a | 8 beds | 30 beds |
| Rx | n/a | n/a | Yes | No | Yes |
| Laboratory | n/a | n/a | n/a | Yes | Yes |
| No. of people attended | 200 | n/a | n/a | 7,568 | 869 |
| No. of surgical procedures | 27 | 45 | n/a | 104 | 821 |

Comments 8 doctors from the Cartagena Navy Hospital  French Navy in partnership with a field hospital and an advanced medical unit  Mexican Navy medical pro- fessionals  A mobile health unit in Petit Goave provided PHC and referred selected patients to the ship, explaining the high number attended U.S. Navy coordinated patient transfers with Haitian, international, and NGO health facilities.

Some observations can be made regarding those ships:

1.  All arrived a week or more after the earthquake;
2.  The USNS Comfort was by far the most technically sophisticated;
3.  Two ships stayed beyond 30 days.

All ships developed their own system of referral; often through one single institution (e.g., HUEH for the USNS Comfort, the French Lyceum for the French vessel Sirico). Teams at other facilities did not necessarily know the criteria used by the hospital ships for accepting patients.

In addition to the self-contained field hospitals, many foreign medical teams (FMT) built their own capacity nearly emulating that of the FFH, the only difference being that services were delivered in local facilities that were conceded or commandeered.

International claims and local reports or interviews about the numbers of FMT could not be easily reconciled. Tracking all FMTs was not feasible, but reconstructing what happened in the University Hospital, for instance, illustrates the situation in many places.

A report from HUEH clearly states that "the important and welcome assistance from the foreign humanitarians arrived the evening of 14 January with two emergency physicians, then three more arrived on 15 January but without material or medicines".

Interviews with international responders and national officials do not always offer the same timeline of events, differing some times by only 24 hours. However, those 24 hours may mean the difference between life and death for some patients. These differences are important to local counterparts: they resent the exaggerated claims of foreign teams while perceiving their own efforts and contributions as being minimized or overlooked. This is representative of a serious communication problem.

Assertions that field hospitals were not operational as early as needed, by no means suggests a deferred or leisurely response. Considering all the logistical, operational, and political constraints, the deployment was massive and remarkably fast. This occurred in spite of problems caused by the restrictive military management of airport access.

Integration of foreign assets with local authorities

The pace of FMT and FFH arrival rapidly accelerated. Following again with the HUEH as example:

"Support from the Emergency Unit of the Association of Haitian Doctors Abroad (AMHE) arrived on 16 January (Day 4) with 60 persons. . . [This association] will set up the first section of post-traumatic emergency care at the University Hospital. . . This team brings material, equipment and medicines as required. . . Ten other NGOs with a total of 200 foreigners will succeed each other in shifts of one or two weeks until the end of March".59

According to interviews conducted with hospital authorities and international actors, some of the non-Haitian teams operating in the first week in the HUEH reportedly commandeered part of the premises, recruited personnel from outside the hospital, and denied the HUEH staff the roles they considered as their own. Instead of assisting local authorities, they displaced them and took over. The same situation was reported under this heading of NGO, the report included bilateral governmental teams such as the Swiss Development Cooperation. Dr. Alex Larsen (HUEH), (nd), Rapport au Ministre de la Sante publique et de la Population. [Translated from the French.]

In other facilities in Haiti. Interviews and reports on the Indian Ocean tsunami and the Pakistan earthquake indicate that the problem is common in the humanitarian community. However, it is less of an issue in larger countries where there is a strong government and institutions have not been directly affected by the event.

The issue of integrating national staff in foreign teams is complex. In fully equipped and well-established military type field hospitals, making room in a trained and homogenous team for local health personnel may cause problems. However, integrating local staff of the hosting facility should be less difficult for teams that are assembled for a specific event or those already working in the country before the event. Most agencies found it easier to recruit local personnel under their direct authority than to share management with local counterparts.

The duration of the presence of the teams and hospitals varied widely: One highly specialized military field hospital was rapidly operational, triaged and treated patients with the fastest possible turnover, and left after 10 days. Some, like the hospital ships, arrived later, specialized in the most difficult cases, and stayed longer. Others, such as the Red Cross hospital, may stay indefinitely and be administered by the local authorities. This is true in the case of some temporary emergency facilities that are built even better than existing government facilities that were intended to last for years (for example, the MSF "container" hospital in Léogâne). This is a matter of choice and the strategic decision of the donor, but that does not always coincide with the Ministry of Health plan.

There is benefit in this diversity as long as, like in an orchestra, there is a score or master plan that all follow. This was not the case in Haiti. Each "musician" played his/her instrument as well as possible with the selected score. There is no surprise that the result was "cacophony" (the term used by Zanotti, 2010).

Quality control

The quality and professionalism of the medico-surgical assistance appeared to be, in the opinion of most interlocutors, relatively satisfactory given the circumstances. There were, of course, noticeable exceptions and examples of possible unethical behavior. But they were by far the exception. As noted by the Handicap International expert who visited 17 hospitals in two weeks:

"The care being administered to patients in most instances appeared appropriate for the resources available. Stumps from amputations were being wrapped; patients were being fed and receiving water; fractures were being either treated by external fixators (until fixators were in short supply) or by immobilization in casts" .

The issue is that there is no accepted standard or mechanism to monitor and assess the quality of the trauma care. Opinions are made based on occasional observation and conversation with colleagues. Reprehensive or dubious practices were not discouraged or penalized.61 Relief assistance remains the "wild west" of medicine where only the Personal communication, Colleen O'Connell, MD, in an e-mail of her findings while working with Handicap International.

Reports of a foreign religious group approaching patients in hospitals to convince them to seek cure through rituals rather than medical treatment was neither investigated nor acted on.

Most experienced and professionalized groups (military, Red Cross, MSF, among others) have developed their own guidelines, standards, and procedures. This situation is not specific to Haiti but is generic in all crises where assistance is on a massive scale.

Changes are overdue, as eloquently expressed in an article by several MSF experts "As an increasing number of actors are becoming involved in the delivery of humanitarian surgery, the need to establish a framework for quality surgical delivery is more pressing. The quality of surgical care may be regulated through a combination of structural, process, and output measures that could include minimum standards for safe surgery, the deployment of appropriately trained surgeons and anesthesiologists for these contexts, protocols for preoperative evaluation, intraoperative management and postoperative care, and standardized databases to record postoperative infection and mortality rates. A simple checklist for each patient can be utilized to ensure compliance. Standardizing data collection can help to evaluate surgical delivery".

As the authors noted in their article, there may be resistance to such measures. Triage of mass casualties

- Some form of triage was used by most of the foreign medical teams. Unlike other disasters, there was no alternative in Haiti as the number of casualties waiting on the front steps of the clinics or hospitals far exceeded the available resources.
- Criteria for triage varied widely. The purpose was to maximize the use of the resources and capacity of each health care provider.

The concept of triage originated in France during the late eighteenth century.62 It focused primarily on mass casualty situations where a systematic sorting process sought to assign priorities in care in order to save as many lives as possible.

Triage is not just one concept. Today there are at least two different scenarios during which triage is applied: 1) at the scene of the mass casualty event, also called pre-hospital care, and 2) in health care facilities.

In the former, the first responder community selects those injured who will be given priority for primary stabilization and transportation to health facilities. Initial medical care might be provided at an advanced health post at the site of the emergency. This is only applicable in localized mass casualty incidents where a medical command center can be established. Its effectiveness lies in the limited number of patients and control of transportation/dispatch by receiving institutions. The dilemma is who is treated first or last.

Robertson-Steel (2006) states that Baron Dominique Jean Larrey, Surgeon-in-Chief to Napoleon's Imperial Guard, was the first to apply a process of sorting around 1792.

Transporting the injured

In health care facilities, injured persons have reached hospitals and health facilities (or the facility's location if it has been destroyed). They are often accompanied by relatives who are vocal in demanding attention. Contrary to what happens during normal situations, in which the severity of a patient's condition determines the priority of attention, in the event of a disaster, the imbalance between the demand and the available resources requires care providers to consider not only the severity of the patient's condition, but other criteria such as the prognosis and the benefit that the action taken (care and/or transportation according to available capabilities) will afford the patient. Those with a poor prognosis (likely to die, in most instances) or those who will not suffer irreversible damage if care is delayed, are placed on hold or denied access to the facility.

Therefore, triage must be more rigorous and selective to the extent that the magnitude of the disaster increases and the disparity between needs and capabilities and resources becomes greater. The dilemma under this scenario remains: Who is going to be treated? This is something not easily understood and accepted by patients and their relatives.

For more than 72 hours in Haiti, the process of transporting injured persons was massive, spontaneous, and chaotic. Hospitals and health centers were surrounded by injured persons and corpses taken there by the population. While local health facilities were not prepared for the systematic use of triage, most of the foreign teams and hospitals had some criteria for screening patients they would accept. Table 5.3 illustrates this point with findings from three hospitals.

Following the earthquake in Haiti,local health facilities supported by MSF Field hospital (Israeli Defense Forces) Hospital ship (USNS Comfort)

Period of performanceOperative in Haiti before the earthquake and continues to be present in Haiti a    Started on Day 4 and continued for 10 days    Started on Day 8 and continued for 40 days

Criteria for accepting patients "In the immediate aftermath . . . it was not possible. . . to carry out systematic triage due to the mas- sive numbers of wounded people flooding hospital grounds"

(MSF 2011)b    Patients with severe injuries (including open and infected wounds); patients with antici– pated short-term treatment (up to 24–48 hours); and patients who had just been rescued by USAR (Merin et al. 2010) Only patients with earthquake-related injuries (e.g., complicated extremity injuries, obstetric cases, and maxillofacial injuries) (Etienne et al. 2010; Criteria for denying care No patients were rejected. Some patients were referred to Santo Domingo for advanced treat- ment and some severe burn injuries were referred to the USNS Comfort Patients with brain injuries; paraplegia secondary to spinal injuries; low score in the Glasgow coma score. Attention to patients with crush injuries was initially denied, but this criterion changed one week later when dialysis equipment was available Less severely injured patients who could be attended in other health facilities in Port-au-Prince.

Cases not accepted included: pelvic fractures, closed head injuries, complete spinal cord lesions, and cases requiring assisted ventilation (Auerbach et al. 2010)

Patients treated 5,707 major surgical procedures (first month: 2,386; second month: 1,902; third month: 1,419) 1,100 treated patients 242 surgical procedures under anesthesia were performed on 205 patients 821 surgical procedures on 446 patients 2010)

Two of the three secondary level health care structures that Médecins Sans Frontières operated in Port-au-Prince were destroyed; only one emergency facility was still functional.

Within a few hours of the earthquake, more than 400 critically injured and dying patients arrived at once. Personnel focused primarily on minor wound dressings of injured persons, trying to organize triage, and providing immediate life-saving surgery and end-of-life-care.

Patients with mild injuries (ambulatory patients) and pregnant women were referred internally to different areas.

Given the shortcomings in information management, it is impossible to establish the number of injured, the number accepted, and the number rejected for injuries classified as too severe, much less to estimate the subsequent morbidity and mortality. Under this scenario, it is therefore very difficult to determine the effectiveness of the implemented triage techniques in the number of lives saved.

What the triage clearly achieved is a better use of the very scarce operating facilities. Theaters and surgeons' time were optimized in most cases. It should be emphasized that surgery is only one critical step in the treatment process.

Independent teams have improved their own performance, but these are initial and facility-centered achievements. The success of one team could imply the failure of other teams not equipped to provide post-operative care or referral with the consequent increase in morbidity and mortality. The impact of triage should also be seen within a health care network that shares information, resources, and capabilities.

In Haiti, a holistic view of the flow of casualties was missing.

Government of Israel (2010), "Triage in mass causality events— taking stock of the Haitian experience" .

Surgical approaches and issues

The 12 January earthquake generated many scientific peer-reviewed articles.64 A significant number address the suitability of various techniques for anesthesia or surgery, subjects which are not part of the scope of this publication. Other topics include advances made in electronic management of medical files and patient registration under emergency conditions, the use of advanced laboratories, point-of-care technology for diagnosis, the application of portable diagnostic devices (ultrasound for instance). The potential for robust, field-tested technologies is important for the future of disaster medicine in poor countries.

Several papers have been published that disaggregate cases by condition, but few offer details on the type of procedures or treatment. Figures 5.2 and 5.3, showing surgical and orthopedic interventions at the University Hospital and at MSF facilities, illustrate what appears to be a common pattern in the first weeks after the earthquake.

The use of health technology in humanitarian response was the subject of a one-day summit between civilan and military experts and NGOs. Baltimore, Maryland, 29 September 2010.

Four medical conditions call for special attention: crush syndrome with its lethal renal failure, spinal cord injury (SCI), amputations, and, more generally, fractures. Interestingly, the general proliferation of humanitarian agencies has also resulted in the emergence of new or increasingly proactive partners offering highly specialized expertise and assistance for some of those conditions.

The "renal disaster"

The expression "renal disaster" used in a scientific article on crush syndrome (Sever, Lameire, Vanholder 2009) illustrates the potential for loss of lives due to shortcomings in diagnosing and treating severe cases of crush syndrome. As noted by the same authors: "Although many crush patients can survive within the first hours or even days until rescue, death will be inevitable for most of them after extrication if emergency measures for the prevention of [acute kidney injury] AKI... are not taken."

Crush syndrome patients and, by extension, the renal victims are usually overlooked or neglected. "According to the general perception, they constitute a relatively minor group requiring complex and labor-intensive therapeutic measures and are rarely included in governmental or local disaster plans" (Sever, Lameire, Vanholder 2009). Informal and empirical enquiries in past disasters in Latin America have shown a lack of awareness of this condition. Either Latin American earthquakes did not produce many crush syndromes or the condition was under-diagnosed.

The Renal Disaster Relief Task Force (RDRTF) of the International Society of Nephrology was established to provide specialized care (including dialysis) for this special group of patients. Strong on expertise but weak on logistics and operational skills, the group partnered with MSF.

A dialysis center with eight units was operational in Haiti on Day 5, in time to prevent fatalities (which generally occur between 4 and 10 days after the trauma). Efforts by the task force to publicize their availability and expertise to other medical partners in Port-au-Prince were limited. In particular, they did not routinely participate in the coordination meetings, and as a consequence, did not receive a large number of referrals to their facilities (only 19). Among the many important announcements of available services published in the Health Cluster Bulletin, no mention was made of crush syndrome and the existing resources for diagnosis (including point-of-care laboratory devices) and treatment. The lack of participation of the task force in the cluster meetings resulted in a facility that could accommodate up to 200 patients a day running at 20% of its capacity.

As expressed in a letter to the editor of Lancet by the Task Force, one of the major lessons it learned from the Haiti disaster is the need for better interagency communication (Vanholder et al. 2010). In this particular case, the full-time assignment of a liaison officer/ technician to participate in the numerous meetings would have been cost-effective. This is one example where it can be demonstrated that participation in coordination meetings would have saved more lives.

Immediate deaths following release from entrapment are caused by hyperkalemia.

There are no data on the number of untreated crush syndromes in Haiti, but it is estimated to be several times more than the 200-patient capacity of the dialysis center.

Another observation is the need for special tagging and medical supervision of patients undertaking periodic dialysis. When mixed with other patients, treating doctors and even visiting medical volunteers from other groups were prescribing treatment incompatible with dialysis or even selecting the patient for immediate transfer to other facilities.

Spinal cord injury (SCI)

Prior to the earthquake, the mid-term survival rate of Haitian patients with SCI was believed to be almost nil. In the aftermath of this disaster, over 150 such cases reached medical facilities, passing through or bypassing the triage system designed to select those patients with more chance of survival at the lowest cost in medical resources, a criterion SCI does not meet. In past disasters, in medically under-developed countries, the prognosis of those patients would have been grim.

In Haiti, early advocacy for action was published in leading professional publications (editorials, invited comments, and forums). Appeals for specialists and physiotherapists were launched and heard. Several groups dedicated special resources to those cases. Among them were the Project Medishare of the University of Miami, which included a spinal care unit in the tent hospital (Ginzburg et al. 2010; Wang 2010); the Haiti Hospital Appeal, a small NGO that transformed their soon-to-be-opened pediatric facility into an adult rehabilitation center for up to 22 SCI (Landry et al. 2010a; Stephenson 2011); Healing Hands for Haiti International, a well-established rehabilitation NGO; and finally, the U.S. Navy hospital ship, the USNS Comfort (Landry et al. 2010a; Burns et al. 2010). Later, other organizations such as the Toronto Rehabilitation Institute assisted with specialist SCI input.

While a spinal cord injury once practically condemned the patient to death within a few years, patients in Haiti are now receiving more appropriate care. It is an area where the disaster has triggered a permanent improvement of the health services.

Treatment of fractures

As noted by physicians working with Handicap International, fractures were the most common diagnosis:

"All modes of fracture management have been reported, including: traction, closed reduction, open reduction, internal fixation, external fixator, slab cast and splint, and complete circumferential casting. Lack of imaging capacity in many facilities limited diagnostic abilities, and doctors noted that some fractures had to be diagnosed by palpation only. Other centers ran out of film and processing agents, resulting in similar limitations".

In the first weeks, it was not uncommon for foreign physicians to repeatedly visit a health facility to examine a particular patient and leave instructions for the facility's local nursing personnel.

Post-operative care

The result of this situation is that months after the earthquake, many of the fractures required a second operation for realignment of the bones.

One issue still debated among emergency professionals is the use of external versus internal fixators, the latter requiring sterile operating conditions rarely found in disaster conditions (Lebel et al. 2011).

Amputations

Amputations may save lives, but they also threaten the social life and economic survival of the patients. It is a procedure that should not be taken lightly. Rehabilitation and support services are below standard in Haiti, as in many countries. Disabled persons, whatever the cause of their disability and their prior status, are rejected by society. They are considered as "punished by god for their sins" and are hidden at home.70 Undertaking an amputation has a very high social and human cost.

After the Pakistan earthquake in 2005, unpublished concern regarding possibly unnecessary amputations had already emerged. In on-site interviews, some medical teams were seemingly presenting the high number of amputations made under difficult field conditions as indicative of the heroism of their intervention.

In Haiti, this issue became publicized following the preliminary report from Handicap International projecting the number of amputees to be over 2,000 and possibly up to "In a country where 10 percent of the population is disabled, you could spend a week here and never see any [disabled persons]," said Josue Joseph, a spokesperson for the Haitian Secretariat for Integration. Accessed at: www.terradaily. com/ afp/100609015616.nv60byyh.html, June 2010.

Patient with external fixators

Later this figure was adjusted to 1,200–1,500. For the purpose of illustration, MSF, the largest provider of emergency surgical care in the first weeks, reported having performed 173 amputations on a total of 147 patients (16 of these patients underwent multiple interventions, possibly involving two separate limbs). Medical teams at the border with the Dominican Republic reported 217 amputations.

As noted in the preliminary survey by Handicap International (O'Connell et al. 2010), there are many reasons why amputations are performed, including: as primary intervention for complex severe wounds and fractures making the limb unviable or as "secondary treatment for infected wounds, compartment syndromes, and poorly treated fractures".

Techniques for amputations were also questioned. Use of the so-called guillotine technique guarantees the need for repeated, corrective interventions on the stump to accommodate prosthesis. This technique is much more rapid (minutes instead of hours) and does not require much skill or instrumentation. Conservative treatment of severe infection requires time-consuming and sustained nursing care (a profession under-represented in the humanitarian response), and its success is far from certain. Most of the interlocutors recognized that under the extreme workload and lack of adequate facilities, often there were no better options than to amputate a limb that could have been saved in better equipped facilities (following the principle of triage to maximize the benefits).

The level of amputation is paramount for indications for prosthesis. In 107 cases reviewed by Handicap International, above the knee amputations represented the largest proportion of lower limb amputations (63%) versus 37% for amputations below the knee (see Table 5.4). There are insufficient data for comparison with other disasters.

Table 5.4 Level of amputation in patients injured in Haiti earthquake

| Level of amputation | No. | Percentage of amputees |
| --- | --- | --- |
| Below knee | 27 | 25% |
| Above knee | 46 | 43% |
| Upper limb | 17 | 16% |
| Unspecified | 17 | 16% |
| Total | 107 | 100% |

Note: Data from Handicap International (O'Connell et al. 2010).

Publicity about this issue had some benefits for the population and offered some lessons:

1. First, it is crucial to centrally register the number of amputations, monitor the use of this procedure, and review their indications.

1. A key step in developing local health systems is the establishment of surgical outcomes monitoring. Such monitoring can optimize patient follow-up and foster professional accountability for the treatment of amputation patients in disaster settings and humanitarian emergencies (Knowlton et al. 2011).

2. The number of amputees is not the same as the number of those wanting or requiring prostheses. Indeed, some amputations may not be suitable for prosthesis and some amputees might prefer to capitalize on their disability. In 2010, Healing Hands for Haiti partnered with Handicap International to provide some 500 prostheses. About half of the recipients had undergone amputations prior to the impact.

3. This intervention should require second medical opinions and, when possible, informed consent of the patient. That was standard procedure for many, but not all the medical teams in Haiti.

4. Finally, rehabilitation specialists must be involved early in treatment, ideally before amputation, and should educate the surgical team in prosthetic considerations. Mental health specialists must be included to help the patient with community reintegration.

Reconstructive surgery

The surgical reconstruction of major injuries is only rarely addressed in the early response phase of earthquakes. In Haiti, this specialized service was made available but remained in short supply despite the massive level of resources deployed for this event. Rather remarkable is the contribution made to treat survivors with craniofacial injuries who required complex and multiple procedures to achieve optimal results. Thanks to the modern facilities on the USNS Comfort, some 34 cases were improved, requiring 93 craniofacial surgical procedures. Average patient hospitalization time was 17 days (ranging from 5 to 38 days) (Ray et al. 2011). These surgeries were also performed at a Brazilian field hospital.

Proximity to North America and French territories, the presence of MINUSTAH facilities, and the very rapid mobilization of some other military facilities were key factors leading to a quality of orthopedic and reconstructive care that cannot usually be expected in emergency response. It is a performance that has rarely been seen in disasters in more remote places.

Post-operative care, referral, and foreign medical evacuations.

- In most disasters, there is much more assistance for surgical care than for follow-up care of surgical patients: too many doctors and not enough nurses.
- Referral of patients to different levels of care was hindered by logistical constraints but above all by a lack of information on specialty services and space available as well as the procedures and criteria for patients' referral.

Post-operative care was an issue from the first few days of the response until late during the recovery. Within a week, it was upgraded to one of the top priorities. Not all foreign field hospitals and medical teams addressed this issue in the same manner. One of the most active field hospitals strictly applied the triage principle to take full advantage of their surgical resources. Turnover was maximized and patients were triaged to achieve the most efficient use of operating theaters. Patients who underwent surgery were discharged, on average, within 39 hours of the procedure. No provision was made for post-operative care, which was not considered a function of this facility.

Field hospitals concentrated on what they do best and what they are equipped for: providing immediate or delayed surgical care. Follow-up and time consuming postoperative care were to be provided by less sophisticated teams or facilities. Unfortunately, those facilities were either not available or overburdened. Although there are no data on the impact of this situation on the outcome of patients, there were doubts about this approach under conditions prevailing in Haiti: that is, no effective coordination among actors, and local health authorities who were not in a position to assume strong leadership. Most components of the medical response system worked efficiently but independently of each other, ensuring serious problems in the overall chain for complete care. There were many examples of excellence, but they were unlinked, "bubbles" of excellence.

Post-operative care is a time-consuming activity requiring a significant number of auxiliary personnel, nurses in particular. There is no lack of interest and dedication on the part of this profession, as was evident in Haiti. Following the earthquake in Pakistan and the Indian Ocean tsunami there was also an insufficient number of nurses compared to the number of doctors volunteering their services. There is often a chronic shortage of nurses in donor countries and institutions providing volunteers.

A successful partnership delivers post-operative care One success story was the partnership developed between a hospital in Jimaní (Hospital Buen Samaritano), an NGO in Haiti (Love a Child), and PAHO/WHO. It provides a model for planning follow-up of patients.

- From Day 3, the pressure on Dominican medical facilities clearly pointed to the need for arrangements for post-surgery care, preferably in Haiti.
- On Day 4, the Dominican Ministry of Health and PAHO/ WHO approached NGOs established in Fond Parisien, on the Haitian side of the border, about developing a facility for discharged surgical patients and their families. A school designed for 400 students and managed by Love a Child was identified as a first-line facility for post-operative treatment of patients discharged from local and Dominican facilities.
- Over the following days, equipment, mattresses, and other supplies were provided by the Dominican Ministry of Health.

- On Day 8, the facility received the first 65 patients.
- On Day 9, the Hospital Eau de Vie in Fond Parisien was evaluated and strengthened to serve as a back-up facility, should the 400 beds of the converted school be insufficient.

To transform an idea into a concrete achievement in the space of one week is a noteworthy accomplishment, made possible by informal partnership between a government, an NGO, and a UN organization, unhindered by bureaucratic obstacles.

Patient flow: evacuation, referral, post-operative care

Patient referral

Post-operative care is only one aspect of the broader issue of referral of patients between facilities.

The flow of patients between levels of care was particularly problematic in Haiti. Problems ranged from lack of transportation to lack of knowledge about options.

Medical teams providing primary or secondary care often did not know of the potential capacity of more sophisticated facilities. Extraordinary work pressure considerably limited the communication between medical teams and hospitals. Few could spare staff to participate in the numerous coordination meetings. The underutilization of the dialysis capacity mentioned earlier is only one example.

A testimony from a trauma expert is revealing:

"The most challenging aspect was a clear plan conveyed to all the responders/groups, as to who was able to manage what, and how to get the patients referred and transferred. A good example is spinal cord injury. It was my experience that at many sites where SCI patients were identified (often lying on mattresses in the street/parking lots, or even on sheets of Flow of patients Lying on plywood), the doctors/ nurses caring for them did not know where to send them. Having been at many of the sites, I knew which centers were accepting SCI patients, and was able to assist in triage, referral and transport organization when I 'found' SCI patients at other sites. This was a very one-off type of approach, and even at centers accepting SCI patients, if the 'wrong' person was at triage when the SCI patient arrived, they could have been turned away."

It was not until four weeks after the impact that a one-page listing of resources for referral was made available. This list offered names and sometimes addresses of specialized services such as burn treatment, pediatric surgery, dialysis, neurosurgery, ophthalmology, cranio-facial surgery, medical evacuations, or simply obstetrics, a need often overlooked in a trauma-focused environment. In future disasters, disseminating a listing of referral facilities should be one of the first priorities.

Problems were not limited to referral from lower level to tertiary level but also in the reverse. The USNS Comfort hospital ship found it difficult to identify receiving institutions for their patients requiring less acute but longer term follow-up care.

Personal communication with Dr. Colleen O'Connell, MD, PMR, 31 January 2011.

Foreign medical evacuations

Evacuation abroad should be an option of last resort to be adopted cautiously and under strict oversight of the national health services. Preference should be given instead to strengthening the capacity of local counterparts.

Unlike the disasters in Indonesia, Sri Lanka, Pakistan, and Iran (Bam earthquake), there was no back-up facility inside Haiti where patients could be evacuated. Evacuating patients into foreign facilities is entirely distinct from redistributing patients within national health services as was done massively in Iran (15,000 evacuated in the matter of a couple of days) and in Sri Lanka.

Transfer of Haitian patients to foreign facilities (mostly in the Dominican Republic, United States, and French territories) was done extensively in the first few days. Quantified data, as for many other aspects of the relief operations, are not easily available. Recipient countries and hospitals often used medical evacuation as a back-up alternative or support for their medical facilities in the field. Criteria for selection, if articulated at all, were not broadly publicized or known.

Selective evacuations of spinal cord injury cases to foreign countries took place early after the impact, but they were soon curtailed (in part due to the realization that those patients would be occupying expensive beds for an open-ended period of time). Returning those chronic patients to Haiti where a suitable receiving facility could not be found was ethically impossible. Economic considerations, especially for institutions caring for patients requiring expensive, long-term care, should be considered at an early stage.

In several instances, relatives did not have information on the whereabouts of injured family members who were evacuated. There were also the issues of immigration and subsistence for the patient's family in the host country.

Foreign medical evacuation of the injured is an expression of solidarity with the affected population but it often causes more problems than anticipated. As experienced in receiving countries/territories such as

Martinique, accepting a patient requiring long-term care is the easiest part, deciding to return him/her raises ethical issues.

National authorities of the affected country or an agency they designate should play a monitoring/tracking role, if not an approval role, in this process. It is an approach that should not be left entirely to the initiative and criteria of foreign teams. Recipient institutions should remain accountable to both families and health authorities of the affected countries and be unambiguous regarding the duration of their commitment.

Almost all injured in the Bam earthquake were evacuated before the first foreign field hospitals arrived.

All nationals injured in the tsunami were treated and referred to third level care in departmental facilities. None needed to be evacuated to the 2,000-bed General Hospital in the capital city, Colombo.

In the U.S., the Government concluded a formal agreement with receiving institutions to reimburse 110% of Medicare rates for approved Haitian patients.

Trenches for mass burials

Disposal of bodies and debris

Disposal of bodies

- In almost all large-scale disasters, mass burials are carried out not for health reasons but for the lack of other practical alternatives. The psychological cost is unknown.
- There are no NGOs and very few bilateral teams with skills and resources for the identification and respectful management of dead bodies. It is a humanitarian niche that has not yet been filled.

There is now extensive literature about the proper disposal of bodies following sudden-impact natural disasters. The humanitarian community seems to have accepted the fact that bodies of victims killed by trauma (earthquake and conflicts) do not represent a significant risk for communicable disease. It is a major step toward more rational and effective public health management of scarce resources.

Not long after the Indian Ocean tsunami and in the aftermath of hurricanes in Haiti, officials, including from experienced relief organizations, were spreading the fear that uncontrollable epidemics were the unavoidable result of decaying bodies. Mass burials, cremation, or other "disinfection" techniques are not justified from a health point of view. It is remarkable that, after an earthquake producing such a large number of bodies left unattended for days, no similar unfounded announcement was made locally by senior health or humanitarian officials. This should be credited to the early formal announcements by WHO that dead bodies are not a source of large epidemics. Nevertheless, this myth was still proliferated in mass media in Europe and Latin America.

Haitians hold their deceased family members in high regard and perform elaborate, costly, and extended funeral rituals to assure the goodwill of the deceased. Deceased family members are still considered to be part of the family. As stated in the WHO publication Culture and Mental Health in Haiti (2010a, 20), "The issue of proper death rites and burial is particularly important in the wake of the earthquake. Many people have not had the opportunity to find and bury their lost loved ones or had to abandon them, or see them buried in a mass grave with no ceremonies. As a result, there may be an increase in ambiguity and uncertainty over the fate of the dead...".

(2004) recommendations that bodies be stored, identified and returned to the family to allow for grieving and ritual burial. Given the magnitude of the losses and the urgency of other life saving measures, this was not a practical option in Haiti. Nor was it following the disasters in Pakistan, Indonesia, and Sri Lanka. Thailand, however, was an exception.

The morgue in the University Hospital which was designed to handle around 30 cadavers rapidly exceeded its capacity and was overwhelmed, according to the report of its Director, "by up to 10,000 bodies". At the same time, MINUSTAH reported on Day 3 that it had collected and buried more than 13,000 bodies in mass graves. How accurate those figures are considering the chaotic and emotional conditions remains to be seen. They are nevertheless illustrative of the overwhelming task that lay ahead. Municipal and state authorities mobilized a fleet of private trucks and worked day and night filling improvised mass burial sites outside the city.

No statistics and sparse documentary evidence (photos or documents) were collected to allow for delayed identification of the remains. The seeming acceptance of this hasty process by Haiti's deeply religious people was remarkable and reflects the sense of shock and the population's focus on the survival challenges ahead. Long-term psychological impacts are unknown.

In Thailand, almost 5,400 bodies were recovered after the tsunami. Special efforts, lasting over one year, were made to identify the deceased, including by photos, finger printing, and DNA analysis. One factor influencing these efforts was the presence of almost 2,000 foreigners among the victims (Sribanditmongkol et al. 2005).

Beyond trauma care

The delayed response (up to 3 months)

During the first two weeks after the earthquake, there were many more health related activities than just rescuing trapped victims and providing trauma care. Water and sanitation, food and shelter, and access to primary health care were among the many needs of the affected population. They became the top priorities of humanitarian agencies once the life-saving interventions were completed, together with surveillance of communicable diseases, rehabilitation, and many-cross cutting issues.

This publication cannot review or analyze in detail the many challenges faced and solutions found for those broad social issues. This chapter addresses selected topics of particular public health interest for future mass-scale disasters.

Clinics and mobile intervention teams in settlements

The terms "clinics" and "mobile teams" covered a large range of services: from the well-established and fully staffed temporary or fixed facility in a large camp to the small tent where a nurse or a doctor occasionally provided minimal care to patients.

The Ministry of Health of Haiti, itself recovering from the impact, realized that it had in fact very little influence on the immediate trauma care process, which, as shown in had its own dynamics and rules. Very early on, the Ministry centered its attention on the establishment of "mobile clinics" to provide primary health care to the displaced populations or to provide a temporary substitute for the facilities destroyed by the earthquake. A chronology of the Ministry's statements regarding the establishment of primary health care clinics after the earthquake is included in the Box.

Ministry of Health targets for primary health care following the earthquake

Within a few days of the earthquake, the President of Haiti established a National Commission for the Management of the Crisis, which included the Ministry of Health. The Ministry's national priorities included "establishing mobile clinics in all the spontaneous camps that have been created, ensuring obstetric care and delivery kits as close to the population concentrations as possible and ensuring that the delivery of health care services is properly coordinated."

- On 21 January (Day 10), the Ministry of Health further asserted its leadership and distributed guidelines on what should be available at primary and secondary level clinics. NGOs and organizations were asked to provide their comments on the basic package proposed by the Ministry. A special working group on primary care/mobile clinics was meeting twice a week in the Ministry.
- On 25 January (Day 14), the Ministry requested partners to focus their attention on primary health care, health centers, and hospitals. The initial life-saving phase was ending. All health partners in Haiti supported this strategy, at least in principle. In practice, the decision to locate those services

on the premises of existing health facilities was ignored by many NGOs.

- On 2 February (Day 22), the Ministry clarified its vision of post-earthquake care, defining the services and human resources required at the three levels of care (see Table 6.1).
- On 8 February, the Health Cluster reported: "mobile clinics are being deployed in 250 spontaneous settlements as identified by the Government."

Source: Health Cluster Bulletins, January–February 2011.

The focus on primary health care was not limited to the area directly affected by the earthquake but also addressed the needs of the many people who were displaced into other departments. On January the Ministry made this statement: "health facilities in the departments outside of the capital are overwhelmed due to internally displaced persons and they do not have the capacity to treat the number of people arriving". The next day, the Ministry reiterated its message to partners: "encouraging Health Cluster partners to move outside the capital area to provide needed services as well as mid- and long-term commitments for health activities" (Health Cluster Bulletin No. 7). This was an important contribution to the linkage of relief with development.

There was no shortage of plans and strategic documents in the response to the earthquake, but they were not always followed by action. Was this concept of mobile clinics implemented and put into practice?

The Ministry defined the minimum package of services it considered necessary at the primary care level (see Table 6.1). To determine the effectiveness of the mobile clinic strategy, The International Rescue Committee (IRC) commissioned Management Science for Health (MSH) in March 2010 to identify sites where there was still a need for mobile clinics.

Components of care     Human resources

- Treatment of minor wounds   A multidisciplinary team, including:
- Prenatal care, normal deliveries, and post-
- Medical doctor (optional)
- partum care
- Nurses
- Contraception
- Students completing training in the health
- Treatment of childhood illness (diarrhea   sciences and dehydration, fever and nutritional
- Social worker   surveillance)
- Psychologist/Social motivator
- Vaccination program
- Treatment of malnutrition

- Treatment for acute and chronic illness (e.g., asthma, hypertension)
- Reception and immediate transfer of rape victims; record cases with allegations of violence
- Regular treatment for HIV and distribution of ARVs

Note: Translated and adapted from Provision des services dans les camps/zones de regroupement de la population (MSPP 2010e).

A survey of 206 of the largest temporary settlements (out of a list of 400 camps provided by IOM) was carried out from 18 to 29 March to determine the existing coverage and delivery of a minimum package of services (Table 6.2). However, it became clear that none of the clinics (fixed or mobile) serving the camps was offering the full set of services. For the purpose of the survey, the minimum package was redefined to include six services: (1) general consultation, (2) prenatal consultation, (3) pediatric consultation, (4) neonatal care, (5) family planning, (6) vaccination.

The survey results were mixed. Out of the 206 settlements hosting 163,000 families, only 72 had local access to health care, i.e., 35% coverage. Of the 79 health posts, 46% of the structures were mobile clinics.78 Only 10% offered the full minimum package (for all six services as redefined for the survey).

Some of the larger settlements had two health centers/clinics.

Table 6.2 Primary health services offered at 79 health posts surveyed in Haiti, March 2010

| Services provided | Point of health service delivery (%) |
| --- | --- |
| General consultations | 96 |
| Pediatric consultations | 94 |
| Prenatal consultations | 87 |
| Neonatal care | 71 |
| Immunizations | 43 |
| Family planning | 39 |

Source: Management Science for Health (MSH) (2010).

Official targets may not have been reached, but there is a consensus that the level, quality, and proximity of primary health care offered were generally superior to that available to most of the affected population prior to the disaster. There were exceptions: Antenatal care was mostly done without any lab testing;79 too many clinics used donated drugs not in the essential drug list; and foreign health workers at clinics worked with translators and did not properly understand the complaints of the patients. Much more important, mobile clinics were often not linked to existing health facilities. This situation hampered the ability to rebuild the health system and to provide care to people closer to their communities.

How sustained this effort was is another issue. A survey commissioned by the Ministry of Health in July 2010 found that out of 286 institutions/mobile clinics considered for the survey sampling, only

171 could be found or were operational at the time field data were collected (MSPP 2010b).

Free care policy

Provision of care and medicines was free of charge for the duration of the emergency.80 This was an important departure from the government policy of fee-based care, which is promoted by international financial institutions. This policy of free care has been extended de facto for several months, although no official policy document was issued by the Ministry of Health.

Promulgating a free care policy had its down side. The fees were used by public health facilities to recruit additional staff and subsidize some of their services. Without this compensating mechanism, the free care policy was detrimental to government facilities that did not have free drugs and funding for basic supplies and services (cleaning material, paper, Internet and telephone fees). The power generators in facilities were also often paid for with these fees. This worsened the situation of public facilities. Communal health offices that received 5% of benefits were in a difficult position. The long-term implication of free basic services is addressed later in the section on the linkage between relief, rehabilitation, and development (LRRD).

Before the earthquake, hemoglobin and urine tests, and tests for HIV and syphilis were free of charge in many dispensaries.

Interviews suggested that the free availability of medicines did not have an economic effect on the private pharmacies, many of which were impacted directly by the earthquake. Most of the income of private pharmacies comes from the wealthier segment of the population. Some even believe that free access to essential drugs for the poorest sector of the population may create awareness of the value of modern drugs and, therefore, a new market.

Post-trauma rehabilitation

- Rehabilitation must be planned very early.
- A survey and campaign should be initiated in the first few days after impact.

The number of people potentially in need of rehabilitation was high; according to Handicap International estimates "at least 7,500 persons may suffer permanent disabilities if not treated correctly".

The strengths of Haiti in this area at the institutional and legislative levels were considerable. Haiti ratified the UN Convention on the Rights of Persons with Disabilities, a national council for rehabilitation was established (Conseil national pour la réhabilitation des personnes handicapées), and a Secretary of State for the Inclusion of Disabled Persons (SEIPH) was created in 2006, but no implementing legislation had been approved. Following the earthquake, there was a rehabilitation working group with 55 agencies declaring activities or interest in this topic.

Among the obstacles was the "inadequate post-operative care. About 10% of the patients required stump revisions to enable a prosthetic to be fitted."83 The conditions under which initial amputations were performed are frequently cited as the cause of this. A more systemic problem is the lack of data and information on disability prior or after the impact.

Disasters also provide opportunities. The public debate on amputations and the cooperation on spinal cord injury had some positive results leading to an animated but overdue discussion of the issue among professionals.

High visibility of the issue is credited for dramatic public and government support or even reversal of individual attitudes and behavior. With the earthquake, both the poor and privileged suffered from disabling injuries. Persons with disabilities who had been hidden from sight and discriminated against are now more readily accepted. Government institutions have been strengthened, and supportive legislation, in draft form before the impact, is moving toward adoption.

There are several important lessons:

1.  The rapid survey carried out by Handicap International was instrumental in bringing about action on the part of the international community and the national authorities. It is one example of an assessment that carried weight in decision making.

2. Success brings its own set of challenges, and it must be managed. A decade ago, the fitting of prostheses was the domain of a very limited number of agencies (fewer than five) who were accustomed to working together. After the earthquake a reported 38 agencies entered this field in Haiti; not all were competent and well equipped. Patients visited several agencies, were discouraged by unavoidable delays in prosthetic design, or were influenced by rumors about a better provider.

3. The donations from the public or donor agencies must be appropriate for local conditions. Electric wheelchairs, of great assistance in developed countries, are unsuitable for Port-au-Prince where many urban roads require four-wheel drive in normal times and are unfavorable for pedestrians, especially for the disabled.

4. International medical and allied professionals need to be prepared to provide continuity and consistency and rapidly educate local staff (especially in the newly recognized specialty of spinal cord injury). It is also imperative that educators speak the local language to reduce misinterpretation and misinformation.

Communicable diseases control

Health officials, humanitarian agencies, and mass media used to overemphasize the risk of outbreaks following sudden-onset disasters.

Massive outbreaks predicted in the aftermath of past earthquakes have failed to materialize in the last 40 years. Declarations on the inevitability of devastating epidemics often result from ignorance of past history, but there are cases when calculated misinformation has been used to mobilize resources for health activities (this occurred in the response to the tsunami in 2004). Unnecessarily alarming an already traumatized public is counterproductive, and when deliberate, it is unethical.

Over the last two decades other agencies have conducted an educational campaign to demystify the topic of disease outbreaks after disaster and to stimulate a more objective and balanced approach to preventing them. On one side, epidemics remain a strong possibility in the absence of any preventive measures. Risk factors include displacement of populations, contamination of water, overcrowding in settlements, and deteriorating sanitation. Dead bodies are not one of those factors (Watson et al. 2007). On the other side, public health measures are implemented more effectively and efficiently because both the public and authorities have a deep-seated fear of epidemics even when these fears are not exacerbated by humanitarian actors.

Emergency surveillance and early warning systems are the first line of defense against communicable diseases and must be carried out flexibly and rapidly after the impact.

*Jeff Benjamin*

Emergency post-earthquake surveillance

An emergency surveillance system must:

- Start within the first few days of the event;
- Include sentinel stations among medical humanitarian actors;
- Be simple, by focusing on a very limited number of the most critical conditions (syndromes).

A surveillance system should be complemented by an alert system where all partners can directly report abnormal health situations.

No major outbreak was detected after the earthquakes in Haiti and Pakistan or after the tsunami in Indonesia and Sri Lanka.

Before the 12 January earthquake, the surveillance system in Haiti focused on six notifiable diseases: acute hemorrhagic fever, suspected meningococcal meningitis, suspected diphtheria, suspected acute flaccid paralysis, suspected measles, and bites by animals suspected of having rabies.

An improved system was required for the emergency. It had to be better adapted to the needs and concerns in disaster situations, more flexible, and capable of being rapidly analyzed and disseminated.

An ad-hoc international working group agreed on the 25 conditions for which new occurrences must be reported nationwide (see Table 6.4). It is now recognized that the number was too high and included conditions of increasingly marginal relevance as time elapsed (for instance, new amputations or crush syndromes). This is a common result of decisions taken by consensus in committees.

The Dominican Republic established its own surveillance and early warning system in Jimaní and neighboring provinces. Within a few days, the system was in place. The Dominican Republic benefited from a more manageable localized emergency and the full backing of its government, which was unaffected by the earthquake.

Countrywide, 51 sentinel stations were selected from the 94 pre-existing health facilities affiliated with the U.S. President's Emergency Plan for AIDS Relief (PEPFAR). The selected sites were due to report daily by e-mail or telephone on new occurrences of the 25 specified reportable conditions. The level of reporting was variable but generally was low. Daily reporting was too demanding even for facilities not primarily involved in humanitarian response.

Table 6.4 Post-earthquake reportable conditions; Haiti

Infectious diseases    Non-infectious diseases
Non-trauma    Trauma related

- Fever of unknown cause
- Suspected malaria
- Suspected dengue fever
- Acute hemorrhagic fever syndrome
- Acute watery diarrhea
- Acute bloody diarrhea
- Suspected typhoid fever
- Acute respiratory infections
- Suspected measles (fever and rash)
- Tuberculosis
- Tetanus
- Acute malnutrition
- Skin disorder
- Renal failure
- Pregnancy complications or 3rd trimester without previous care
- Mental health or psychological health
- Chronic diseases not accounted for in other conditions
- Other, not specified
- Trauma
- Fracture
- Cerebral concussion from head injury
- Laceration from weapon or dagger injury
- Burns
- Infected wounds
- Crush injury syndrome

- Amputation
- Other, not specified

On 24 April (over three months after the impact), the U.S. Centers for Disease Control and Prevention (CDC) assumed responsibility for analysis of data (Magliore et al. 2010).

Considering the difficult conditions of its inception, the system inevitably had serious defects such as a late start, chronic underreporting, unclear definitions, and limited laboratory support or field supervision for quality control. More important, foreign medical teams and facilities that were providing most of the earthquake related services were not included in the reporting system, which was based on pre-existing, primary level institutions active in AIDS programs.

Nevertheless, the network did provide some basis to rule out any unexpected increase of the notifiable conditions, especially infectious syndromes. Day after day, the system reported that no unexpected or abnormal increase in diseases was detected.

With the lingering concern shared by most actors of possible epidemics and a higher density of medical personnel ever seen by Haiti, the absence of any significant outbreak is worth noting.85

85 A major cholera epidemic started in October 2010. It was unrelated to the earthquake disaster as it started in a department not directly affected by the event. Furthermore, the morbidity/mortality of cholera was lower among the displaced populations attended by humanitarian organizations than in groups not affected by the earthquake. Had the emergence of this unrelated cholera epidemic coincided in time and place with the earthquake response, the myth of inevitable post-disaster epidemics would have been considerably more difficult to dispel.

The three most reported conditions for the period 25 January to 24 April were: acute respiratory diseases (16.3%), suspected malaria (10.3%), and fever of unknown cause (10%) (Magliore et al. 2010). These are common findings in developing countries.

Laboratory support

Strengthening the laboratory was a major success in Haiti.

The limited capacity in public health and clinical laboratory service was severely reduced by the impact. Several agencies partnered with the Haitian Government to restore capacity of the Haiti National Public Health Laboratory. Among them, CDC in collaboration with USAID began sending laboratory supplies including microscopes, rapid diagnostic tests, and other critical equipment and reagents by the end of January. Subject matter experts were also provided for the post-disaster disease surveillance (malaria, typhoid, measles, cholera, dengue, etc.).

Training of the laboratory staff began on 8 February and the National Laboratory test-ed the first dengue sample on 10 February, less than a month after the earthquake hit.

Two months after the impact, the National Laboratory began sending consolidated reports to the Haitian Ministry of Health.

Immunization programs

- In Haiti, the Ministry of Health refrained from endorsing improvised or indiscriminate mass immunization campaigns as had occurred following some other disasters.
- Instead, the Ministry recommended targeted vaccinations of vulnerable groups to meet specific risks. Private actors did not consistently follow these guidelines.

Because a widespread, lethal outbreak is not a reasonable scenario, improvised emergency immunizations programs generally have no place in the immediate aftermath of the disaster. This does not, however, preclude the need for specific and carefully planned immunizations to respond to a specific threat or to take advantage of population displacement to improve routine immunization coverage.

Specific factors required attention in Haiti:

- An increased incidence of tetanus was anticipated due to the high number of injuries (many wounds had not been cleaned and were becoming infected);
- A DPT immunization campaign had been planned for the week of the earthquake in response to an ongoing diphtheria outbreak in Port-au-Prince;
- Finally, the opportunity (and risks) of a large population with very low routine immunization coverage (the lowest in the Region of the Americas) living in temporary settlements served by NGOs or donors.

Tetanus

There are no reliable estimates of the number of post-injury tetanus cases in Haiti. As of 8 February 2010, 16 cases were reported by the surveillance system. Cuban and Dominican medical teams also periodically reported cases.

Tetanus vaccine and serum were available in sufficient amounts in PROMESS, the pharmaceutical warehouse administered by PAHO/ WHO. Surprisingly, many foreign medical teams arriving to treat the injured did not have those essential products available. A campaign was initiated to inform all teams of the need for and availability of vaccine and serum.

Diptheria, pertussis, and tetanus (DPT)

In most countries, DPT is part of the routine child immunization program. In Haiti, it was estimated that 50%-60% of the new cohort (under one year old) was not covered at the time of the earthquake.

Having passed the acute emergency, the Ministry of Health decided to plan a campaign at the end of February (6 weeks after impact) for DPT and measles, mumps, and rubella (MMR). Some major NGOs opposed this move and abstained from collaborating. In addition, logistical problems appeared rapidly in the first cycle (maps of temporary settlements printed in English) followed by vaccine fatigue in the second cycle.

Measles

Although there had been no confirmed cases of measles since 2001, the risk of outbreaks remained present due to low immunization coverage. In 2007 coverage was estimated at only 58% in children under one year old. New cohorts of children were potentially at risk.

In a briefing document prepared for Haiti responders, WHO recommended that all displaced persons between six months and 35 years old who were living in an overcrowded camp be vaccinated against rubella and measles (WHO 2010b). As indicated earlier, a national strategy to improve the coverage in the camps was adopted in February but was not supported by some of the largest NGOs.

No case of measles has been reported since the earthquake.

Water, sanitation, and hygiene (WASH)

- Water and sanitation are rapidly emerging as a major public health priority in all disasters where there are massive displacements of population.
- The Ministry of Health, although often not responsible for the delivery of services, should assume quality control of water and sanitation.

All houses in the metropolitan area were GPS-referenced prior to the earthquake. With the massive displacement of population after the earthquake, this technical prowess was of little use for immunization campaigns.

Water and sanitation is not an issue that is as popular or easily funded as providing medical care to the injured. Media coverage of the topic was modest. Out of 258 health publications listed in a Medline search (May 2011), only one specifically dealt with water and sanitation while almost 50 addressed trauma management. Fortunately, funding and donor support were more even-handed in the response.

Health implications of water, sanitation, and hygiene (WASH) are obvious. In the aftermath of disasters in Haiti prior to 2006, the management of those two public health issues—health care and WASH—was integrated under single national and international leadership for both development and humanitarian response. Recently, following the "Humanitarian Reform" adopted by the United Nations, the emergency management of these two sides of the same coin has been separated at the international level.87 Water and, to a lesser extent, sanitation, were issues frequently debated at Health Cluster meetings.

A remarkable feature of the response in WASH was the early leadership and assertiveness of DINEPA, the Haitian agency responsible for water and sanitation

(Direction Nationale de l'Eau Potable et de l'Assainissement). Unlike many other Haitian institutions such as the Ministry of Health, DINEPA suffered only very limited damage to its offices and management capacity. In addition, DINEPA was already strongly supported by development donors who had allocated specialized support staff (French Cooperation—AFD) and funds (Spanish Cooperation [AECID] and the World Bank) prior to the earthquake.

These donors continued this support to ensure that DINEPA could fulfill its role during the response phase. The Inter-American Development Bank (IDB) was particularly flexible in allowing the immediate reprogramming of development funds for emergency response. DINEPA was in a better position to reclaim its role as coordinator of the international response by assuming the lead of the WASH cluster with support from UNICEF.88 Noteworthy is the fact that within a few weeks of the impact, reports and meetings were mostly in French, facilitating the participation and leadership of a national institution in this process. In other sectors, English remained the only language used throughout the response and recovery.

Water supply

- The Haitian water authority set a positive example by asserting early on its primacy in coordination.
- Pragmatism is required in setting minimum standards for humanitarian response. The "triage" principle of providing services to the largest number of beneficiaries should apply.
- Sources of drinking water in Port-au-Prince were atypical: retail distribution outlets of mostly high quality (and expensive) water. The response primarily involved private, commercial providers.

This split was the result of the new coordination structure (clusters) set by the Humanitarian Reform. In the opinion of a large number of interlocutors, the selection of a clusters structure and "lead agencies" reflected and accommodated the mandates of the UN agencies rather than of the national authorities.

The impact of the 12 January earthquake on water supply in Port-au-Prince was rather atypical. In urban earthquakes, attention normally focuses on the damage to water and sewage pipe systems resulting in a shortage of water and the risk of cross-contamination between both networks. Reports of people breaking into pipes to access water have been common in past disasters.

These were not major issues in Haiti where drinking water distribution was largely based on three systems: an extensive commercial distribution network of high quality water (reverse osmosis and other techniques); the establishment of networks delivering water at collective delivery points (bornes et fontaines) managed by local committees (Comités de l'eau); and water delivered at the house level by networks functioning under the municipal company (CAMEP).

The challenge was therefore to restore these three networks and ensure the availability of drinking water at no cost to the beneficiaries. Four days after the impact it was estimated that the commercial sector was in the position to produce 1 million gallons of water per day. The challenge was how to distribute it. The commercial sector played a major role in this distribution, first spontaneously then later as contractors who were funded or subsidized by DINEPA and many humanitarian organizations.

On the operational level, the water response was pragmatic with the objective of providing as many people as possible with a bare minimum of water. Although all interviewees in Haiti were aware of the "minimum humanitarian standards" established by the Sphere Project (2011) (for example, 15 liters/person/day), none spontaneously mentioned them in our interviews. Instead, they focused on slowly raising the initial amount of drinking water to be made available to all (from 3 liters to 5 liters of drinking water) over a matter of weeks and months.

This approach is a considerable improvement on the frequent misuse of Sphere standards by donors as compulsory, quantified goals to be achieved under risk of penalty. This was observed in other disasters (natural or human-caused) where agencies opted to limit the number of their beneficiaries receiving an unrealistically high "minimum" standard or requirement in order to avoid criticism by evaluators or donors for not being in compliance. This was in fact exactly the contrary of the triage principle: the best benefit for the greatest number.

As reported in the Health Cluster Bulletin (No. 20) nearly five weeks after the impact:

"The WASH Cluster continues to provide safe drinking water (5 liters per person per day) to over 780,000 people through water tankers and water treatment plants at 300 sites across Port-au-Prince, Léogâne, and Jacmel. The Cluster aims to scale up provision of safe drinking water to a total of 1.1 million persons per day. Approximately

2.1 million liters of water are delivered per day to about 500,000 displaced persons in 184 sites."

Twelve months after the earthquake, there was still a large amount of water being delivered to camps and sites with dozens of bladders being used every day, underlining the difficulties of finding solutions "beyond water trucks". Provision of safe water in Haiti is a never-ending humanitarian task.

Environmental health in temporary settlements

New approaches are needed for excreta and waste management in temporary settlements in dense urban areas.

Sanitation and hygiene (waste disposal, human excreta, etc.) often fall outside the responsibility of the Ministry of Health, but are nevertheless critical for public health. On 28 January (Day 17), the WASH Cluster shifted its priority from water to sanitation: a change reflecting the relative progress in provision of water and the lingering fear of possible outbreaks in overcrowded settlements without even rudimentary sanitation. Rapidly, the provision of latrines rather than the distribution of water became the preeminent priority and challenge.

Sanitation conditions in Haiti including in the capital were very poor prior to the earthquake. Normal overcrowding in Port-au-Prince is such that few open spaces (parks, squares, green spaces, etc.) exist. After the quake they were quickly packed with displaced populations. In an urban environment, installing traditional latrines (trenches, for instance) at a safe distance from tents and shelters was not possible. During the first three months, more than 3,000 portable latrines (chemical or not) were installed by NGOs in targeted camps in metropolitan areas. The major challenges were to find unoccupied spaces where they could be positioned, and to organize an ongoing system of collection and disposal of urban excreta. This was not solved during the period under review (Grünewald, Binder, Georges 2010).

The objective of waste disposal has largely benefitted the commercial sector. It was only partially met in part due to lengthy difficulties with customs clearance and the registration of UNICEF trucks.

Despite efforts to install latrines, progress was slow 30 days after impact:

"Sanitation continues to be a major challenge of utmost concern. It is currently estimated that less than 5% of the needs for latrines is being met (one latrine per 50 people). This poses huge challenges for public health in temporary settlement sites."

This challenge was, however, alleviated by a progressive reduction in the number of families in temporary settlements. However, for many of those interviewed, it appears that the services provided by the international community were ultimately better than those available to the general population, although far short of the "minimum" standard of one latrine for 20 people as set internationally.

Reported in the Health Cluster Bulletin No. 18. The figure of one latrine for 50 persons was seen as too optimistic by some interviewees who believed that the number of users actually was around 200 per latrine for at least three months.

See the Sphere Project standards for excreta disposal at: www.sphereproject.org/content/view/43/83/lang,english.

Environmental health in medical facilities

Medical and hospital waste is a major problem in all disasters. It is a costly issue that must be addressed early on.

The need for safe water in hospitals (existing or new facilities) was brought to the attention of decision makers at a very early stage. Coordination between DINEPA and the Ministry of Health as well as quality control by PAHO/WHO-trained personnel ensured that this problem was addressed beginning one week after the impact.

The provision of medical care by thousands of health professionals or volunteers created a significant need for safe disposal of human as well as medical waste (dressings, syringes, needles, expired drugs, etc.). The Swedish Civil Contingency Agency (March 2010) estimated that 15%–20% of health care waste was hazardous or infectious (including discarded human tissues or limbs).

The need for "a clear strategy for dealing with health care waste" was identified as a priority from Day 6 and remained so for weeks. On Day 13, a system was launched to collect medical wastes and dispose of them in a landfill. Progress was noted in the main hospitals but the issue lingered due to the carelessness of some independent teams or facilities.

Lack of prior planning for safe disposal of medical waste is a recurrent problem in disasters and need not be rediscovered by humanitarian organizations in each emergency situation.

Food and nutrition

No widespread malnutrition was noted in Haiti or in other disaster-affected countries. This may be due in part to the massive food distribution and strengthening of nutritional activities but also to the fact that earthquakes do not affect food availability at the national level. The issue was one of lost income that might be addressed by direct financial assistance to households.

Prior publications from PAHO/WHO on natural disasters outlined that the impact of earthquakes on food supply and malnutrition is distinct from that of hydrological disasters such as floods, hurricanes, or drought. Earthquakes do not directly affect crops or food stocks at the national level. They may have an indirect and delayed impact on nutritional levels by reducing the access of some of the affected population to existing stocks because of lost income or logistical problems.

Haiti was not an exception. Food stores and markets were closed only temporarily (1–2 weeks at most). Food and basic supplies were rapidly available provided one could afford them. Prices increased but not to the point of affecting those lucky enough to have maintained their business and income. The destruction of the harbor in Port-au-Prince and other logistical challenges (blocked roads) were only temporary, aggravating problems affecting both the humanitarian and commercial flow of goods.

The most important impact from a nutritional point of view is the fact that an already inadequate access to a proper diet for those economically most vulnerable was drastically reduced by the loss of their means of survival. Loss of meager livelihoods was only partially compensated by the sharp increase in remittances from abroad, and 89% of the recipients used those remittances before the earthquake to procure food. Some donors and experts suggested early after the impact that if the primary cause was a loss of income, cash assistance should partly replace the importation and distribution of food after the initial emergency response (WFP 2010).

Prior to the earthquake, the "cluster" structure was seen as very peculiar (Binder and Grünewald 2010): nutrition, food aid, and food security after sudden-onset disasters were considered distinct, albeit related, issues that are coordinated separately. The Nutrition Cluster under UNICEF, the Food Aid Cluster under WFP, and Food Security Cluster under FAO were three different and disconnected entities. Yet prevention of acute malnutrition in the aftermath of a geological disaster, the end result of food insecurity, is mostly beyond the responsibility of the health sector.

The re-activation of the Nutrition Cluster offered UNICEF an opportunity to strengthen the capacity of its counterpart in the Ministry of Health by providing an instrument to exercise leadership over humanitarian actors. The priorities as established by the Nutrition Cluster, which convened on 20 January (Day 9), included:

- Protection and support for women who are breastfeeding;
- Monitoring breast-milk substitutes and other milk products coming into the country;
- Monitoring the provision of breast-milk substitutes and other milk products;
- Complementary feeding of children above six months old;
- Treatment of global acute malnutrition.

Between 40 and 50 agencies participated in the meetings of the Nutrition Cluster. Only 25 of them had professional nutritional expertise while some 15 were regarded as "amateurs, without any idea of the nutritional value of food." Rapidly, the nutritional offers and requests were critically reviewed and filtered, ultimately focusing more on therapeutic products. The department of the Ministry dealing with nutrition was the only one that had updated guidelines in an electronic version, which were generally respected by all partners. However, specific guidelines on breast milk substitutes were often violated.

The Food Aid Cluster, led by the World Food Programme, focused in February on supplementary feeding of children (6–59 months) and pregnant or lactating women in temporary shelters in Port-au-Prince. The program was based on distribution of high-energy biscuits or ready-to-use foods to 88,000 beneficiaries. In March 2010, the supplementary feeding program was extended to the same vulnerable groups in departmental urban areas having received large numbers of internally displaced. At the same time, the biscuits and ready-to-use food were progressively and partly substituted with the usual WFP supplementary ration made of corn-soya blend (CSB), oil, and sugar (WFP 2010).

The normal activities of prevention and treatment of acute malnutrition within the Ministry of Health with UNICEF, which were inadequate prior to the impact, were resumed in March (6 weeks after impact).

General food distribution was of a much greater scope than targeted nutritional programs. At the peak of activity, food was reportedly distributed to over 4 million beneficiaries. It should be noted that the PDNA estimated the affected population at 1.5 million. According to a WFP external evaluation, "political factors influenced the input and stance the Haitian government took with respect to program implementation, including the phasing out of general food distribution to more targeted safety net activities" (WFP 2011).

Other experts are of the view that the large-scale food aid was largely a response pushed by some governments, and by and large terminated on time in order to avoid negative effects. Some donors interviewed also mentioned their only partly successful efforts to promote greater cash-based programs (not merely the traditional cash- or voucherfor-work but also direct, un-earmarked cash allocations). Yet, as recommended by some studies, many aid actors finally moved away from food-based and engaged in cash-based relief activities, especially cash-for-work programs (e.g., removing debris and improving the urban environment and sanitation).

The provision of milk products was also a point of interest. The unsupervised donation of powdered milk is strongly discouraged in the aftermath of sudden-impact disasters. Its use outside well-managed programs is often unsanitary and a potential cause of diarrhea. The quality of water being a special concern in Haiti, it was necessary to repeatedly remind NGOs and health care providers not to distribute powdered milk. Success was only partial.

In conclusion, further surveys indicated that malnutrition did not increase as a result of the earthquake. Considering the scale of food distribution and supplementary feeding, this outcome was to be expected. More than that, the flow of remittances from the diaspora increased significantly thus increas-ing the purchasing power of the affected populations and their access to food. Food markets became very active in a few weeks time and the flow of products from rural areas to affected urban zones increased rapidly. There are no data available regarding the cost-effectiveness or the possible negative

impacts (for example, on local food production and markets, dependency, etc.) of the massive distribution of food compared to other measures. Whether financial assistance to households would not have been more effective from the point of view of nutrition and well-being has not been sufficiently debated in the case of Haiti. It definitely would have helped to maintain the sense of dignity and pride that is so important to Haitian culture.

Instead, ready-to-drink tins were provided, contributing to the tons of waste produced daily and clogging most of the drainage system in Port-au-Prince.

Mental health and psychosocial assistance

- Needs for psychosocial assistance should not be overlooked on the assumption that poor communities are more resilient.

- The psychosocial field is currently attracting too many emergency actors who may not have the necessary expertise and resources.

- Specialized programs in the aftermath of sudden-onset disasters should serve as the point of entry for the provision of mental health services at primary health care and community levels.

In past sudden-onset disasters, the mental health impact on the affected population has been the subject of debate, leading to diverse interventions. These range from the dispatch of unprepared young social workers from Western urban areas into the conservative Islamic, rural environment of Bam (Iran) to the excessive medicaliza tion of an otherwise common reaction in the aftermath of a sudden disaster.

- Aid agencies outside the health sector tend to speak of "supporting psychosocial well-being". Health sector agencies tend to speak of "mental health". Exact definitions of these terms vary between and within aid organizations, disciplines and countries.

- Mental health and psychosocial problems in emergencies are highly interconnected yet may be predominantly social or psychological in nature (rather than medical).

- Significant problems of a predominantly social nature include:

- Pre-existing (pre-emergency) social problems (e.g., extreme poverty);
- Emergency-induced social problems (e.g., family separation; disruption of social networks; destruction of community structures, resources, and trust; increased gender-based violence); and
- Aid-induced social problems (e.g., undermining of community structures or traditional support mechanisms).
- Similarly, problems of a predominantly psychological nature include:
- Pre-existing problems (e.g., severe mental disorder; alcohol abuse);
- Emergency-induced problems (e.g., grief, non-pathological distress, depression and anxiety disorders, including post-traumatic stress disorder [PTSD]); and
- Aid-related problems (e.g., anxiety due to a lack of information).

Psychosocial support to relief workers, an important topic, is not addressed in this section.

A survey conducted six months after the tsunami in Sri Lanka found that 56% of the internally displaced population suffered from post-traumatic stress disorder (PTSD). In other words, more than half of the population was suffering from a pathological disorder (Wickrama 2008).

The key point of the WHO/IASC guidelines is that "mental health and psychosocial problems in emergencies encompass far more than the experience of PTSD." This point was well understood by the Sri Lankan authorities who recommended "listening to victims [of the tsunami] without offering opinions and not diagnosing or labeling people as suffering from post-traumatic stress disorder" (Mahoney et al. 2006).

Disasters are highly emotional events. The State of Minnesota handbook on disaster recovery offers a layman's description of the various phases in the affected population's reaction to disasters. It is noteworthy that this scenario can be applicable to most cultures.

| Phase | Usual length of time | Actions | Emotions |
|---|---|---|---|
| Heroic phase | Prior to impact and up to a week after- wards | Struggle to prevent loss of lives and minimize property damage | Fear, anxiety, stunned |
| Honeymoon phase | Two weeks to two months | Relief efforts lift spirits of survivors; hopes of quick recovery run high; optimism is often short-lived | Euphoria at being alive, grateful, grief, disbelief |

| | | | |
|---|---|---|---|
| Disillusionment phase | Several months to over a year | The realities of bureau- cratic paperwork and recovery delays set in; outside help leaves; survivors realize they have lots to do themselves and their lives many never be the same | Frustration, depression, self-doubt, loss/grief, isolation |
| Reconstruction phase | Several years | Normal functioning is gradually reestablished | Satisfaction with progress; emotions appropriate to current events |

Source: Minnesota Department of Public Safety (n.d.) Recovery from disaster handbook

Mental health interventions in Haiti

There is a lack of quantified or objective information regarding the importance of the mental health impact on the affected Haitian population.

Mental health was not an orphan topic in the Haiti earthquake response; it had sev-eral parents. Immediately after the earthquake, meetings of a Cross-Cluster Working

Abaakouk provided insight into mental health care services available prior to and following impact in Haiti. Mental Health and Psychosocial Support were convened first by UNICEF and later by IOM to assist in coordinating the many organizations present in the field. The Ministry of Health, with WHO support, also led a Mental Health Working Group with selected actors (mainly psychological and psychiatric service providers) that focused on specific strategic issues related to the mental health model for intervention at the national level. This included: essential psychotropic drug list, mental health protocols, mental health data collection, drafting a plan for training health and mental health professionals, etc.

In order to guide the initial response, WHO provided some tentative projections or estimates of what might be expected in the aftermath of disasters:

- "The percentage of people with a severe mental disorder (e.g., psychosis and severely disabling presentations of mood and anxiety disorders) increases by 1 per cent over and above an estimated baseline of 2–3 per cent.
- "In addition, the percentage of people with mild or moderate mental disorders, including most presentations of mood and anxiety disorders (such as post-traumatic stress disorder, or PTSD), may increase by 5–10 per cent above an estimated baseline of 10 per cent.

- "In most situations natural recovery over time (i.e., healing without outside intervention) will occur for many—but not all—survivors with mild and moderate disorders" (WHO/ IASC 2007,123).

No attempt was apparently made to validate those figures in the context of Haiti, a country showing extraordinary resilience over the years but also submitted to a considerable shock (the earthquake, the mass casualties, the amputations, the management of dead bodies, and the side effects of an international response not always addressing the perceived priorities). Resiliency, a survival trait, does not reduce the emotional stress and need for psychosocial support.

The extent of the mental health response is better documented. In addition to local human resources, additional assistance poured into Haiti. Among them were 10 psychiatrists, 4 psychologists, professionals from the Cuban Medical Brigade working at the community level, three mental health trainers from International Medical Corps, experts and clinical practitioners from the major medical NGOs (MSF, Médecins du Monde) as well as from many Red Cross societies.

Yves Lecomte (2010) gave the following account:

"According to a census conducted by the Working Group of the Ministry of Health, there would be 100 NGOs working in mental health, or 1% of the NGOs currently active. Seventeen intervention methods are available, [including]: psychological as individual counseling, group psychotherapy, medication, social issues advocacy, skills development, vocational training, social support, etc."

More than 110 organizations provided mental health services

Such a proliferation of actors is not always in the best interest of the affected population. Not all responders were as professional or effective as should be expected. The first priority in humanitarian assistance is "do no harm." External mental health and psychosocial support is an important means of helping people affected by emergencies but has the potential to cause harm because it deals with highly sensitive, cultural issues.

Lecomte expressed reservations regarding the nature of some of this assistance:

"Despite the fact that since the seventies, it is said that mental health is not a priority of the State and that 'Haiti does not support the mentally ill,' everybody has been doing mental health since 12 January 2010. In fact, some say, 'Haiti was invaded by a disparate variety of mental health experts who are neither doctors, psychiatrists, nor psychologists.'. . . Many do not speak French or Creole. Suddenly, mental health in Haiti has become a coveted item internationally."

On the positive side, the same author noted that "many international organizations intervened in the camps and hospitals and provided training for mental health practitioners."

Those mixed findings were also observed in the aftermath of major disasters attracting considerable assistance and funding (earthquakes in Bam, Iran, in 2003, Pakistan in 2005, and the Indian Ocean tsunami in 2004).

In spite of those occasional excesses, the response has produced significant changes in Haiti's approach to mental health.

Response in Haiti

Establish one overall coordination group on mental health and psychosocial support

Two parallel processes: one managed by the UN and one by the Ministry of Health. Priority should have been given to strengthen the leadership of the Ministry.

Pay attention to gender differences    Appears to be a concern attended by most the actors.

Learn about local cultural practices and use a mix of local and external methods as appropriate    WHO published a literature review on this topic early on. A genuine local approach and strategy was a priority of the working group established by the Ministry of Health.

Build government capacities and integrate mental health care for survivors in general health services International NGOs and actors stressed capacity building and training. The strategy developed by the Ministry of Health working group focuses on decentralization and integration of mental health in health services (away from specialized psychiatric hospitals). Mass media gave visibility to this approach.

Integrate psychosocial considerations into all sectors of humanitarian assistance. The meetings organized by UNICEF and later by IOM included thematic sessions on education, children, religion, etc.

Response in Haiti

Do not conduct duplicate assessments' or accept preliminary data in an uncritical manner   A weak point as no quantified and objective assessment was available. Lack of clear criteria on the mental health needs and more pressing, competing issues may explain this shortcoming.

Do not assume that everyone is traumatized, or that people who appear resilient need no support   The services of many seasoned agencies appeared to be tailor-made for the needs of the population.

No excessive medicalization and use of PTSD definitions were noted. Emphasis was on psychosocial assistance and community approaches.

Do not use a charity model that treats people in the community mainly as beneficiaries of services    From interviews, the response has contributed to problems of dependency and frustration among "beneficiaries." The self-centered institutional focus of many actors is claimed to have contributed negatively.

Do not provide psychotropic medication without training and supervision    Except for occasional unconfirmed or undocumented observations, use of medication was limited and believed to be under supervision.

Do not institutionalize people unless institutionalization is a temporary and indisputably last resort    A major achievement was the shift from an institutionalization-based approach prior to the disaster to a community and health services focus.

"Ultimately, international experts are encouraging the Haitian Health Ministry, which they say is receptive and eager for help, to incorporate mental health care into the primary health care system and to make it available throughout the country."

All information clearly points toward a significant improvement in the approach and priority given by the Ministry of Health to a long neglected issue in Haiti. A window of opportunity has been used.

## Reproductive health /gender-based violence

Reproductive health emergencies should be attended from the early days of response.

While trauma care may be the dominant and most visible concern in the immediate aftermath of an earthquake, deliveries and obstetrical emergencies continue to occur and require uninterrupted attention to save lives. Increases in gender-based violence are also routinely reported in the aftermath of most disasters. Attention to these particularly vulnerable groups is critical.

## Reproductive health care

The rate of deliveries often increases temporarily in the first days and weeks after a sudden-impact disaster (one might speculate that this is the result of stress). Although no data are available on the number of deliveries, informal reports tend to confirm this observation in Haiti. Similarly, the number of pregnancies after the impact often increases. This was noted in a survey in temporary settlements conducted by the Ministry of Health.

The reported rate of pregnancy in a post-earthquake study was 12%.98 Prior to the earthquake, this rate was 6% nationally (4% in urban areas and 8% in rural areas) (MSPP 2006). The very high rate observed in the camps may reflect increased promiscuity in these settlements, increased incidence of unprotected sex in a context of disruption, and/or inadequate supply of family planning services. The desire for pregnancy or having a child could also be explained by psychological reasons, as is often observed after major disasters (MSPP 2010b).

Within days after the impact, the groups specializing in reproductive health intensified their efforts to ensure proper attention was given to women's health. This was in a context dominated by the dispatch of military trauma field hospitals or polemics on amputations and crush syndromes.

Within one week, the Reproductive Health Response in Crises Consortium (RHRC) urged responders "to establish services to treat pregnancy complications, including emergency C-section, to provide immediate access to clinical care for survivors of sexual violence, to resume HIV prevention, as well as to reestablish the usual family planning methods."99

A reproductive health working group was set up in Port-au-Prince to address these issues and a Minimum Initial Service Package for

Reproductive Health was promoted through the timely distribution of emergency kits by UNFPA.

A sample size of 2,391 women, 15 to 49 years old was used in this study.

The Reproductive Health Response in Crises (RHRC) Consortium consists of seven members: American Refugee Committee (ARC), CARE, Columbia University, International Rescue Committee (IRC), John Snow Research and Training Institute (JSI), Marie Stopes International (MSI) and Women's Refugee Commission.

A survey of 171 clinics100 serving temporary settlements in July 2010 suggests that five months after the impact, there were still significant deficits in terms of the range of services (minimum package) provided. According to the authors of the survey, the deficits observed were probably related to the disorganization of health care services and non-adherence to standards set by the Ministry of Health regarding the minimum package of services. In addition, the survey authors note that lack of availability of certain services for obstetric and neonatal emergencies and sexual health may be due to the specialized nature of these interventions (MSPP 2010b).

The same survey confirmed that access to reproductive health care although not yet meeting minimum standards had improved considerably in the temporary settlements compared to the situation prior to the earthquake.

Gender-based violence

- Increased gender-based violence is routinely reported after most disasters. Although the problem was better documented after the Haiti earthquake, the lack of quantified evidence about this issue should be addressed.
- A cross-sectoral strategy to address this chronically overlooked issue must be developed and implemented under the leadership of the Ministry of Health.

In addition to the need for urgent restoration of normal reproductive health services, an "epidemic of gender-based violence" was reported in the media and in technical reports.

How significant and evidence-based this post-earthquake outbreak of gender-based violence was is unclear.101 Amnesty International (2010) observed: "Protection mechanisms for women and girl victims of sexual violence were deficient before the earthquake, now they are totally absent. This is a major cause for under-reporting." The report provides numerous observations of tragic cases, but it lacks quantified evidence.

Sexual violence is a much more difficult or elusive issue to document than amputations or communicable diseases, but lack of statistics is no reason for inaction. In Haiti, the magnitude of the problem before and after the earthquake prompted a large array of initiatives from provision of specialized medical care, increased policing of the camps by the UN and National Police, to the adoption of protective measures such as the installation of 200 durable streetlights in 40 of the camps.

In March 2010, the Ministry of Health launched a national program for attention to the victims of sexual violence. According to interviews, the protocol proposed by the Ministry met with resistance from some NGOs who were unwilling to change their own protocol and response kits, insisting instead that the national program be amended to adopt their approach.

100 In the survey conducted by the Ministry of Health (MSPP 2010b), 171 institutions were visited in the 12 municipalities affected by the earthquake to assess the provision of care and services. Of these, 86 were functioning inside the temporary settlements and 85 outside. The facilities were providing general health care, and not exclusively reproductive health.

101 The household survey carried out by the University of Michigan (Kolbe et al. 2010) estimated that "in the six weeks after the earthquake, 10,813 people (95% confidence interval, 6,726–14,900)

were sexually assaulted, the vast majority of whom were female. In the same period 4,645 individuals (95% confidence interval 1,943–7,347) were physically assaulted."

There are valuable lessons to be learned from the efforts to respond to or prevent sexual violence in the aftermath of the earthquake.

- As noted after the tsunami, it is impossible to find out whether gender-based violence has actually increased (Felten-Biermann 2006). It does not, however, mean that it does not exist.
- A national strategy, whether for gender-based violence or other public health priorities, cannot be implemented unless all health actors, foreign or national, accept the technical leadership of the health authorities.

As is the case for other neglected problems, the high visibility of the response and funding available has shed light on ongoing deficiencies and put into motion a reform process. This reform most likely will benefit future victims of gender-based violence in Haiti.

Supplies

- Inappropriate health donations is a serious issue in all large disasters; however, this occurred to a lesser extent in the case of Haiti.

- The existence of a central pharmaceutical warehouse managed by PAHO/WHO has been an asset unmatched in other disaster-affected countries.

How did the Haiti response compare to recent global disasters in terms of incoming health supplies and procurement capacity?

Haiti response faced logistics problems similar to those in other major humanitarian deployments in the past:

- The amount of incoming supplies (and personnel) increased rapidly over the first weeks.
- Transport into Haiti was a major limiting factor. The management of the airport in Port-au-Prince and the control of Haitian air space were rapidly assumed by the U.S. military which had its own set of security and bilateral priorities, distinct from those of the humanitarian civilian community. Critically needed medical equipment, including some field hospitals and health teams, were rerouted through Santo Domingo in the Dominican Republic.
- Transport within Haiti was complicated by the destruction, rubble in the roads, and the lack of vehicles to accommodate the surge of experts and other personnel arriving in increasing numbers. The considerable transport assets of MINUSTAH were not made available to the humanitarian community or even to UN agencies until the Security Council adopted a

resolution mandating MINUSTAH to assist in this regard (Day 7).

UN Security Council Resolution 1908 was adopted on 19 January 2010 to "increase the overall force levels of MINUSTAH to support the immediate recovery, reconstruction and stability efforts".

PROMESS distributed essential medicines and supplies to hospitals and international and local NGOs.

The lack of medical supplies rapidly became a major obstacle in the treatment of the injured. The items missing were the same reported in short supply in any earthquake: dressings, gauze, disinfectant, suture material, casting supplies, and X-ray film. Standard emergency kits (including trauma kits) were rapidly made available, but according to several interlocutors they did not adequately satisfy the most common shortages in the aftermath of a massive earthquake.

One item in short supply not often mentioned in other disasters was external bone fixators. The demand for this orthopedic equipment was unexpectedly high as conditions for the use of the internal fixators (surgical skills and sterile environment) were rarely met in the first weeks. PROMESS (see below) could not meet demand for this unusual item (unusual in the sense that it is not part of the "normal" list of essential articles).103 Stockpiling this item globally seems to be the only practical approach.

PROMESS

PROMESS, the central health procurement system managed was an unusual but invaluable international asset in the first weeks. PROMESS facilities had not suffered critical damage. Its stock had just been replenished at the end of 2009 and its personnel were serving not only in public institutions but also in eligible nonprofit facilities or organizations. This efficient and well-tuned mechanism was in place for support to all humanitarian health actors. However, local public health offices that were running out of stocks were not universally aware of this service.

With the urgent and large demand for external fixators, PROMESS placed an order for 2,000 units. The amount was not excessive considering the number of fractures. However, the procurement system (centralized in PAHO/WHO HQ) was unfamiliar with sources for this specialized item, which is not routinely in stock at the usual suppliers. Ultimately, 50 units were delivered but they arrived far too late.

In the immediate aftermath of the earthquake, PROMESS saw an average of 30 clients per day, such as public hospitals and international and local NGOs. During the first 45 days, PROMESS distributed more than 345,000 boxes of essential medicines and supplies, including antibiotics, vaccines, drugs for mental health conditions, drugs for treatment of TB, diabetes and malaria, and anesthetics. In March,

100 mobile clinic kits were distributed in all priority areas. In early April, the Ministry of Health extended free access to medicines until 12 July 2010 and PROMESS continued to partner with the Ministry for the distribution of health packages to most mobile clinics, public hospitals, and NGOs.

Several factors limiting the effectiveness of PROMESS were addressed with the support of the U.S. Government:

- Repair of walls surrounding the facility and improved security;
- Updating the inventory of supplies;
- Organizing the chain of distribution to accommodate the increased number of clients and the urgency of the deliveries;
- Creating access to and space for storage areas by clearing rubble. Drug donations

According to responses to specific questions during interviews and the review of technical reports, there is general consensus that the quality of drug donations has improved. WHO guidelines on donations of pharmaceuticals (WHO 1999) appear to have been followed more systematically than in past disasters or in other regions. Progress, however, does not mean satisfactory performance. On Day 15, as noted in the Health Cluster Bulletin (No. 8), "The majority of medicines arriving into Haiti are well classified; however, there are still a lot of medicines without labels, expired or arriving as assortments, thus hampering distribution."

Although PROMESS required detailed information (listing, expiration date, analysis certificate) before accepting donations, rejected supplies usually found another point of entry. The department for regulatory authority of pharmaceuticals in the Ministry of Health remained too weak to veto unsolicited and inappropriate donations. This office did not receive support from the international community.

Inappropriate donations were usually from new humanitarian actors (groups with no prior experience) or new donor countries, including from the Americas. Overall, traditional donors and established bilateral agencies seem to have exercised stronger leadership in controlling the quality of donations from their countries and constituents.

Linkage with early recovery and development

- It is never too early to initiate recovery and "build back better" in the health sector.
- Disasters offer opportunities for change, however incremental they may be. Some are being used in Haiti.

In this section, the outlook will project beyond the initial three-month period. It will attempt to determine the impact of the early response on the recovery and reconstruction process in Haiti.

Initial relief activities have a justification and dynamic of their own. Designed to save lives, they can truly do so or also evolve into development-like activities. They may be carried out in a manner that either prepares the ground for, and blends into recovery and reconstruction processes, or that complicates that process.

Early recovery represents the undefined border or transition between emergency relief and reconstruction. Whether it is an extended humanitarian function or an initial step toward post-impact development is a matter both of perspective and origin of funding: that is, humanitarian/emergency or development (World Bank 2008, 31–32).

Over the last decade, development actors have become more proactive and rapid in triggering the reconstruction process, overlapping in time with the immediate response. The economic valuation of damage developed by the Economic Commission for Latin America and the Caribbean (ECLAC) used to be launched more than a month after impact; it is now promoted within a few weeks. In Indonesia, the international financial institutions initiated economic assessment within three weeks, involving a large number of experts supported by recent local graduates. There were more experts compiling, scrutinizing, and validating financial and cost data from all sources than were employed to gather and compile response intelligence. A similar effort was launched in Sri Lanka and Pakistan.

In Haiti, the same approach resulted in early planning for a Post-Disaster Needs Assessment (PDNA). Twenty years ago, early recovery and reconstruction were an afterthought once relief was near completion; in Haiti it was pushed to early in the agenda. On 19 January (Day 7) the Early Recovery Cluster was activated in Haiti.

The two processes (response and reconstruction) may run independently or be closely linked together. The linkage between relief, rehabilitation, and development (LRRD) was a feature present in this emergency. This linkage is an asset for agencies with both a strong development mandate and an emergency response capacity.

There were strengths as well as shortcomings in this linkage. Success stories in LRRD

Reconstruction, which is development, is meeting considerable obstacles in Haiti. The most brilliant schemes cannot succeed without some modicum of efficient government with authority regarding its partners.

While most "ambitious new ideas" articulated by the PDNA process have not been implemented, the seeds of many incremental thematic changes have been planted in Haiti. Preexisting but dormant initiatives for change were reactivated, promoted, and in some cases funded. Progress in some initiatives may not last but others will change public health in Haiti. The initial successes are listed below. Most have been discussed earlier. None is revolutionary, but development is always incremental.

- Free access to primary health care— the SIG and the SOG: Before the impact of the earthquake, modest efforts were under way by WHO to conclude compensation agreements with individual non-profit institutions willing to provide free obstetric care (Soins Obstétricaux Gratuits, or SOG) (WHO 2010d). It was a strong departure from a rigidly enforced, albeit poorly controlled user-fee policy on which local health facilities became dependent for most of their operations. The SOG program was made operational again after February 2010 with a simplified activity reporting mechanism. It not only continued to provide free-of-charge obstetric care to pregnant women right after the earthquake, but during 2010 it expanded the content of the health package, becoming the SOG-2 in July 2010. Sixty-three health institutions are currently providing services under the program all over the country. As a result, the number of institutional deliveries has increased from an average of 2,953 per month in 2007 to an estimated 6,828 per month in 2010 in participating institutions (PAHO/WHO 2011a).104

The SIG program (Soins Infantiles Gratuits) provides free care for children under age 5 thanks to a financial agreement with public and private hospitals similar to that of the SOG. It was launched and implemented after the earthquake in order to ease the financial difficulties being experienced by both the general population and the health facilities. Twenty-seven of the largest hospitals in the country engaged in SIG between July and November 2010. During this time more than 15,000 children beyond the base line numbers had the opportunity to access quality care with dignity.

The temporary support for these programs from humanitarian funding was substituted by a development grant ensuring the sustainability of free access to care for those groups.105

- Mental health: As discussed above, a new community-based approach is complementing the traditional third level hospital-based care of mental health. This represents a change of attitude and approach which is likely to last.
- Rehabilitation and acceptance of disabilities: The earthquake also induced a significant change of perception and policies regarding disabilities in Haiti. It is a profound and permanent modification of public behavior. Institutional changes will follow.
- Awareness of gender-based violence: The emergency provided an opportunity for the Ministry of Health to develop a strategy, albeit still under debate, to provide standardized care for victims of gender-based violence. It has shed light on this long-standing problem that has largely been overlooked.

- Communicable diseases surveillance and control: The establishment of a surveillance system based on 51 sentinel stations is a first for Haiti. Although late and fraught with serious quality issues, this experience has reinforced the Epidemiology Department of the Ministry of Health. The importance of further strengthening this department was demonstrated in the cholera outbreak late in 2010.

104 Some NGOs, as a matter of internal policy, were delivering free care without formally adhering to the SOG.

105 On a more international scale, the SIG and SOG programs contributed to the IASC Global Health Cluster position recommending removal of user fees for primary health care during humanitarian crises. See IASC (2010b).

- Water services: DINEPA, a relatively strong institution responsible for water distribution in Haiti, has emerged stronger from the disaster response. The quality of services offered to internally displaced populations (IDPs) by international partners exceeded that available in non-affected areas. The long-term benefit has been shown again during the subsequent cholera outbreak. Morbidity and mortality rates in temporary settlements were considerably lower in the IDP settlements.

- Nutrition: According to UNICEF, the emergency gave nutrition issues higher priority at the Ministry of Health and provided opportunities to strengthen programs at the department level.

- Decentralization of management and services: The response to the emergency contributed to revitalizing the trend toward decentralization of services to departments and the community level. The central level may have been weakened by the international response, but the local level has probably benefitted in terms of visibility and direct access to the international community. This has led to a renewal of the debate at the national level.

- Reduction of vulnerability to earthquakes: As is common after major earthquakes, awareness and commitment to disaster risk reduction increased considerably.

The new health facilities (repaired or reconstructed) will comply with safety norms in the process of review. A joint World Bank and PAHO/WHO project will promote and monitor the development of guidelines and the implementation of the concept of safe hospitals as part of the reconstruction process.

In Haiti, the tragedy offered an impetus for incremental change in the medium-term. Shortcomings in LRRD

Several aspects of the response in the first months were not supportive of a successful and rapid recovery. The most noticeable were the lack of NGO support to Ministry of Health strategic and policy initiatives, the practice of "poaching" human resources, the closure of a private for-profit hospital, and the weakening of the role and potential leadership of national institutions.

- The Ministry of Health had little leverage over the immediate response by NGOs and other actors. It focused pragmatically on recovery planning. Strategies and norms were developed only to be ignored or in some instances contradicted by NGOs that were supposed to be implementers. While reconstruction and development cannot be dictated by overly detailed planning at the central level, neither can it come about when there is systematic disregard of the technical norms and standards provided by line ministries.
- The practice of recruiting national health professionals from local health services, or "poaching," is common in all major natural disasters or conflicts. In the medium-term, as indicated earlier, this practice seriously weakens the recovery capacity of the country.

Attempts by the Ministry and the Health Cluster to agree upon a standard approach regarding this recruitment and salaries were never seriously considered by the major medical NGOs that were competing among themselves (and with the UN) for the services of the few local health professionals available. It was a market where the demand far exceeded the local offer. Qualified personnel were recruited not only from the public sector but also from the dedicated local NGOs unable to match salaries offered by international NGOs. There is no easy solution when the humanitarian industry operates in an unregulated, free market mode.

- The bankruptcy of a major private facility has ended an era of opening the for-profit sector to poor patients. The Centre de diagnostic et traitement intégré (CDTI) closed on 1 April, a situation in which everyone loses. Since the first hours after the impact, this hospital offered free emergency care to the affected population. CDTI reported treating 10,500 patients and performing some 2,000 surgical interventions in 10 weeks.106

In an interview with the Nouveiiste, the main newspaper in Haiti, the CDTI director claimed "We did not receive any emergency funds during the three months of services that we offered." However, this institution did receive an important amount of assistance in the form of essential medical supplies, equipment, and human resources. In fact, CDTI experienced severe economic difficulties long before the earthquake. The issue is not one hospital's fate but the fact that the international community is ill-equipped to deal with the issue of monetary compensation for the care provided at no cost by the for-profit sector. This issue should be addressed especially in situations where the role of a particular facility is critical.

- The weakening of health institutions will be discussed in more detail in the section on national coordination in.

Interestingly, some NGO interlocutors praised the quality of care and noted that it was one of the few facilities with a proper balance in the number of doctors and nurses.

The Nouvelliste. 6 April 2010.

Information management

- Information management, including in the health sector, appears to be one of the weakest points of response in past disasters. The situation is compounded by the proliferation of general actors as well as agencies addressing highly specific needs.
- Considerably more human resources should be dedicated to intelligence gathering: the one who is best informed is the one with the moral authority to coordinate.
- Coordination cannot be effective in the absence of actionable information.

Disaster management is essentially information management. The main difference between decision making in crises versus in normal situations is not so much the humanitarian consequences but the higher levels of uncertainty. Decisions in sudden-onset disasters need to be made with limited or no accurate factual information. Therefore, emotions, institutional interests, or political considerations often prevail.

The Global Health Cluster led by WHO developed a list of suggested core health indicators.108 Few of them were collected and monitored before the impact, least of all under the chaotic conditions and extreme pressure for immediate action.

See IASC, Global Health Cluster (2009), "Global health cluster suggested set of core indicators and benchmarks by category."

Information needs

Information needs are not limited to the traditional indicators of number of dead (a figure of no practical immediate value), the number of injured (when compiled, it is often too late for action), the number of homeless or IDPs (elusive but actionable data), and the number of damaged buildings/houses. What is needed is relatively specific information on the extent of additional and critical human needs caused by the disaster, and the amount of resources already on site or in the pipeline to address them. Too often, the assumption is that local capacity is overwhelmed or non-existent. This perception was unfortunately more accurate in the case of the 12 January earthquake in Haiti than for the disasters in Indonesia, Pakistan, and Sri Lanka, where local resources and solidarity were severely underestimated or discounted by the international community.

What matters are not the needs per se, but those needs that cannot be met with existing resources.

The initial rapid assessment

- In the initial "rapid" assessment, speed should prevail over perfection.
- Democratic consensus on all indicators and inclusiveness are incompatible with speed. Leave well enough alone.
- Assessments must lead to decision-making by comparing observed needs with existing capacity in light of practical constraints.

In catastrophic disasters such as the Indian Ocean tsunami or the earthquakes in Pakistan and Haiti, humanitarian partners will immediately deploy their assistance, before any data can be compiled and validated.

Needs can take many forms and change rapidly over time and place. Response (local or international) may rapidly meet some of the needs, rendering further intervention off target or counterproductive; some life-saving needs or vulnerable groups may be overlooked. An intersectoral (interagency) initial rapid assessment (IRA) should be the first step before more decisive and specific action is taken. It is potentially a critical tool for setting up broad priority areas to guide the global humanitarian response.

Speed is more important than comprehensiveness or high accuracy. Information from a "quick and dirty survey," to borrow an epidemiological term, should be available before donors and agencies have made all their decisions. It is better to have 60% confidence in data before the decision, than to wait two weeks for 95% statistical probability.

The IRAs in Haiti and in the tsunami-affected countries present both extremes. In the case of the tsunami, the initial assessment was rapid but so sketchy (a few pages) as to be of little use. In Haiti, the pursuit of technical perfection resulted in data that were too complex and too late to assist partners with operational decision making.

In Haiti, a specific IRA, called the Rapid Initial Needs Assessment for Haiti (RINAH), was launched on 23 January. To speed up the process, pre-agreed international templates for IRAs were developed—and not used. Attempts to achieve consensus on areas of concern and priorities of all key actors led to lengthy negotiations among partners. As often is the case, the large number of parties in the discussion resulted in an inflated questionnaire including something for every agency's concern regardless of its relevance (in terms of importance or timing) for the beneficiaries.

Committee-driven design is particularly slow, as can be seen from the sequence below:

- Day 12 (23 January): The actual fieldwork for the assessment began; it concluded on 6 February.
- Day 29 (9 February): The Health Cluster reported: "the Rapid Initial Needs Assessment for Haiti (RINAH)109 evaluated several sectors including water, hygiene, security, and sanitation, visiting 108 locations within Port-au-Prince and 98 locations outside of Port-au-Prince. Data are still being assimilated and analyzed and will be made available soon."
- Day 39 (19 February): Announcements were made that a Revised Flash Appeal (the joint process for emergency fund raising) had been issued. It would be assumed that the preliminary results of RINAH, although not officially released, were used in this process. At the same time three other assessments of interest to the health sector were completed or launched:
- Key health partners who maintain networks of service providers in Haiti conducted an assessment of the impact of the earthquake on their service delivery;

- A rapid assessment was carried out by the Ministry of Health with support from UNAIDS on the delivery of services for prevention of mother-to-child transmission of AIDS in West Department;

- The Post-Disaster Needs Assessment (PDNA) was being organized by the Haiti government to guide recovery.

- On Day 45 (25 February), results of the RINAH (data with hundreds of tables and graphs) were released to all partners. Meanwhile, at the request of the Ministry of Health, an "emergency health information cell" was meeting within the Health Cluster to "assemble clearer information on the health situation in the country."

The methodology suffered from some design flaws: a questionnaire unsuitable for the Haitian context and language; a list of questions that were far too long (interviews lasted three hours); and some confusion between an assessment of the impact of the earthquake or of the ongoing poverty (CDC 2010a). The "severe security restrictions imposed by the UN." were also seen as an important factor delaying this and other rapid assessments (ACAPS 2010, Grünewald and Renaudin 2010).

The financial costs (estimated at US$ 3 million) and the resources required (128 workers, 18 evaluators, 23 helicopters, and 51 vehicles) were disproportionate in view of Assessment Capacities

Project (ACAPS), Rapid initial needs assessment for Haiti (RINAH). Conducted 23 January-6 February 2010.

Health Cluster Bulletin No. 19, 11 February 2010.

The revised flash appeal did not make mention of the RINHA but expected more information on longer term needs to be included in the Post Disaster Needs Assessment (PDNA), which had not yet been launched.

The lack of use of the results. The RINAH was only the first of 10 cross-sector surveys.

But more serious is the fact that these exercises systematically forget that needs assessment is not enough: Capacity assessment (existing resources and those in the pipeline) and proper analysis of constraints are essential components if the initial assessments are to be of any value to decision makers. These two elements were mostly missing in initial assessments carried out in the disasters under review.

These issues and problems were not specific to Haiti. After the Indian Ocean tsunami, the evaluators for the Tsunami Evaluation Commission (TEC) found that most of the interagency assessments failed to influence decision makers and donors. It should be noted that in past disasters investments in time and resources for the rapid assessment have been far more modest. Adding resources and funds did not contribute to better information or benefit the response in Haiti.

## The Post-Disaster Needs Assessment (PDNA)

- Government ownership is essential: The PDNA is a valuable exercise to the extent that it builds on the capacity of the Ministry of Health and focuses the Government and its partners on health sector reconstruction early on. It should determine the shape of the health system that will emerge after the disaster.
- Broad participation of the health sector in the cross-sectoral recovery process is critical to ensure that basic health needs and priorities receive adequate attention in the rehabilitation and recovery process.

The PDNA process is comprehensive and therefore also time-consuming. It pulls together information on the physical impacts of a disaster, the economic value of the damage (replacement cost) and losses (income or services), and the human impacts as experienced by the affected population.

One of the assets of the PDNA is its ownership by the government of the affected country. Although promoted and supported by the international community (UN, the World Bank, regional financial institutions, the EC, and others), the PDNA should be requested and led by the government.

In Haiti, as early as on Day 7 initial approaches were made for a scoping mission before the end of January. However, the formal request was delayed until 16 February as the Government required changes in the Terms of Reference in order to assume true ownership.

As is often the case, balance shifted excessively towards infrastructure when many of the challenges were in the development of human resources and institutional building. The PDNA was also influenced (some said "carried away") by the anticipation of pledges, which, as seen from past disasters, do not fully materialize.

In Haiti, the initial draft of the health section required the full time efforts of several experts from UNICEF, UNFPA, the Interim Haiti Recovery Commission (IHRC), the Clinton Foundation, and CIDA as well as three professionals from WHO for up to four weeks. Over 15 professionals from the Ministry of Health were involved on a daily basis, one almost full-time.

The effectiveness of the document itself (rather than the process) in guiding and influencing donors is seen as limited. Key donors participated proactively in the process, but most had probably already established their own priorities.

According to some interlocutors, the product was an "inspirational document with ambitious new ideas and horizons." However, most of these "new" ideas were already piloted somewhere in Haiti. In the health sector, an effort was made not to introduce policy directions that were completely alien.

Success stories in recovery (LRRD) such as decentralization of services, provision of some health services at no cost (obstetric and pediatric), and others were advocated in the PDNA and therefore facilitated. A positive result of this exercise was reaching consensus in the health sector on the interim (six-month) health plan developed by the Ministry of Health.114

The experience gained in Haiti will be valuable to guide the health recovery process in future disasters.

Specific assessments

- Consolidated information management should be the utmost priority in future disasters.
- Considerable human resources are required to transform the numerous surveys and assessments into collective strategic planning.

In Haiti, as in countries affected by other major disasters, there was a proliferation of specific surveys and assessments, almost as many as there were actors or problems to be addressed. The challenge of compiling and interpreting the results was overwhelming. A working group on information management was established within the Health Cluster, a Google group on assessment was led by OCHA to set up and update a "Survey of Surveys,"115 while as noted before, an "emergency health information cell" was established by the Ministry of Health.

The need for timely information was insatiable: Who is doing what, where (3Ws)? Are the existing health facilities operational? Which key supplies are needed? What donations have been received and are potentially available? Where are the field hospitals and what are their capabilities? How many temporary settlements and with how many people (when new ones were spontaneously created every day)? How many people migrated toward departments and what is the absorption capacity of their services? What is the impact on food stocks, income, and availability and needs? What is the water availability and quality in camps and hospitals?

The list of queries fluctuated and expanded day-by-day. Agencies and clusters attempted to respond separately to many of those questions. Have provided the comprehensive view required for strategic orientation at the macro level, but in most instances they met the needs of the agency carrying out the survey.

It remains a question as to how often the better-targeted and specific assessment reports and the information compiled were timely and convincing enough to influence operational decisions of other partners in the humanitarian community.

Information on incoming assistance and actors Information on incoming human resources (the responders)

* Information on available (or soon to be) resources is essential to determine unmet needs.
* The capacity to monitor the arrival and potential contribution of incoming health teams (lacking in past disasters) was further weakened by the proliferation of organizations in Haiti.

As shown in Chapter 4, an unusually high number of individuals, teams, field hospitals, and organizations flooded the affected areas. Efforts made at the international level to monitor, if not influence, this flow were far from effective.

As a first measure, incoming actors were required to register. This otherwise sensible approach was complicated by a duplication of efforts and processes required by national institutions. Health organizations had to register, in principle, with the Ministry of Planning, the Ministry of Health, the Health Commission established by the President, and finally the Health Cluster. When the Health Cluster was reporting over 200 agencies registered, the number complying with registration at the Ministry of Health was only. A much larger but unknown number of (smaller) actors were not registered with any institution.

A valuable information product is the so-called 3W list: "Who is doing What and Where" (or in the 4W version: "When" and for how long). Compiling this list is time-consuming, and depends on the collaboration and transparency of actors (in absence of pro-active surveys or systematic visits). It is in constant need of updating so as not to quickly become obsolete. For months, only very rough 3W maps were available. The compilation of these lists, however incomplete, was an appreciated achievement in Haiti, although no evaluation of the actual use made of the information (or its effectiveness) is available.

The same can be said of the numerous maps developed for the health sector with the support of WFP and OCHA. Health actors frequently cited difficulties due to the lack of precise mapping of health services present in the camps and temporary settlements.

Quality assurance is indispensable for proper response management, especially in the health field. Information provided at registration or in 3W lists is based almost

Many of the NGOs registered with the Presidential Health Commission (or the Cluster) believed that they were automatically registered with the Ministry of Health. This was not the case, which reflects the tension between administrative and political branches of the sector.

This was the responsibility of the agency in charge of Camps Coordination and Camp Management, not of the health sector. It is another result of the piecemeal international approach in the health sector.

Or entirely on what the actors say they do (or intend to do). It does not cover information on their operational capacity or professional competence. Since there were no provisions or resources for quality control of the incoming actors, the information provided by actors could not be validated. This has been a serious issue in all recent disasters, only made worse in Haiti with the exploding number of partners.

Information on incoming supplies

The Logistics Support System (LSS/SUMA) has proven its value as a management tool of humanitarian supplies in recent disasters. In Haiti, it was one of the few international instruments directly managed by national authorities.

In most disaster situations, the management of incoming supplies is one of the major bottlenecks in the humanitarian system. In the health sector, large amounts of unsolicited and inappropriate supplies (expired medicines, used and unsuitable equipment, etc.) compete for scarce storage and transportation facilities. In past conflicts or natural disasters in Haiti and elsewhere, safely discarding unwanted medical supplies has been done at significant expense.

The main challenge is not only dealing physically with those inappropriate donations, but to know what has arrived where, and for whom. In major disasters it is common for agencies and authorities to make public appeals for urgent donations of medical items that are already available in large amounts in warehouses at an airport or at government or NGO facilities. The cross-sectoral coordination agency (Directorate for Civil Protection) and Ministry of Health had no general decision-making authority on the flow of donations in Haiti.

Many interlocutors had anecdotal horror stories of unethical or incompetent behavior, ranging from disaster "tourism" to the unannounced closure of one organization's project and office in Port-au-Prince, leaving field staff stranded in departments without information or support.

Timeline of LSS/SUMA activities in Haiti;

January–March 2010

12 January    Impact of the earthquake

15 January    Arrival of the advance team (Haiti and the Dominican Republic)

16 January  Begin activities in Haiti and Santo Domingo; coordinate with Logistics Cluster and OCHA

23 January  Open a warehouse in Jimaní (Dominican Republic) for medical supplies in transit

1 February  Support from the White Helmets (Argentina); cooperation with IOM

10 February  Inventory starts at Port-au-Prince port facilities (recently reopened)

17 March  Meeting with Directorate for Civil Protection about lessons learned; development project initiated

Ongoing Project to support capacity of the Haitian Directorate for Civil Protection

An important feature is that LSS/SUMA counterparts were primarily in the Haitian Directorate for Civil Protection. The Government of Haiti owned and managed the information rather than the UN or another external agency. Having some post facto information on the supplies already on site was, however, not sufficient to influence and filter the donations themselves. The Directorate for Civil Protection played the lead role in activating and installing LSS/SUMA at two entry points (the airport and later the seaport); it was one of the very few international initiatives directly managed by this Haitian institution. The organization of LSS/SUMA in Haiti and categories of supplies inventoried are -In the health sector, LSS/SUMA supported PROMESS, the main channel for distribution of medical supplies on behalf of the Ministry of Health.

LSS/SUMA operates during emergencies by mobilizing dedicated volunteers from neighboring countries (in this case from the Dominican Republic, Nicaragua, and Argentina). Its deployment capacity is impressive due to the thousands of volunteers trained in Latin America and the Caribbean (as well as outside the Americas). It is a true example of regional solidarity in action.

Counterparts and local experts are trained in all countries of the Americas, Haiti included. As often occurs in major disasters, trained nationals faced competing demands and few were immediately available for what was perceived a less critical (not life-saving) activity.

LSS/SUMA supply coordination in Haiti and the Dominican Republic

Categories of items arriving at Port-au-Prince airport,

16 January–25 February 2010

Water and sanitation
1%

Food and drink

35%

Unclassified items

46%

Personal needs/education

1%

Shelter/housing/electrical/construction

5%

Pharmaceutical

11%

Health (non-pharmaceutical)

1%

Logistics/management

0.5%

Percentages by category of supplies arriving at Port-au-Prince harbor

Non food

Personal needs/education

846

Logistics/tools

54


Medical

1,080


Unclassified items

1,188


Food

43,956


Water

4,680

12,762


Category Weight in Tons


Haiti


Collecting and interpreting meaningful and timely information can be an almost impossible challenge in disasters. This has been noted in the aftermath of all disasters involving large numbers of actors. To influence decision making and effect changes, information must be available in the format that meets the specific requests and needs of the intended users.

In Haiti, the HIC was not formally activated in spite of the much greater flow of visitors and general enquiries. Sectors were basically left with the task of briefing all incoming visitors regardless of their potential to contribute positively. This distracted health experts from more serious and productive tasks. Another significant source of distraction was the constant demand on the time of coordinators and field staff to repackage the same information (or lack of) in distinct formats and styles according to the specific purpose of the request (administrative, information for the agency's executive management, fund raising, public relations, or merely to justify a request for support).

While efforts were made to improve the immediate dissemination of information to operational partners, less attention has been given to preserving this perishable data for future use. There was no single point when key documents produced in the first few months in Haiti were systematically saved in electronic format for public or academic access. Of particular interest would be access to the e-mail "inbox" and "sent box" of the clusters so as to appreciate the changing patterns and flow of requests and action. Early cluster e-mail exchanges were not available for research purposes (lost or corrupted files for the health sector and access not granted for others). As a matter of transparency and for the sake of collective memory, cluster files and archives should be in the public domain.

To address this lack of institutional memory, several data rescue projects have been launched, almost as an afterthought. Those projects are no substitute for a policy of systematic, long-term preservation and sharing of files.

Mass media and social media

- Haiti response confirmed the preeminent role of the mass media. In light of their influence on the flow and nature of assistance, the health sector would benefit by involving them more closely in its information management activities.
- For the first time, social media played a large role in information dissemination. Its potential should be explored and, if possible, harnessed before the next disaster.

Both traditional mass media and new social media played a critical role in encouraging generous support for Haiti. It was a double-edged sword: it was positive when it motivated the public and governments to provide financial and operational support, but negative when it incited a deluge of well-intentioned but unsuitable supplies or personnel.

This became the main raison d'être of the numerous meetings.

The Emergency Operations Center (EOC) was close to filling this role internally. It has a remarkable collection of documents, situation reports, and documentation related to health. Its function, however, is not for document preservation and access.

The University of Haiti (UEH) and Tulane University Disaster Resilience Leadership Academy (DRLA) have conducted a review of over 500 documents related to the earthquake, 94 of which have been classified in a database (available at www.drlatulane.org).

During the first two months after the earthquake there was no local coverage by traditional news media in Haiti (national television news or newspapers) due to the extensive damage to communications and transport infrastructure and serious deficiencies in utilities services. Foreign outlets included, among others, CNN, the New York Times, and Los Angeles Times.

Mass media

In past humanitarian crises foreign news outlets carried extensive coverage from the first day of impact. Their capacity to react quickly and obtain information is impressive. Their ability to deploy resources is far superior to that of most humanitarian agencies.

It is difficult to gauge to what extent official allocations of funding and deployment were influenced by the public perceptions shaped by the rapid media coverage rather than by formal assessments from UN and other humanitarian agencies. Interviews in Haiti and similar studies of past disasters suggest that the media play the major role in this regard, although not always with the most reliable or objective information.

In all major disasters, the accuracy of the information in the mass media may be determined by the need to oversimplify complex situations. The perception is that the public prefers black and white stories. Accuracy is also influenced by the quality of briefings provided by partners and stakeholders. Pacifying comments such as the "situation is under control" are generally poorly received. Alarming information even if intended to generate support for a special group or issue usually finds a more receptive audience. The responsibility to improve the quality of media coverage lies with the humanitarian actors who should give higher priority to informing the public about effective response than to securing favorable coverage for their activities.

When the objective of media briefings is to inform the public on health impacts or educate it, for example, on the need for sanitation or the absence of risk caused by dead bodies, the message is generally understood.

In Haiti, relations between health actors and the media appeared predominantly directed toward the impact on public relations (the agency image) rather than on a partnership to better inform and educate the public on what actions were likely to be effective. Greater benefit for the affected population would result from improved collaboration between humanitarian agencies and the media, for instance by embedding selected journalists in initial assessment missions.

Social media

On 22 January a reporter for the BBC (MacLeod 2010) commented:

"New and emerging media played a key role in breaking news to the outside world of the Haiti earthquake. Citizens turned to a range of networking tools in a bid to share the news and personal stories from microblogging on Twitter and video-sharing on YouTube to the internet telephone application Skype, and the social media site Facebook. For over 24 hours after the quake, countless reports and images came not only from big, established news organizations but from ordinary people on the spot.

Authors of an evaluation of the response to the Indian Ocean tsunami make this observation: "The mass media, not the UN or another humanitarian body, was able to provide early and 'convincing' comprehensive formal assessment of immediate needs" in the aftermath of the tsunami. "The quality of this information, and especially the tendency to pick up the most negative, frightening or outrageous statements from any unqualified source, has long been a matter of legitimate complaint from responsible and professional disaster managers" (de Ville de Goyet and Morinière 2006; 14, 58).

"However, aidagencies, charities and others pointed out that while news was being broken and getting out of the country via new and emerging media, such platforms were often unable to provide practical assistance to victims."

It is too early to conclude what may be the role of social media in the management of future disasters. As noted in regard to Haiti, social media were "calling into question the ingrained view of unidirectional, official-to-public information broadcasts. Social media may also offer potential psychological benefit for vulnerable populations gained through participation as stakeholders in the response" (Keim and Noji 2011).

However, this new form of peer-to-peer information collection and sharing played a significant role in identifying needs. Web-based platforms such as Ushahidi became information providers linked to geographic information systems, and produced interactive maps through Google maps. There may be caveats for these emerging systems, but they proved very useful at the time to direct ambulances to the injured or sick and to allocate relief.

Official reports from the government and humanitarian organizations are unlikely to remain the only source of information (apart from the mass media) and may be increasingly challenged in the future by a "bottom-up" flow of information.

The shortcomings noted do not reflect a lack of dedication or concern on the part of the coordinators and managers, but rather the complexity of fast evolving, multifaceted needs and response unmatched by corresponding institutional investment.

The Health Cluster Coordinator in her one-month report clearly identifies information management as one of two pillars for future activities. It was defined as: "The construction of an information management system/situation room that allows for decisions on actions via a clear presentation about the initial needs, trends, service provision, epidemiologic alerts, status of the national health system (facilities, staff) and international cooperation, so as to see where are the priorities and gaps, to define actions, to monitor implementation, and to evaluate results" (Van Alphen 2010).

Ushahidi (which means "testimony" in Swahili) is a data-mapping platform that was first used in 2007 in Kenya. The developers used it "to collate and locate reports of unrest sent in by the public via text message, e mail and social media . . . Ushahidi quickly became the world's default platform for mapping crises, disasters and political upheaval. [By May of 2011] Ushahidi, which is free to download, had been used 14,000 times in 128 countries to map everything from last year's earthquake in Haiti to this year's Japanese tsunami. . . . "(Perry 2011).

One of the biggest challenges faced by Dr. Alex Larsen, then Minister Lom psum doe t m of Health (middle), during the first months of the response was keeping track of all the different organizations that were in Haiti:

Coordination

- The primary responsibility for coordination lies with national authorities.
- Although direct external coordination may be required for a short period after a sudden-onset natural disaster, it cannot exercise the same authority over humanitarian partners that a legitimate government can.
- A mechanism and set date for transfer of responsibility were lacking in all recent disasters.

Coordination has been discussed in several places in this publication. Overall, there is a strong consensus that the response from all sectors was chaotic and poorly coordinated in Haiti.

However, in the aftermath of Haiti, several editorials and articles in professional journals raised serious and fundamental issues regarding the current status of international response. Abstracts of titles are illustrative of the malaise: "Growth of aid and the decline of humanitarianism," "Unintended consequences of humanitarian volunteerism," and "Cacophonies of aid." The fact that these critiques were published in peer-reviewed scientific publications and not only in the mass media is significant.

"Disaster relief in post-earthquake Haiti: unintended consequences of humanitarian volunteerism"

What is coordination and who is responsible?

Coordination has a distinct meaning for every actor. Some see coordination merely as a forum to learn what others are doing, while for others it is the authoritative setting of priorities by the coordinating body, with resources being allocated and activities permitted accordingly. For many, it is also a mechanism of quality control whereby the "mushroom" operators (popping up overnight) without experience and resources are weeded out.

All profess to be willing to coordinate with others. Few accept being coordinated. Many operational partners, while decrying the vacuum of authority as a major impediment to effective relief, in fact see it as convenient.

There is not always a clear understanding about who has the authority to coordinate the health response. That should not be the case: the UN

General Assembly Resolution 46/182 acknowledges clearly that the Government has primary responsibility in organizing humanitarian assistance in a disaster. In the aftermath of a natural disaster in a country with a recognized government, the authority for all health issues should remain with the Ministry of Health of the affected country, not with international, ad hoc structures. The issue may be blurred or debatable in conflict situations or in failed states. The latter situation was not the case in Haiti.

Whether a weak institution in a country so severely crippled by a disaster could coordinate the highly complex web of agencies and actors alone is another matter. Specialized UN agencies and mechanisms play a key role in assisting the health authorities and in some instances temporarily accept the burden of de facto coordinating the response. In the same way that the Government of Haiti formally delegated its authority over airport operations and Haitian airspace to the United States, it implicitly delegated overall or sectoral coordination of the external response to the UN. As was the case in Pakistan, the authorities initially welcomed the establishment of the UN Clusters on the understanding that they would strengthen the capacity of line ministries while they readied themselves to assume leadership.

National coordination

Cross-sectoral national coordination

- Weak and poorly performing national organizations tend to be marginalized and further debilitated by the international response while the stronger ones may emerge strengthened.
- In the same way that the most vulnerable individuals among the affected population should receive special attention from the humanitarian responders, the weak or "vulnerable" national institutions should benefit early from special support from the international community and donors. This is particularly important when the mandate of those institutions is critical for survival and recovery, as in the case of the Ministry of Health.

The coordination mechanisms for dealing with disasters are relatively complex in Haiti. The operational arm of the system is the Directorate for Civil Protection (DPC). DPC presence at the provincial and municipal levels is uneven.

In emergencies, the Government activates the Emergency Operations Center (Centre d'Opération d'Urgence—COU), which brings together the relevant institutions. Surprisingly, this center was not activated after the earthquake. This had consequences, as many of the national institutions felt relatively lost in this "institutional vacuum."

In the first months, external funding and logistics support for overall coordination kept flowing to the UN and international agencies, bypassing the DPC coordinators. DPC staff were left almost without personal or professional means while young, inexperienced, foreign volunteers had transport facilities, internet and communication access, food, and accommodation.

The adoption of English as the working language of all coordination and briefing meetings, the location of those meetings in the MINUSTAH base ("Logbase") with restricted access for Haitian nationals, and the sheer imbalance in number of attendees ("one Haitian official versus 150 internationals" as said by an interviewee) made it extremely difficult for the DPC to reclaim leadership and assume its coordination role.

For affected populations the benefit of international agencies assuming the lead in the first weeks is not questioned. Those agencies have had greater experience and have the skills for this task. Their leadership was necessary in the immediate response when speed meant lives saved. However, the fact that their control persisted throughout the recovery and rehabilitation process with only token participation of the DPC is of concern.

The Presidential Commissions

An ad hoc mechanism was established a few days after the earthquake to assert Haitian State leadership in the response: the Presidential Commissions. Directly linked to the President and perceived as "double pouvoir" by some line ministries who felt deprived of their administrative responsibilities, these commissions contributed to blurring lines and weakening tested links of the normal mechanisms.

In the health sector, one of the added values of the Presidential Health Commission was the participation of academic and other national health actors in addition to the Ministry staff. The first location of its office in the vicinity of the airport (the de facto center of all humanitarian coordination activities and temporary headquarters of most UN agencies) greatly facilitated closer contact. Opinions vary regarding the value of setting up this Health Commission in an atmosphere of protracted tensions between political decision makers and administrators within the health ministry, a problem mentioned by several key interlocutors. Some see this initiative as alleviating the problem while others see a third stakeholder as a complicating factor.

Ministry of Health

Being a line Ministry in a very specialized and regulated area (rather than a central directorate, as the DPC), one would expect that the Ministry's authority would be less challenged. It was not challenged—it was mostly ignored.

The caliber, seniority and experience of inter-Cluster coordinators, as well as the speed of their arrival were questioned in interviews and external evaluation reports.

The situation is reportedly similar 18 months after impact.

Being part of the military peacekeeping headquarters, access to Logbase was first denied and later merely difficult for Haitians who were not employees of international agencies, including officials of the government.

Over 70% of the health budget is externally funded. Most of the health resources (facilities, staff, and budget) are not under the control and management of the State but of donors and NGOs, who are often critical of the lack of leadership and governance in the sector. A vicious circle is sustained as key decisions are ultimately taken outside the Ministry.

The Ministry of Health had not invested seriously in its preparedness for major emergencies. The Disaster Preparedness Unit remained grossly understaffed and was ineffective and marginalized in this mega-crisis. With the loss of its main building with staff, files and equipment, the Ministry was ill-equipped to exercise leadership over an unruly humanitarian community. A weak institution further weakened by the impact was no match for financially independent NGOs that felt they had the backing of the UN, the donors (cooperation agencies and/or public opinion), and their own constituencies. NGOs could and regularly did opt out from any policy or strategy set by the Ministry.

This marginalization persisted throughout the year in spite of UNICEF and WHO support to the Ministry. Strengthening the Ministry's ability for strategic planning and its capacity to deliver, areas of greatest weakness in the eyes of the partners, was not a priority for the international humanitarian community. This situation was far from unique to Haiti. It was noted in Indonesia and Sri Lanka (although the Cluster approach had not yet been adopted in 2004) and in Pakistan. However, in those countries dependence on external assistance was minimal and institutions were able to reassert their authority to a considerable extent. This was due to the efforts of national authorities, not as a planned strategy by international actors.

A success story: the water and sanitation agency

DINEPA, the water and sanitation institution in Haiti, offered an example of how a national entity could reclaim and assume its leadership and successfully coordinate the partners in its area of competence.

How easily this could have been duplicated in other sectors—in health in particular— is debatable. Water and sanitation is far less emotional and visible (and consequently less political internationally) than medical care. DINEPA, a relatively well organized and efficient institution prior to the earthquake, was already receiving direct funding from major donors and it did not suffer significantly from the impact of the earthquake.

To conclude, a comment published on 3 February (three weeks after impact) by an NGO working in Haiti says it best (Ivers and Cullen 2010):

"The international community needs to prioritize medium- and long-term investment in the health care system of Haiti, which was weak before the earthquake. Support must be sustained and promises kept if Haiti is to be rebuilt not only with stronger buildings, but also with a greatly strengthened ministry of health that sets the priorities. NGOs must then adopt these priorities and work in part-

In fact, WHO experience during the crisis has been one of a much closer association and more open dialogue with the highest authorities than ever before.

A common critique is the proliferation of strategic official documents or plans that are never implemented by the Ministry of Health. However, resources and means for implementation were often not in the control of the Ministry but of its independent minded partners.

A unique partnership with the Haitian government was formed to achieve this. Partners in Health—which has worked in Haiti for 20 years—continue to believe that the Haitian people can be empowered to take care of one another if they are given monetary support and solidarity."

International coordination

Humanitarian Reform and the health sector

The Inter-Agency Standing Committee (IASC) is the inter-agency forum for coordination, policy development, and decision making involving the key external UN and non-UN humanitarian partners. It was established in June 1992 in response to United Nations General Assembly Resolution 46/182 on the strengthening of humanitarian assistance. General Assembly Resolution 48/57 affirmed its role as the primary mechanism for inter-agency coordination of humanitarian assistance.

Members are the UN operational agencies and selected non-UN humanitarian agencies are standing invitees. There is no representation or input from disaster-affected countries.

In 2005, the IASC adopted an ambitious Humanitarian Reform covering several areas: financing of assistance, strengthening the function of the Humanitarian Coordinator in the UN, and more systematic and predictable attention to all main sectors of response ("the Cluster Approach") (Holmes 2007). The cluster approach is of more direct concern to the health ministries in affected countries.

The cluster approach intends to introduce a system of sectoral coordination agreed upon among external humanitarian actors. It is intended as a mechanism that can help to address identified gaps in response and enhance the quality of humanitarian action.

In September 2005 the IASC agreed to designate global "cluster leads" in nine sectors or areas of activity. These global sectors (clusters) as defined by the IASC closely reflect the distribution of mandates among main UN agencies:

Technical areas:

1. Nutrition
2. Health
3. Water/Sanitation

Emergency Shelter

International Committee of the Red Cross (ICRC) and International Federation of Red Cross and Red Crescent Societies (IFRC) are standing invitees. NGOs are represented by the International Council of Voluntary Agencies (ICVA) or Inter Action which are associations of NGOs.

Summarized from the IASC Guidance Note on Using the Cluster Approach to Strengthen Humanitarian Response (24 November 2006).

Cross-cutting areas:

1.  Camp Coordination/Management
2.  Protection
3.  Early Recovery

Common service areas:

1.  Logistics
2.  Emergency Telecommunications

Health, which is an all-inclusive concept, was thereby split into three technical areas (nutrition, health, and water and sanitation).

The IASC principals (the head of agencies) agreed that at country level the cluster approach should be applied, with some flexibility, in all new emergencies.

The nature of the links between clusters and the host government "will depend on the situation in each country and on the willingness and capacity of each of these actors to lead or participate in humanitarian activities." According to the procedures for field activation of the clusters, the UN Resident Coordinator, following consultations with the Humanitarian Country Team, submits the decision for approval by the UN Under Secretary-General and Emergency Relief Coordinator.

The host Government and all other partners are then informed of the decision taken.

Global, regional and local coordination

- Disasters triggering a global response call for global coordination.
- Priority setting and actual coordination must take place in the affected country to ensure that the response is relevant to the unique local context.

International coordination must be done where the action is taking place and where all humanitarian partners are: at national and sub-national levels.

Regional and global levels should be in a support mode. Country offices of development agencies are designed for long-term cooperation and are not always particularly suited for managing emergency information and coordinating a massive response of "new actors" in the aftermath of a sudden-onset disaster. The national office, regardless of its sectoral mandate, should be offered and accept strong reinforcement of management staff with humanitarian experience.

In Haiti, the magnitude of the disaster and the global nature of the response called for strong participation of global coordination mechanisms. In spite of their efforts to play a lead role, regional organizations (political or technical), did not have the critical mass to assume this leadership. The contributions of OAS, CARICOM, and CDEMA, among others, were most valuable but were dwarfed by the sheer volume of the international assistance. As a regional health body, did not have the capacity to quickly mobilize a sufficient number of experts, especially given the desirability of French language skills and familiarity with Haiti, which is uncharacteristic of other countries in the region.

The most valuable asset of a regional office remains its closeness to the health authorities, the health services, and the health conditions. This familiarity with the local context is an important asset to ensure that future coordination strengthens rather than hampers the capacity of the Ministry of Health.

Cluster application and health implications in Haiti

- Clusters in a given country should reflect the mandate of the line ministries.
- When necessary, participation should be limited to those in a position to offer a significant contribution.
- At the early stage, a small executive committee and technical work groups should be established under the leadership of the Ministry of Health.

At the global level, the normative work of the Global Clusters resulted in an array of technical guidelines that facilitated and guided the field work (for instance, on user fees in emergency situations, mental health and psychosocial assistance, gender-based violence, etc.).

At the country level, Haiti already had experience working with clusters during the response to the tropical storms and hurricanes that hit the country in August and September 2008. Many of the findings and recommendations in the Cluster Evaluation for Haiti (Binder and Grünewald 2010), which was carried out before the earthquake, remain pertinent. Some of the most relevant are:

- "Undermining of local ownership due to a top-down approach and a membership excluding local NGOs and government or donors;
- "Lack of clear criteria for activation and deactivation;
- "Improved identification of existing gaps but no evidence of those gaps being better filled;
- "Improved information sharing but poor information management (lost or untimely information);
- "Weak inter-cluster (cross-sectorial) coordination..."

In the case of the 12 January earthquake, the devastating impact on the weak capacity of the Haitian Government made activating the clusters the most promising approach for some measure of coordination at least during the first few weeks of the response.

An original and much appreciated initiative from CDEMA has been to sponsor short periods of rest in Jamaica for key staff of Haiti's Ministry of Health. The initiative was very similar to the statutory "Rest and Recuperation" (RR) leave with full pay granted to international UN staff who were required to work for extended periods at the duty stations under hazardous, stressful and difficult conditions.

The number of sectors/clusters activated in Haiti exceed the number initially envisaged by the Humanitarian Reform: agriculture, camp coordination/management, early recovery, education, emergency telecommunications, food distribution, health, logistics, nutrition, protection (which included two sub-clusters: child protection and gender-based violence), shelters, non-food items, and finally water, sanitation, and hygiene–a total of 12 clusters and two subsectors. All clusters were led by an international agency with the exception of the water, sanitation, and hygiene cluster, initially assigned to UNICEF but actually led by DINEPA at its own request.

The structure adopted did not seek to match the structure of the Haitian State that the system was designed to assist. For instance, the responsibilities of the Ministry of Health were distributed to the three clusters but also to a higher number of working groups, several under additional clusters (camp management, protection, etc.). This should be avoided in future disasters by matching the clusters structure to the scope of mandate of the line ministries.

The section below focuses on the Health Cluster. It was responsible for everything health related for which another cluster had not been set up.

The initial implementation of the Health Cluster met considerable challenges and had a slow learning curve. The challenges included:

- Severe logistics limitations, among which were security restrictions. As noted by the UN Humanitarian Coordinator in May 2010, "there has been ongoing discussion of protecting 'humanitarian space'. Yet Haiti is not the [Democratic Republic of the Congo]; the humanitarian response is not taking place in a war zone, in an environment of civil conflict between warring factions." This statement is supported by evidence that "between 2007 and 2009 collective violence had dramatically declined even if other forms of violence— that is, sexual and gender-based—began to appear more visible" (Muggah 2010).

- A randomized household survey (n=2,940) in the months after the earthquake indicated that crime and victimization rates were lower than announced in the global media.

"Contrary to media claims of widespread looting and organized theft, the vast majority of Port-au-Prince residents reported that neither they nor any members of their household had had property stolen from them or intentionally destroyed by others since the earthquake"(Muggah 2010). Only 20% of the respondents considered insecurity/crime a very serious or serious problem after the earthquake compared to 62.9% prior to the earthquake. (Kolbe 2009, Kolbe and Muggah 2010).

These findings are supported by the lower number of gunshot wounds treated by MSF in the first month after the earthquake. As noted by MSF, interventions for gunshot wounds are part of everyday life in Haiti, but they were less frequent in the first month following the earthquake.

The distinct perception at international level and the resulting restrictions, which were perhaps due to unrealistically alarmist scenarios and extraneous considerations, further alienated the UN actors from their counterparts and the population. A new UN Security Management System was intended to move decision-making away from "go/no-go" to balancing risk and opportunity. Its application was not felt yet in Haiti.

- A large number of organizations performed far above expectations but a significant number were minor actors without significant experience or resources and therefore unable to offer added value. The Health Cluster meetings became an opportunity to claim visibility (flag waving) or for newcomers to collect basic information on what to do and where to go. The strategic coordination objective was lost. To keep clusters from collapsing under their own weight in future disasters, filtering or "triage" of participants may be required. Cluster support should be directed to those agencies and actors most likely to provide significant benefits for the

health of the affected population.

The early and excellent decision of WHO to move into PROMESS facilities rather than to the MINUSTAH base ("LogBase")—as instructed by UN security—had a positive impact on its future activities, offsetting the disadvantages of being relatively far from the clusters' meeting place.

This shift from risk aversion to risk management represents the culmination of the past decade's evolution in thinking and methodology for programming in insecure conditions. Key to this shift is the concept of the enabling security approach, i.e., an approach that focuses on "how to provide services" as opposed to "when to be grounded". Under this new approach, the use of military or armed escorts for humanitarian agencies is purely a security risk mitigation measure to reduce security risks from one acceptable risk level to another (rather than reducing risk from an unacceptable to an acceptable level as remained mostly the case in the response to the earthquake).

A slow learning curve resulted from the extreme pressure on the few senior staff involved in the cluster process. Responding to urgent needs delayed important decisions. Among the positive measures taken belatedly were:

- Setting up a select group of agencies working in Haiti before, during, and after the earthquake to agree upon strategic options and collectively guide the process: The cluster was initially conceived precisely to provide this guidance. Democratic consensus-building among all participants proves not to be effective in acute response management. After several weeks this "small committee," where keys options and decisions were debated, was quietly set up among 19 larger agencies that have a long-term commitment in Haiti.

- Organizing technical working groups where specific thematic topics could be discussed at the level of practical details: Ultimately those working groups included the following topics: hospitals, mobile clinics, mental health and psychosocial support, vector control, epidemiology, disabilities, and information. Experience has shown in the disasters in Haiti, Indonesia, Sri Lanka, Pakistan, and others that the work in thematic sub-groups was far more concrete and productive than in the large forum. In future disasters, establishing some or all of those groups from the early stage of the emergency should be considered.

- Decentralizing the Health Cluster to departments (away from the capital): a very efficient measure that should be planned earlier in future large disasters.

514

In addition to coordinating the outcome from all those sub-groups, the health sector was also attempting to maintain coherence in public health activities that were being coordinated by other clusters (nutrition, hygiene and community health education, reproductive health, HIV/AIDS, and gender-based violence, among others).

As noted in the 2009 evaluation of clusters in six country studies (including Haiti, Hurricane 2008), inter-cluster coordination was ineffective in most cases and did not lead to integration of cross-cutting issues (IASC 2010a, 6). This observation was still accurate in 2010.

In spite of the serious shortcomings in terms of national ownership, this donor-supported approach has considerable value in the first weeks especially when those national coordinating bodies which are severely affected are still under the shock of the impact. If coordination was difficult to achieve, it is due to the absence of legal or formal authority over the "partners," normally the exclusive prerogative of the State, and the chaotic and exponential escalation of humanitarian assistance rather than to the faulty design of this gap-filling coordination model.

It must be said, however, that in disasters of the scale of Haiti's, effective coordination is almost impossible to achieve.

*Jeff Benjamin*

The clusters rapidly outlived their usefulness—and their welcome—with Haitian counterparts. The failure of the humanitarian community to implement an early albeit progressive and monitored transfer of leadership and responsibility to the national Directorate for Civil Protection, the Ministry of Health and other line ministries rapidly eroded the tenuous legitimacy of the clusters in a country with an established and recognized government. The result has been a weakening of the institutions: The principle of "First, do no Harm"

Unfortunately the Ministry of Health was not systematically invited to participate in the "small committee" meetings.

Unfortunately, the situation after the earthquake in Haiti was no exception. This has been observed and reported in past major disasters.

The argument of the inherent inability of the Haitian authorities to manage such a crisis has been proven fallacious in view of the role played by DINEPA. It demonstrated that such a transition or sharing of power was indeed possible even in the difficult environment of Haiti.

The coordination by lead agencies, mostly UN agencies, left room for considerable improvement. However, challenges and obstacles to coordination were not limited to the international system. The response taxed the coordination mechanisms of the largest donors as well. In the health sector, the U.S. Department of Health and Human Services (HHS) worked in an environment in which the Department of State served as the lead for the fatality management mission, USAID served as the lead for public health and medical care to the Haitian population, the Department of Homeland Security was the lead for repatriation of U.S. citizens, and the Department of State with the Federal Emergency Management Agency (FEMA) coordinated patient movements. That was just for Health and Human Services' own activities. In addition, health assistance was provided by the Department of Defense and Department of State agencies.

If achieving effective communication and coordination in the response from one country was difficult, the task of coordinating all actors was far more complex and ambitious.

The health sector's ultimate goal during a disaster remains reducing all possible

avoidable deaths, disabilities and suffering. The focus is on strategic lessons of global use. Among sudden-onset disasters, earthquakes pose a particularly difficult challenge to the international community. Speed and professionalism during the response are critical. Among earthquakes, Haiti was an exceptional situation. Consequently, not all the lessons from Haiti will be relevant to the next catastrophic earthquake.

The magnitude of international response has increased dramatically from one disaster to the next. This growth has many positive aspects:

- First, many developing countries, neighbors or not, are now joining the more traditional humanitarian donors to respond to disasters. A number of specialized agencies are filling small niches neglected in the past and new NGOs are providing collective services to other partners (communications, information, logistics, etc.). There are now numerous organizations active in a variety of health disciplines, creating the potential for great diversity and coverage of services.

- This rapid growth has come with a lot of pain and changes. In the health sector, a two-fold process is emerging: On one side, the established humanitarian organizations are becoming more professional by developing their own standards and norms and training their staff.

On the other side, the number of inexperienced newcomers (NGOs, universities, countries, and others) is rising rapidly. Some of these new actors plan to remain in the humanitarian field, which justifies the investment made by more established agencies in guiding their first steps. In the very distinctive health vacuum of Haiti, they did contribute positively and will improve their performance. However, a rising minority of new actors, with doubtful health competence or with questionable motives, were definitely more a hindrance than help. They should be filtered out by the health authorities.

Few of the lessons from the health response to the Haiti earthquake are new or groundbreaking. Most have been "learned" in a variety of regional workshops and published in formal evaluations. Consider the regional workshop following the Indian Ocean tsunami (UN 2005), the analysis of response to the Haiti earthquake published by ALNAP (2010), an evaluation of the health sector in Haiti one year after the earthquake (Merlin 2011), or the notes on preliminary lessons learned from Haiti (Fisher 2010).

The humanitarian community seems to have little institutional memory or capacity to change.

Is a better organized response possible?

Lack of information sharing and coordination (two intertwined concepts) is the most common criticism in the aftermath of disasters. It is easily documented by external evaluators, eagerly conveyed by mass media, and conveniently used by lead agencies to call for more resources and staff.

There are two relevant questions: 10 Is it possible to significantly improve the information? 2) Is it possible to effectively coordinate such an unruly world of humanitarian organizations?

Is it possible to significantly improve the information? In the health field, the response is a definite "yes."

The first step is to identify (conservatively and pragmatically) what must be known to improve relief and what can be collected in time for this information to have the proper impact (not what we would love to know). In matters of immediate trauma care, which is a rapidly changing field, perhaps not much can be known and disseminated before it becomes obsolete.

The second step is to deploy qualified human resources in time. This implies interagency agreements and the capacity to share rosters of experts. It supposes a significant investment in deployment of human resources and logistic support at the time of the crisis and a shift of lead agencies' priorities from visible delivery of "hard" services to "soft" information management.

Is it possible to effectively coordinate such an unruly world of organizations? In the health field, the response is a more qualified "yes."

More human and financial resources and definitely more meetings are not necessarily the solution. Coordination should not be an end in itself. Some level of chaos is an integral part of the initial response to large disasters. To what extent "more" coordination will improve the fate of the affected population deserves scrutiny. A high-level UN official in Haiti concluded privately that the lack of coordination in the first two months may have in fact permitted meaningful, community-level contributions from the many small or marginal actors. The same actors were seen as a major burden in past disasters in countries with more national capacity. Response and coordination must be determined by the context.

A particular area that may benefit from quality control and improved coordination is that of foreign medical care assistance. The next disaster may require a substantial and rapid mobilization of senior managers and thematic experts, with significant logistical support, which is very problematic in the first days when needed most. WHO and its regional offices need to seek partnerships with bilateral and other institutions to develop a roster of experts and considerably increase their surge capacity to coordinate the incoming flow of medical responders. The Global Outbreak Alert and Response Network (GOARN) may serve as a useful model. Many bilateral groups and NGOs have demonstrated a high level of technical competence and critical analysis. Their support and participation will be most valuable.

The efforts of INSARAG to improve search and rescue assistance may provide some additional clues to the way forward in the health sector. An independent review of its impact in Haiti is, however, still lacking (i.e., "What would have happened if this sustained investment had not been made by INSARAG?").

In other words, we need to shift from outcome indicators ("more coordination is better") to impact appraisal by demonstrating that diverting funds from relief activities toward coordination and quality control actually does save more lives.

Ownership of the disaster

Mobilizing more external coordinators will not, in itself, improve coordination. Coordination without meaningful participation and leadership of the national health authorities is ultimately doomed to fail.

One of the key findings of the self-evaluation of the UN Country Humanitarian

Team in Haiti was the need to ensure national ownership of the disaster response.

"Governments however weak, has to play a central role in humanitarian leadership

and coordination of post-natural disaster. We as humanitarian leaders and actors have to accept and facilitate this."

To follow up on those findings, the IASC recommended that:

- "Wherever possible, international humanitarian actors should then organize themselves to support or complement existing national response mechanisms rather than create parallel ones which may actually weaken or undermine national efforts.

- "Where appropriate and practical, government leads should be actively encouraged to co-chair cluster meetings with their Cluster Lead Agency counterparts. As with all co-chair arrangements, respective responsibilities should be clearly defined from the outset" (IASC 2011).

Sudden-onset disasters are creating a wave of generosity (and therefore a high number of volunteers who are in need of coordination, and strong competition for funding and visibility among actors which is in need of arbitration). In such disasters, the cluster approach must be implemented differently to ensure national ownership.

Asserting the national government's primary role in coordinating and selectively filtering external assistance is not an easy matter for national authorities even when local health resources have the capacity to respond effectively. The perception held by the public that the international community is better suited to coordinate response guarantees that weaker national institutions will continue to be marginalized, and further weakened. Coordination should be a key feature of national disaster preparedness.

A formal agreement on the cluster approach with governments prior to the disaster is an indispensable preliminary step.

As part of joint preparedness efforts, a formal agreement for sectoral coordination (cluster approach) should be discussed with those countries most vulnerable to large-scale, sudden-onset natural disasters. Many potential worst-case, urban earthquake scenarios have already been identified and those countries are receiving technical cooperation in preparedness from the UN and bilateral agencies. Under this agreement:

- The Government will determine the number and scope of responsibility of the sectors/clusters at the national level in order to better reflect the organization of the government and respective mandate of the line ministries. Adjusting the clusters to national structure is a requirement to facilitate the early and smooth transfer of responsibility to the government. The sector/cluster structure at national level will vary from country to country (in line with the flexibility recommended in the 2006 IASC guidelines recognizing that "one size does not fit all").
- The Government, in consultation with the UN Humanitarian Country Team, will designate in advance one or more (co-lead) agencies to assist the national institution (line ministry) responsible for each sector. Those lead agencies

may or may not be the same as those at global level (another recommendation of the IASC

Following the earthquake in Mexico City (1985), hospital bed occupancy never exceeded 95% and the ample resources of this large country were mobilized. The Government initially declined external medical assistance.

Within one day, however, a campaign launched by the international media forced the Government to withdraw its decision and open its borders to foreign medical teams.

The Port-au-Prince metropolitan area was severely affected. Eighty percent of the town of Léogâne (17 km southwest of Port-au-Prince) was destroyed.

guidelines). It would not affect the role of the cluster lead agency at global level. It is also understood that in the immediate life-saving phase, the co-lead UN agencies may have to actually manage and coordinate the entire response in exceptional situations such as in Haiti.

- The agreement will endorse the existing 24-hour activation mechanism for the clusters but ensure explicit participation of the government in the UN decision-making process (beyond merely informing authorities).

- Finally, a clear end-date (for example, three weeks) will be set for either transfer of responsibility to the national institution or a formal request for extension of the lead role of the international agencies for a specified period, should the national authorities deem that necessary.

In brief, the humanitarian community must acknowledge that in order to strengthen the capacity of national authorities it is worth taking the risk, in the short-term, of having less "efficient" or "experienced" coordination. Indeed, the risk of additional chaos might be less than anticipated considering the poor performance of external coordination in the first few months in Haiti and other disasters. Instead of managing the crisis themselves, international partners should accompany and build the capacity of their counterparts— admittedly a more demanding and difficult task.

Quality control in the medical sector

Many agencies that regularly provide medical teams and field hospitals are dedicating considerable effort to improve the quality of their performance by carrying out systematic evaluations and training. Some have gone a step further to analyze the cost-effectiveness of their interventions in terms of development and relief. However, not all groups have a high standard of quality assurance.

Medical care is one of the most regulated service sectors in all countries, even in less developed ones. Accrediting medical doctors, paramedical technicians, and pharmacists or licensed facilities is one of the key functions of a ministry of health in "normal" times. In the aftermath of a disaster, any medical team or individual can claim (accurately or not) competence and the qualifications to amputate limbs or undertake major surgery. The medical humanitarian business has grown too much not to be better regulated. There must be a balance between the current laissez-faire approach and rigid accreditation. Regulations must be adapted to fit the magnitude and urgency of needs that cannot be met nationally.

Some definitions are useful at this stage:

- Registration is merely a process of filing information into a register or database. It does not validate the competence of the entity registered.
- Certification involves a technical evaluation of compliance with pre-established requirements or criteria. An independent third party normally does this evaluation. In light of the potential liability for the certifying agency, INSARAG has adopted the term "external classification."
- Accreditation is "a formal process by which a recognized body recognizes that a health care organization meets applicable, pre-determined, and published standards." In normal, non-crisis situations, "An accreditation decision about a specific

health care organization is made following a periodic on-site evaluation by a team of peer reviewers, typically conducted every two to three years. Accreditation is often a voluntary process in which organizations choose to participate, rather than one required by law and regulation" (Rooney and van Ostenberg 1999).

- Licensure is a process by which a government authority grants permission to an individual practitioner or health care organization to operate. In normal situations, organizational licensure is granted following an on-site inspection to determine if minimum health and safety standards have been met.

At this stage, registration is the only process that can be realistically considered in the medical sector.

According to one analysis (Gosselin et al. 2011), the costs saved per disability-adjusted life year (DALY) in short surgical missions for elective surgery and those in post-earthquake relief missions in the same country were unexpectedly very similar.

As endorsed by the Global Health Cluster, setting up a worldwide registry of providers of such services and developing predetermined and published norms and standards for deployment of medical teams and hospitals are the initial steps toward improved quality control of the health response.

The ministry of health must be provided with this basic information about the capacity of foreign medical teams and field hospitals prior to the occurrence of a disaster.

## Learning from the past

There were many evaluations of the response to the earthquake in Haiti; more than a few interlocutors said that there were too many. Nevertheless, it is hard to note a significant improvement or change of attitude in the response. One of the main shortcomings is, perhaps, the scope of those evaluations: How efficiently and effectively are the objectives and policies pursued? How did we mobilize our resources and coordinate what we set out to accomplish?

Whether the objectives pursued were desirable and achievable, or if the policies were in the best long-term interest of the beneficiaries were beyond the scope of the terms of reference of most evaluations.

Some of those strategic and policy topics are best left to researchers rather than hired evaluators. However, to do proper research, scientists would benefit from greater access to documents and internal reports (including electronic mail) than is allowed by the current level of transparency of main actors.

Finally, to paraphrase Nigel Fisher, the Humanitarian Coordinator in Haiti, the "lessons learned tend to focus on resolving what did not work so well. But again, we should not forget the many considerable achievements of the humanitarian community." In Haiti, many lives were saved, people were fed and sheltered, and they received much better care than before. The disaster brought significant positive changes in mentality, behavior, and attitude. It is up to the Haitians and the international community to ensure that those changes endure.

Prior to the earthquake, nearly two-thirds of all Haitians made their living in the agricultural sector, mainly from small-scale subsistence farming, making them more vulnerable to natural disasters.

The Republic of Haiti occupies the western third of the Island of Hispaniola, which it shares with the Dominican Republic. The country is divided into 10 departments and has an estimated population of 10 million.

Nearly half of Haiti's population (47%) lives in urban areas, the largest being the Port-au-Prince metropolitan area (which has a population estimated at 2.3 million). The metropolitan area has expanded considerably in population but not so much in size in the last 20 years, leading to overcrowded, improvised settlements on the steep slopes surrounding the old city.

In terms of population density, Haiti ranks second after Barbados (and a few island territories in the Caribbean) in the Region of the Americas. The density is particularly high in Port-au-Prince.

Social, political, and economic determinants

Haiti was the first country to gain sovereignty in Latin America and the Caribbean and in 2004 it celebrated 200 years of independence. With nearly two centuries of dictatorship and intermittent attempts at democracy beginning in the late 1980s, the country has suffered recurrent periods of political instability. Following the 1991 military coup, an OAS/UN embargo was enforced in 1993. The ousted President Aristide returned to the country in 1994. One of the first decisions of this new Government was to dismantle the army, leaving the police forces as the only national security institution.

Following a political crisis, in March 2004 a new transitional government was installed with the support of the United Nations Stabilization Mission (MINUSTAH), paving the way for presidential and parliamentary elections in February 2006. Presidential elections were scheduled to take place in 2010 and the country was entering into the electoral period at the end of 2009. The government was in a weak position when the earthquake struck in January 2010.147

The vast majority of Haitians continue to live under precarious conditions, in poverty and marginalization. This poverty especially affects women heads of households, as they are often the primary breadwinners.

The UNDP Human Development Report issued in 2010 (with data from 2007), illustrates the pre-earthquake situation in Haiti:

- Ranks 145 out of 169 countries for the human development index. This index improved slightly since 2005, but remains the lowest among Caribbean and Central American countries;
- In Latin America and the Caribbean multidimensional poverty affects from 2% of the population (Uruguay) to 57% (Haiti);
- Among the few countries doing very poorly both on gender equality and human development are the Central African Republic, Haiti, and Mozambique.

Income distribution is inequitable: 4% of the population has 66% of the nation's wealth, while 10% has practically nothing. Foreign commercial investment is minimal and manufacturing or service employment is practically nonexistent for the majority of the population. Imports (including food and fuel) exceed exports by a factor of four.

Deficient farming practices on steep terrain have accelerated soil erosion, as the run-off from tropical rains flushes arable land toward the sea, further obstructing urban drain-

Compiled from various sources, including: Institut Haitien de Statistique et Informatique (IHSI 2010); World Bank, Haiti at a glance (2006); Health in the Americas (2007); Haiti health profile

(2010); United Nations, World population prospects: the 2008 revision (2009).

The presidential elections finally took place at the end of 2010, but there was an international challenge of the results. A second round of elections were completed in 2011.

The UNDP Multidimensional Poverty Index (MPI) complements income poverty measures by reflecting the deprivations that a poor person faces all at once with respect to education, health, and living standard. It assesses poverty at the individual level, with poor persons being those who are deprived in multiple areas, and the extent of their poverty being measured by the range of their deprivations.

Heavy deforestation is noticeable from the air, almost delineating the border between Haiti and the Dominican Republic. Sanitation management is ineffective or nonexistent, so excreta and household waste heavily pollute surface water.

An estimated 25% to 50% of national income comes from remittances from the approximately one million Haitians living and working abroad, mostly in the United States, Canada, and France. According to the 2010 Population Survey of the U.S., in 2009 nearly one-third of Haitian immigrants in the U.S. belonged to households that earned more than US$ 60,000. In comparison, less than 15% of the immigrants from Mexico, Dominican Republic, and El Salvador in the U.S. had that level of household income. A quarter of Haitian immigrants, especially women, are reportedly in the relatively higher paying health care and education sectors; only a small number of them are in the construction sector (Ratha 2010). Emigration of highly qualified health personnel is a serious issue.

Salaries of civil servants in Haiti, health professionals included, remain unpaid for months at a time. This leaves professionals little option but moonlighting or charging fees for services to make a living.

Governance, or rather the lack of it, is often cited as one of the most serious shortcomings in Haiti. In 2008, Transparency International's "Corruption Perception Index" ranked Haiti 177 out of 180 countries (the last five were Afghanistan, Haiti, Iraq, Myanmar, and Somalia). In 2010, that score (on a scale of 10) improved from 1.1–1.7 (2008) to 2.2, moving Haiti's ranking to 146 out of 178.

It is undeniable that poor national governance is a major obstacle in Haiti, but the international community should assume its share of responsibility for bypassing the government—thereby weakening it—for most decisions and projects. An international "blank check" (financially and politically) written to NGOs that often have their own agenda and shortcomings is legitimizing a culture of unaccountability in the public service sector (Zanotti 2010). Officials who are not meaningfully consulted and have no authority over the resources assigned to foreign implementing agencies (NGOs) cannot feel responsible.

It is estimated that between 3,000 and 10,000 NGOs are operating in Haiti, one of the highest densities of NGOs per capita in the world. According to the U.S. Institute for Peace (2010), USAID budgeted some US$ 300 million for Haiti in fiscal year 2007–2008, all of which was implemented through NGOs. These projects often had more money than the entire Haitian Ministry of Planning. For this reason, Haiti has been called "the Republic of NGOs."

Health status

Core health indicators are, indeed, alarming. Mortality rates are by far the highest in the Region of the Americas, with the crude mortality rate of 12 deaths per 1,000 population; under-5 mortality rate of 76 deaths per 1,000 live births; infant mortality rate of 57 deaths per 1,000 live births—that is, 1 in every 12 children dies before her/his first birthday; and the maternal mortality rate of 670 deaths per 100,000 live births.150 Life expectancy at birth, estimated at 61.5 years (59.7 in males and 63.2 in females) is the lowest in the Americas. Birth rate remains high, at 25 per 1,000 in urban areas and 30 per 1,000 in rural areas; the average number of children per woman is 3 in urban areas and 4 in rural areas.

Quantified data on communicable diseases are limited in normal times. Disaggregated data on morbidity or mortality by cause, gender or age are mostly unavailable except for malaria, which has an annual parasite incidence (API) three times that of the Dominican Republic.

Acute diarrheal disease is highly prevalent: 2 out of 5 children aged 6 to 11 (40%), and 1 out of 4 children under 5 years old (25%) experienced one or more episodes of diarrhea in any two-week period. All other age groups are also disproportionately affected. However, the last outbreak of cholera had been reported in Haiti over 100 years prior to the earthquake and the disease was totally absent until the outbreak in late 2010.151 In spite of the poor sanitation and lack of access to safe water, Haiti was spared during the 1991–1993 cholera outbreak that started in Peru and killed over 4,000 people in the Western hemisphere.

Haiti has the highest incidence of tuberculosis in the Americas (about 30,000 new cases per year); it is reportedly the seventh leading cause of death in the country. TB/ HIV co-infection rate is close to 30%.

Mortality statistics in normal times are very incomplete: under-registration is estimated to be 94.7%. Death certificates are filled out for only 1 in 20 deaths (5% coverage), and yet 1 in every 3 death certificates records an ill-defined cause of death.

A national epidemic of cholera started in October 2010 in the Artibonite department, an area that was not affected by the earthquake.

HIV/AIDS and sexually transmitted infections (STIs) are common in Haiti. According to the 2005-2006 Mortality, Morbidity, and Service Utilization Survey for Haiti (EMMUSIV), estimates put HIV prevalence at 2.2% (2.3% among women aged 15–49 and 2%

among men aged 15–59). Haiti's HIV/AIDS program is cited as one of the most successful in the world, on the way to providing universal treatment for HIV/AIDS nationwide (Koenig et al. 2010).152

Vaccine-preventable diseases such as diphtheria and neo-natal tetanus are all too common. Grave concern arises from the extremely low immunization coverage rates for measles (54%); diphtheria, pertussis and tetanus (68%); and polio (66%) in children under 1 year old. In 2009 an epidemic of diphtheria with 29 confirmed cases affected Port-au-Prince and rural departments. By the end of the year WHO epidemiologists feared an explosive outbreak in the shantytowns of the Port-au-Prince metropolitan area (including Carrefour). In the past, Haiti has led several measles vaccination campaigns, the last one in 2007 against measles/rubella for children and adolescents between 1 and 19 years old. The last case of indigenous measles reported in Haiti was in 2001.

Tropical diseases such as leprosy and lymphatic filariasis remained prevalent in spite of progress in their control.

Dengue was first confirmed in Haiti in 1964, but national surveillance of dengue has not taken place. According to the CDC, a study of 215 children in Port-au-Prince in 1996 showed that 85% had been previously infected with one or two dengue virus serotypes. Studies during prior foreign military operations found "minimal numbers of symptomatic community cases or hospitalizations, while high attack rate and severe cases were reported among foreign military and foreign civilian personnel in Haiti" (CDC 2010b).

The delivery of health services

Health services delivery is mostly private with a small public component. An estimated 75% of health care is provided by NGOs, faith-based groups, and other foreign medical providers.

The public health services network in Haiti is organized in three levels:

1. The primary level comprises ± 600 clinics with and without beds, and 45 community hospitals;
2. The secondary level includes nine department hospitals;153
3. The tertiary level represents the six university hospitals (five are in Port-au-Prince; the principal one is the University Hospital—HUEH).

This success is tied to a strong foundation for HIV care that was in place before external funding became available. This includes national guidelines prepared by the Ministry of Health; political commitment at the highest levels of government; NGOs that had been providing high quality care in Haiti for decades; and the assistance of the Global Fund to Fight AIDS, TB, and Malaria, the U.S. President's

Emergency Plan for AIDS Relief (PEPFAR), and other private donors (Koenig et al. 2010).

There are 10 departments in Haiti, but the West department, where the capital is located, has only university hospitals. Since 2009, five integrated diagnostic centers have been established to serve as a bridge between first and second care levels, but they have not yet been integrated with the rest of the system. A decentralized organization was also formulated through Communal Health Units (one CHU for 80,000–140,000 people) but this had not been effectively implemented at the time of the earthquake. Decentralization is still in its infancy and being implemented very slowly. As a result, most of the functions are still very centralized with the roles and responsibilities between levels poorly defined. There is no framework for the participation of communities in management of the CHU. There is also major confusion about roles and responsibilities among levels of care (i.e., the CHU provide primary level care as well as serving as departmental hospitals).

According to 2007 reports, nearly half of the population lacked access to basic health care. Financial barriers were seen as the main problem. There was a fee for services and local health facilities were heavily dependent on this income to pay for part of their staff and services. When accessible, services were poor due to lack of quality control, infrastructural deficiencies, poor communication equipment, electrical blackouts, water problems, and general deterioration of the facilities.

A joint initiative of the Ministry of Health, PAHO/WHO, and CIDA was launched in 2007 to provide access to free obstetric care (Soins Obstétricaux Gratuits, or SOG). Following the earthquake, a similar free program was instituted for children under age 5 (Soins Infantiles Gratuits, or SIG).

Specialized services such as rehabilitation for persons with disabilities or mental health care are far behind the level and quality in neighboring countries.

The National Blood Safety Program (NBSP) was created by the Ministry of Health to establish standards for safe blood transfusions, increase voluntary blood donations, and facilitate access to safe blood for patients. Between 2004 and 2009, blood collection rose by 250%, the number of blood units increased from 9,000 to 22,000, and voluntary blood donations rose from 47% to 70%. The NBSP hoped to reach the goal of 100% voluntary donations by 2010.

Inequities are widespread in health service delivery: 68% of women in the wealthiest quintile deliver in a health facility while only 6% of the poorest quintile does. A high majority (90%) of the urban population is within 30 minutes of a health facility, but this is the case for only about 50% of people in rural areas.

In a review carried out in 2007 on governance of the health sector, leadership and regulation functions were seen as "weak or very weak," at central, departmental, and periphery levels. Most of the services are operated or delivered by a mix of public and private not-for-profit entities without an effective pre-existing policy dialogue/ coordination mechanism with relevant development partners.

On the positive side, numerous health NGOs and faith-based organizations that have played a major role in humanitarian response in other major disasters were already present with ongoing programs in Haiti at the time of the earthquake. Their familiarity with the situation and the existence of a support and logistics mechanism will be critical as Haiti rebuilds after the impact.

The private for-profit sector is small (< 5% of services), is not regulated, and provides services to higher income patients often pending their referral to foreign facilities.

In addition to a thriving, private pharmaceutical industry, PROMESS (Programme de Médicaments Essentiels) is the central procurement facility and warehouse of essential drugs for the Ministry of Health and most of its non-profit partners. Established in 1992 during the embargo after a coup d'état, this program, managed by the Pan American Health Organization, serves as the national pharmacy, offering essential supplies and drugs at or below cost thanks to the support of donor agencies. A well-stocked and managed central warehouse has proven to be an invaluable asset in past disasters striking Haiti. However, because PROMESS is dependent on outside funding and completion of agreements between the Ministry of Health and all its partners, it has not evolved into a national system offering the complete range of items required for health care.

Governance problems in Haiti are well-known but they cannot be attributed solely to government shortcomings: As noted at the multi-sectoral level, the fragmentation of services is also due to donor policies resulting in several vertical programs being well funded while others are poorly supported if at all. Self-funded health NGOs are reluctant to respect Ministry norms and procedures because they are pursuing their own objectives in line with their own policies, standards, and protocols. "Leading" such a sector under such conditions is, indeed, almost an impossible task.

In terms of information management, there is inadequate information to support decision-making at strategic and operational levels. The existence of many parallel or vertical health information systems based on projects financed by specific donors has not contributed to streamlining the information.

Water and sanitation

While only 58% of the general population has some access to improved drinking-water sources, in urban settings access is estimated at 70% (Schuftan et al. 2007). In urban areas, safe drinking water is provided, for a fee, by a commercial (or in some instances subsidized) distribution network of treated water (reverse osmosis mostly). Even the poor urban population in the capital will invest their limited resources for high quality, industrially processed water sold retail, by the gallon. Small individual plastic bags sold as high quality water are believed not to come from safe industrial sources. Piped public distribution system is rudimentary and limited even in Port-au-Prince. According to the Haitian Institute for Statistics (IHSI), only 8% of houses have piped water and they are mainly located in limited areas of Port-au-Prince. Piped water in Haiti is not fit to drink.

Only 19% of Haitians have access to improved sanitation and disposal of excreta (29% in urban areas and 12% in rural). Those who have access to a septic tank or latrine use the services of a group of specialized workers called bayakou, who manually empty excreta. Dedicated sites for discharge are mostly absent, a situation that induces high environmental and health risks. As a sewage system is nonexistent in most poor suburban areas, accumulated solid and liquid waste are flushed away periodically by the rains through an unmaintained storm drainage system.

Nutrition

The pre-earthquake global acute malnutrition (GAM) rate was estimated at 4.5% for the affected areas, with severe acute malnutrition at 0.8%.154 At these levels, an estimated 17,500 children under 5 years old are suffering from acute malnutrition and 3,100 of these are severely malnourished and in need of life-saving assistance. While high, these levels are markedly under those considered a humanitarian emergency (10%). Stunting rates are significant (30% in 2005).

Nutrition interventions have been scarce, and the lack of coordination at central and departmental levels have had important negative effects on the efficiency of these interventions. In an article published by the World Bank, the author made the following observations about deficits in nutrition programs prior to the earthquake:

- "There was no structure in place to address nutrition security comprehensively. The approach was patchwork, with small, mostly donor- and NGO-run programs operating in distinct areas.
- "The health system had serious coverage gaps and was not oriented, nor endowed with the human and material resources, to address nutrition issues.
- "Programmatic coordination was an enormous challenge. There was little communication across implementers or with government.
- "Program focus was not sufficiently aligned with Haiti's priority nutrition security problems or with international best practices. The majority of nutrition programs in Haiti focused on the treatment of acute malnutrition because the problem is more visible" (Bassett 2010).

It should be pointed out that in 2009 national guidelines to address malnutrition were developed, including a National Protocol for the Management of Acute Malnutrition. This was undertaken through the concerted efforts of the Nutrition Department of the Ministry of Health, several NGOs, and donors (in particular the EC's Directorate-General for Humanitarian Aid). Following hurricanes that hit Haiti in 2008, a Nutrition Cluster was set up by UNICEF, which was replaced in 2009 by the National Nutrition Committee led by the Ministry of Health.

Malnutrition in Haiti is the end-result of extreme poverty associated with low education level. It is primarily an economic and equity issue rather a health one. In addition to economic and equity issues underlying causes of malnutrition such as food insecurity, infant feeding practices, maternal and child health, health care access, and water and sanitation conditions and practices are strong contributing factors.

154 Nutritional survey carried out by the Haitian Ministry of Health and Action against Hunger (December 2008– March 2009).

155 World Bank, Haiti at glance, 2010.

Mental health

The Centre de Psychiatrie Mars et Kline and the Hospital Psychiatrique Défilé de Beudet are the only two government-run, psychiatric facilities in metropolitan Port-au-Prince. No public institution offers mental health services outside the capital, but several small, private centers have emerged. The Mars et Kline center is the sole national facility for treatment of acute (short-term) cases while the Hospital Défilé de Beudet is dedicated to severe chronic cases.

Mental health approaches in Haiti were centered on medical and hospital interventions far from the community-based approach recommended by WHO. There is widespread belief that mental illness is caused by supernatural forces, which further complicates a modern approach.

Figure A.1 shows that the ratio of psychiatrists per 100,000 inhabitants in Haiti is the lowest in the Caribbean and Central American regions.

Gender-based violence was a well-known issue prior to the earthquake. A study carried out by the Inter-American Development Bank in Haiti in 2006 reported that one-third of women and girls reported incidents of physical or sexual violence. The Inter-American Commission on Human Rights (OAS) reports that more than 50 percent of those who had experienced violence were under the age of 18. A 2006 survey study attests to the rampant use of rape as both a tool and outcome of violence, documenting that 35,000 women were victimized in the area surveyed (Kolbe and Hutson 2006). The real scale of the problem is not fully known because of a lack of central figures on rapes.

Gender-based violence is often considered to be most common in poor slum areas where overcrowding, poverty, and lack of education are factors. In Haiti, it is also a serious problem in more wealthy segments of the society:

"Poor, mostly rural families send their children to cities to live with wealthier families whom they think will provide the children with food, shelter and an education, in exchange for some work. Sadly, the parents' dream is often a nightmare for these children known as restaveks.... Sixty-five percent of the victims are girls between the ages of six and fourteen. They work excessive hours, receive little or no schooling, are unpaid and are often physically and sexually abused" (Cde Baca 2010).

The importance of addressing gender-based violence in time of disaster was acknowledged during the response to the cyclones of 2008. The Inter-Agency Standing Committee issued a three-page summary of the information available on gender-based violence prior to the earthquake...

# SPECIAL THANKS TO:

The Haitian Government, Libraries and Archives Acknowledgments

The author express their gratitude for all those who have shared their experience, their views, and observations during numerous meetings and field visits. They helped us to appreciate the dedication of so many facing an insurmountable challenge.

Our appreciation goes first to the Haitian health professionals who candidly described their odyssey in the first weeks following the earthquake, and their gratitude but also frustration with well-intentioned but sometimes counterproductive assistance. Among those who have influenced our thinking are: Ariel Henri, Cabinet Chief of the Ministry of Health; Daniel Henrys, senior consultant; Jean Hughes Henrys, Dean of the Medical School, University of Notre Dame; Alix Lassegue, Director, University Hospital of Haiti; Claude Surena, Haitian Medical Association; and Yolene Surena, Directorate for Civil Protection/World Bank Project.

In the international community, among the many who helped us to reconstruct the complex patterns of the response, special recognition is due to Edmond Mu-let, Special Representative of the UN Secretary-General. A remarkable diplomat with sound judgment on our collective lackluster coordination, Mr. Mulet reassured us in our quest for additional critical insights. The support and contributions of

UNICEF staff in the initial interviews but also in the review process were also outstanding. Representatives, Henriette Chamouillet and Lea Guido; Dana Van Alphen, the Health Cluster coordinator; and Cristian Morales, Health Services Advisor. They helped us to navigate between the two occasionally clashing worlds of the life-saving humanitarian response and of the long-term, capacity building of the national counterparts.

This document would never have come to fruition without the visionary support from Jean-Luc Poncelet's encouragement and ability to mobilize resources for the preparation and publication of this document, Sam Vigersky and Cristina Estrada's management support, and Liz Stonaker's editorial contributions were most valuable.

In addition we would like to acknowledge the contributions made by the following people who served on the review committee: Ellen Wasserman (Johns Hopkins School of Public Health); Shannon Strother (Disaster Resilience Leadership Academy, Tulane University); Alana Officer (WHO); Andre Griekspoor (WHO); Jon Andrus (PAHO); Jean Luc Poncelet (PAHO); Sylvain Aldighieri (PAHO); Cecilia Acuña (PAHO); Peter Graaff (PAHO); and Nicolas Lagomarsino (PAHO). Naming a few can be an injustice for the many others who helped us. Few of the ideas and key findings are ours. They all have been revealed to us by one colleague or another. Our appreciation and our gratitude go to those anonymous thinkers from NGOs, UN or other agencies. We hope that these lessons, their lessons, will be learned and put in practice in future disasters.

United States Centers for Disease Control and Prevention

Government Agency: The Centers for Disease Control and Prevention is the national public health institute of the United States.

U.S. Department of State, Primature d'Haïti,BBC Broadcasting House, Time Inc.

The Bibliothèque nationale de France (The National French Archives)

The Museo del Prado (Spanish Museum)

# BIBLIOGRAPHY

Abaakouk Z. (forthcoming). Mental health in Haiti in 2010: a public health need, an added value within health care practice and a cornerstone for reconstruction. In PAHO/WHO, Mental health and psychosocial support in emergencies in the Caribbean. Washington, D.C.: PAHO/WHO.

Active Learning Network for Accountability and Performance in Humanitarian Action (ALNAP)/ProVention. 2009. Responding to urban disasters: learning from previous relief and recovery operations. Available at: www.alnap.org/pool/files/alnap-provention-lessons-urban.pdf.

―――. 2010. Haiti earthquake response: context analysis. Available at: www.alnap.org/pool/files/haiti-context-analysis-final.pdf.

Adams P. 2010. Rainy season could hamper Haiti's recovery. Lancet 375(9720):1067–9.

Afshar, M., M. Raju, D. Ansell, T. P. Bleck. 2011. Narrative review: tetanus—a health threat after natural disasters in developing countries. Ann Intern Med 154(5):329-35.

Alkire, S., M. E. Santos. 2010. Multidimensional Poverty Index: 2010 Data. Oxford Poverty and Human Development Initiative. Available at: www.ophi.org.uk/policy/multidimensional-poverty-index.

American Medical Association. 2010. Medical and public health responders: preparing for the Haitian earthquake disaster relief efforts. [Web-based training program.] Available at: www.ama-assn. org/ama/pub/ news/news/haiti-earthquake-response.page.

American Red Cross. 2011. Haiti earthquake relief, one-year report. Available at: www.redcross.org/wwwfiles/Documents/pdf/ international/Haiti/HaitiEarthquake_OneYearReport.pdf.

Amnesty International. 2010. Haiti: after the earthquake: initial mission findings, March 2010. London: Amnesty International Publications. Available from: www.amnesty.org/en/library/info/ AMR36/004/2010.

Anderson, A. J., C. L. Powell. 2011. "The role of humanitarian efforts: lessons from Haiti." Lecture, 45th Annual Uniformed Services Pediatric Seminar, American Academy of Pediatrics. Washington, D.C., 12-15 March.

Archibold, R.C. 2011. U.S. reduces estimates of homeless in Haiti quake. New York Times, 31 May.

Assessment Capacities Project (ACAPS). 2010. Rapid initial needs assessment for Haiti (RINAH). Conducted 23 January-6 February 2010, Port-au-Prince. Available at: www.acaps.org/img/documents/ rinahreport-final-rinah-report-feb2010.pdf.

Association of Schools of Public Health. Haitian earthquake relief: schools of public health respond. Accessed 20 July 2011. www.asph. org/document.cfm?page=1141.

Auerbach, P. S., R. L. Norris, A. S. Menon, et al. 2010. Civil–military collaboration in the initial medical response to the earthquake in Haiti. N Engl J Med 362(10):e32.

Babcock, C., C. Baer, C. Bayram, et al. 2010. Chicago medical response to the 2010 earthquake in Haiti: translating academic collaboration into direct humanitarian response. Disaster Med Public Health Prep 4(2):169-73.

Bajkiewicz, C. 2009. Evaluating short-term missions: How can we improve? J Christ Nurs 26(2):110-4.

Bar-On, E. E. Lebel, Y. Kreiss, et al. 2011. Orthopaedic management in a mega mass casualty situation: the Israel Defense Forces Field Hospital in Haiti following the January 2010 earthquake. Injury, Apr 18. [Epub ahead of print].

Barrera, G. 2010. Regreso al país del buque ARC Cartegena de Indias procedente de Haiti [Radio Santa Fe broadcast, interview with Commander Guillermo Barrera, Colombian National Navy]. Accessed 20 May 2011. www.radiosantafe.com/2010/02/10/regreso-al-pais-el-buque-arc-cartagena-de-indias-procedente-de-haiti.

Basauri, V. 2010. Rapport de Mission: La Santé mentale et le soutien psycho-social in Haïti (PAHO/WHO Mission Report, 3–6 February 2010). Unpublished.

Bassett, L. 2010, Nutrition security in Haiti: pre- and post-earthquake conditions and the way forward. World Bank En Breve Series No. 157 (June 2010). Available at: www.worldbank.org/enbreve.

Bennett, J., W. Bertrand, C. Harkin, et al. 2006. Coordination of international humanitarian assistance in tsunami-affected countries. London: Tsunami Evaluation Coalition.

Binder, A., F. Grünewald. 2010. IASC Cluster approach evaluation, 2nd phase. Country study: Haiti. Groupe URD (April 2010). Available at: www.gppi.net/fileadmin/gppi/GPPi-URD_Cluster_II_Evaluation_HAITI_e.pdf.

Born, C.T., T.R. Cullison, J.A. Dean, et al. 2011. Partnered disaster preparedness: lessons learned from international events. J Am Acad Orthop Surg 19 (suppl 1): S44-S48.

Burns, A. S., C. O'Connell, M.D. Landry. 2010. Spinal cord injury in post-earthquake Haiti: lessons learned and future needs. PM&R Vol. 2, 695-7.

Calvot, T., A. Shivji. (Forthcoming). Haiti, du Traumatisme au Relèvement, Quelles Perspectives? In Conoir, Y. (ed.). Laval, Canada: Presses de l'Université Laval.

CdeBaca, L. 2010. Best practices: human trafficking in disaster zones. Keynote remarks to the Harvard Kennedy School's Ash Center for Democratic Governance and Innovation, Washington, D.C., May 24, 2010. Available at: www.reliefweb.int/node/355692.

Centre for Research on the Epidemiology of Disasters (CRED). Emergency Events Database (EM-DAT). Available at: www.emdat.be.

Chu, K. M., M. Trelles, N. P. Ford. 2011. Quality of care in humanitarian surgery. World J Surg 35(6):1169-72.

Cochran, J. 2010. Statistics without Borders assists with Haitian data collection project. Statistics Without Borders/Amstat News, 2010. Accessed 1 January 2011. www.magazine.amstat.org/blog/2010/05/13/ swb5_10.

Cosgrave, J. 2007. Synthesis report: expanded summary. Joint evaluation of the international response to the Indian Ocean tsunami.

London: Tsunami Evaluation Coalition. Available at: www.alnap.org/ pool/files/ Syn_Report_Sum.pdf.

DARA. 2010. Climate vulnerability monitor. Report. Available from http://daraint.org/climate-vulnerability-monitor/climate-vulnerability-monitor-2010.

de Ville de Goyet, C., L. Morinière. 2006. The role of needs assessment in the tsunami response. Tsunami Evaluation Coalition. Available at: www.alnap.org/initiatives/tec/thematic/needs.aspx.

Doocy C., C. Robinson, C. Moodie, G. Burnham. 2009. Tsunami-related injury in Aceh Province, Indonesia. Global Public Health 4(2):205-14.

Dowell, S. F., J.W. Tappero, T.R. Frieden. 2011. Public health in Haiti: challenges and progress. N Engl J Med 364(4):300-1.

Eckes-Roper, J. 2010. Operation Haiti relief: South Florida health/ medical response. Philadelphia Public Health Forum: Current Issues in Public Health and Preparedness.

Etienne M., C. Powell, B. Faux. 2010. Disaster relief in Haiti: a perspective from the neurologists on the USNS Comfort. Lancet Neurology 9(5): 461-3.

Farfel A., A. Assa, I. Amir, et al. 2011. Haiti earthquake 2010: a field hospital pediatric perspective. Eur J Pediatr 170(4):519-25.

Farmer, P. 2011. Haiti after the earthquake. New York: Public Affairs.

Felten-Biermann, C. 2006. Gender and natural disaster: sexualized violence and the tsunami. Development 49(3):82-6.

Ferris, D. 2010. Pharmacist's assistance after Haiti earthquake. Am J Health Syst Pharm 67:1138-41.

Fisher, N. 2010. Notes on preliminary lessons learnt from Haiti. Address to IASC Principals Meeting, 6 May 2010, New York. Unpublished.

Florida Department of Health. 2010. Recommendations/guidelines for initial infection control, medical screenings and vaccinations of Haitian earthquake evacuees. February 3, 2010.

Florida Hospital Association. National Disaster Medical System Overview and Contact Information, Feb. 5, 2010. www.fha.org/Article.html?ArtID=8774.

Food and Agriculture Organization and World Food Programme. 2010. Evaluation de la Récolte et de la sécurité alimentaire en Haïti.

[Special Mission Report, 21 September 2010]. Available at: www. fao.org/ docrep/012/ak353f/ak353f00.htm.

France. Embassy of France in the United States. 2010. Earthquake in Haiti—update on French effort (02/04/10). Accessed 20 May 2011. http://ambafrance-us.org/spip.php?article1504.

Galeckas, K. 2011. Dermatology aboard the USNS Comfort: disaster relief operations in Haiti after the 2010 earthquake. Dermatologic clinics 29(1):15-9.

Gerdin M. and J. Von Schreeb. 2011. Presentation at the 17th World Congress on Disaster and Emergency medicine in Beijing, May 2011.

Ginzburg E., W.W. O'Neill, P. J. Goldschmidt-Clermont, et al. 2010. Rapid medical relief—Project Medishare and the Haitian earthquake. N Engl J Med 362(10):e31.

Goodman A. 2010. Ministry of touch—reflections on disaster work after the Haitian earthquake. N Engl J Med 362(11):e37.

To all the Haitian people for you help in writing this amazing story.

# ARIMA BOYS ROMAN CATHOLIC SCHOOL (TRINIDAD & TOBAGO)

The Arima Boys' RC School celebrated its 125th anniversary at the conclusion of 2011, a very historic feat for a prestigious school. In this 125th year of serving the community and the country, Arima Boys RC has continued to achieve outstanding successes in keeping with its illustrious past.

The school was established in 1886 by Monsignor de Martini.

Today the school hosts 700 students with a staff of 32 lead by Principal Brian Brooks.

**The Mission Statement of the school:**

Arima Boys R.C. School will teach children respect for God, Life, family and country in a secure Roman Catholic environment. It will make use of sound pedagogy to ensure the curriculum provides for the development of well rounded pupils imbued with the values and skills that create life- long learners and patriotic citizens.

Dr. Jeffrey Anthony Benjamin is a proud alumni of this wonderful institution in his primary years of learning.

***** Deeds Not Words******

*AuthorHouse™ LLC*
*1663 Liberty Drive*
*Bloomington, IN 47403*
*www.authorhouse.com*
*Phone: 1-800-839-8640*